Those Earnest
VICTORIANS

Those Earnest VICTORIANS

By Esmé Wingfield-Stratford, D.Sc., M.A.

*"In tragic life, God wot,
No villain need be! Passions spin the plot:
We are betrayed by what is false within."*

WILLIAM MORROW & CO.

PRINTED IN THE U. S. A.

TO

LIEUT. COL. F. H. L. ERRINGTON, C.B.

PREFACE

The period with which this book is mainly concerned is that of the middle class supremacy in England, and comprises, roughly, the four mid decades of the nineteenth century.

More than once I have drawn on my own memory and on private information. And I must apologise for the necessity that I have been under of suppressing certain names of those not so long dead, out of respect to the feelings of the living.

CONTENTS

Those Earnest
VICTORIANS

CHAPTER I

THE SETTING

OLD-FASHIONED history affords the same sort of view of human development as you get, on ship-board, of the sea. The most magnificent of all spectacles unrolls itself before your eyes—the innumerable laughter of wavelets kissed by the sun, the Almighty's form glassing itself in tempests, more than a Swinburne could sing or a Turner paint, but not the movements of tide and current, the age long work of erosion under the cliff-face, the dark and measureless depths beneath the keel.

Until well on in the last century, the storm raised by the French Revolution, the surge and thunder of the Napoleonic wars, riveted men's attention to the exclusion of all else. You have only to read as much as you can endure of Sir Archibald Alison's ten portly volumes on the History of Europe from 1789 to 1815, to realise what constituted that history in the eyes of the ensuing generation. Nothing but the monotonous tramp, tramp, in prose equally monotonous, of men in red and blue, in white and green, beneath the dust and through the slush of all the roads from Moscow to Lisbon, with occasional pauses to line up and blow each other off the face of the earth. Kingdoms rise and wither like Jonah's gourd, the map changes like a kaleidoscope, some two millions of lives are snuffed out, and things end up to all appearance where they started, with France back in the old frontiers under the old dynasty, and the sovereigns of Europe putting back the clock to the eighteenth century and nailing the hands to the dial.

We have learnt a little more about that war than was apparent to the industrious Sir Archibald. Our eyes are no longer dazzled by the sunrise of Austerlitz or the sunset of Waterloo. It was an American admiral who, towards the close of last century, pointed to the "far distant, storm-beaten ships" of the British blockade, "on which the grand army never looked, and which stood between it and the domination of the world." But even he may hardly have realised that the decisive function of these ships, hells of human misery as most of them were, was to build a wooden wall round the new English factories, where employers, ruthlessly competing, with no other thought than that of making fortunes or averting ruin, organised hordes of overworked, underpaid, and villainously housed human beings, to turn out the cheap and often shoddy products, against which Napoleon and all his legions were powerless, in the long run, to contend. Salvoes of cannon thunder quicken the pulse more than the gradually increasing hum of power looms, and the smoke that darkened Moscow forms a spectacle more impressive than that which has never ceased to darken Salford.

Like a storm had the spirit unchained by the French Revolution swept over Europe, with the Man of Destiny seeming to ride it, and like a storm it had died away, leaving the shores strewn with wreckage, and men's hearts glad because they were at quiet. But the main currents were neither hurried nor diverted in their drift, the work of erosion went on unperceived, and far beneath were depths hardly conscious of tumult and agitation on the surface.

Perhaps when, if ever, the time comes for us to view these events in their true perspective, the whole Napoleonic episode will strike us as an enormous—an enormously mischievous—irrelevance. For its precise importance lay in the fact that, at the most critical of all periods in human history, it diverted men's minds and energies from the things that really mattered, to the miserable squabble as to who should rule who—such nice questions as whether his tatters and vermin would sit less honourably on the back of a Spanish peasant under the rule of a rather silly Buonaparte than under that of a wholly blackguardly Bourbon, backed by the Inquisition; whether a bearded moujik would be happier having his grain requisitioned by a party of famishing conscripts, or the seignorial rod applied to his bare buttocks in the course of holy Russian routine. Whichever way these grave matters were ultimately decided, both peasants would probably be made to give up the ghost, not without agony, in the course of the debate. And all the while the Sphinx was putting her riddle, whose answer, if a better one could not be found in time, would be death for human civilisation. But nobody had time to listen.

In England, not even the surface of life had been violently disturbed by the storm that had swept over Europe. Whatever might happen abroad, John Bull was not to be hustled out of his genteel eighteenth century way of conducting war by professional armies, and even the press gang confined its attentions to the poor. Not only the business, but the amenities and amusements of life went on undisturbed. During the year of Albuera, when Napoleon's power was at its height and our prospects at their gloomiest, the streets of London were blocked by crowds cheering home the hero, Tom Cribb, who, before upwards of 20,000 spectators, had succeeded in fracturing the jaw of the negro Molineaux. It was during the ensuing year that the Goodwood Cup was first run, the Gold Cup at Ascot having been started in 1807, the time that Wordsworth was penning his lines:

"We are left, or shall be left, alone,
    The last that dare to struggle with the foe!"

And when Miss Austen wrote her immortal studies of English provincial life, so placid, and as trivial as if painted on china, it seems to have quite slipped her memory that there was a war on.

The invincible obstinacy with which our ruling class had persisted in the struggle against half a continent in arms, was born of a deep, subconscious determination to keep things as they were, to preserve intact the constitutional order of English society and the balance of European power. This purpose seemed to have been finally achieved when Napoleon stepped on to the deck of the *Bellerophon,* and the gentlemen of England, as magnanimous in victory as they had been relentless in their will to obtain it, might now peacefully devote themselves to the enjoyment of its fruits.

The problem presented by the French Revolution and its child Napoleon had only been brought to an effective, if rather tardy solution, by shelving one of far greater moment, though of less immediate urgency. For England, thanks to the new machinery by which she had conquered Napoleon, was transforming not only her own, but the rest of Western civilisation. In the blind pursuit of wealth, she had dictated new conditions of life that might, or might not, turn out to be compatible with the existence of a creature with a brain and physique by no means superior to that of the cave man, at his best. Of an age of gamblers, it was the supreme gamble.

Such considerations were not of the kind likely to penetrate the hard skulls of lords and gentlemen during the Regency. As a class, they were little disposed to philosophise, and they were profoundly satisfied with themselves, the social order they adorned, and a constitutional system guaranteed to perpetuate it. Few of them, probably, either had, or desired, any personal acquaintance with the new and extremely unattractive towns that were coming into existence in the Midlands, and in the valleys on either side of the Pennines. As for what we should now call social reform, that sort of thing smacked too strongly of Jacobinism to make it safe to meddle with. To genteel palates, the old wine was better than such new, effervescent stuff.

But the social question was not to be burked so easily. Nobody had had time to attend to it during the war, nobody, that is, who counted, for agitators like Will Cobbett could be lumped under the genial designation of "blackguards." There was certainly young Lord Byron, who could protest to his fellow peers that never in his travels among the most despotic infidel countries had he beheld such squalid wretchedness as he had seen, since his return, in the very heart of a Christian England. But Byron's voice, destined though it was to reverberate through Europe, was not loud enough to disturb the complacency of the British House of Lords, and the condition of the people was not, after all, a subject about which Byron himself was to manifest any very sustained interest. The home front had remained unbroken throughout the war—nobody had so much as dreamed of its breaking. There might be rioting and machine smashing reported now and then from the industrial districts, but the victories of Wellington, not to speak of Tom Cribb, provided news more exciting.

No doubt the general feeling among comfortably off people after the crowning mercy of Waterloo was that of the reader of conventional novels, who comes to the marriage in the last chapter, and closes the book in the blissful assurance that they will live ever happy afterwards. But it happens not unfrequently in real life that the chapter of accidents concluded at the altar is followed by a chapter of miseries that begins there. Hardly had the bonfires smouldered to ashes and the carillons died upon the breeze, than the condition of the people began to obtrude itself in a way not to be ignored even by Tory statesmen. The year after Waterloo was one of unprecedented misery. Industry was no longer doped by the demand for munitions, the labour market was flooded, and England's customers abroad were either too much impoverished to pay for her goods, or were beginning to use the new machinery on their own account, and protect their home markets against British competition. To crown all this, the harvest was one of the worst ever known. Unemployment, distress, discomfort, were everywhere rife. The fruits of victory had no sooner been grasped, than they turned to ashes.

"The climax of misery," ran one workingmen's manifesto, "is complete, it can go no further. Death would now be a relief to millions."

Or as Shelley cried a few years later:

> "Nay, in countries that are free,
> Such starvation cannot be
> As in England now we see."

With the menace of a European tyrant English rulers had often had to deal, but here was something new and ominous, quite beyond the mental scope of the well-meaning and usually kind-hearted gentlemen to whom the King's government was entrusted. It is not surprising that it found them without any constructive remedy whatever. The spectre of revolution was more apparent to them than that of starvation. Their duty, as they understood it, was to keep order, and most of them had the genial, eighteenth century faith in a Deity who, in some unexplained way, imparted a favourable tilt to his universe, and, if not too much interfered with, would make everything come right in the end.

So the menace of Jacobinism was sternly fought down, and after a few years the social crisis seemed to be mastered. The governing class still held all the cards. Its constitutional ascendency seemed to be as impregnable as human contrivance could make it, when seats in Parliament were almost as much a matter of genteel patronage as livings in the church. As for anything the mob might do, the position had never been so secure, now that there was a veteran standing army, whose rank and file, despite the inhuman conditions of its barrack life and the arbitrary torture of flogging, were sufficiently a caste apart to go anywhere and do anything at their officers' orders.

And after all, however hard might be the conditions of life in mills and mines, however merciless might be the competition between the new employers, it was not fashionable in those romantic days to look on reality naked. The fact that a labourer might here and there be found starved under a hedge, or that men and women were harnessed like beasts to the parish carts, did not prevent the England of Constable's landscapes from being an earthly Paradise to those who owned her soil. Thanks to duties on corn, that soil yielded comfortable incomes, and never, since the days of Nimrod, had there been better hunting.

CHAPTER II

THE SQUIRE AND HIS RELATIONS

THERE is nothing more remarkable in the whole of English history, than the breakdown of aristocratic dominance within seventeen years of Waterloo, and this not by bloody revolution, but by peaceful surrender. The very Parliament whose franchise was so arranged as to make it the mouthpiece of the landed interest, voted another class into supreme power by what was finally an overwhelming majority, and the great nobles, little kings in their own sphere, with the mighty Wellington at their head, stood aside to let the hated measure pass.

How are we to account for this almost unbelievable sequel to the great victory, unless by an extension of Napoleon's dictum that in war the moral is to the physical as three to one? And indeed, in dealing with social movements, one is tempted to put it even higher. The Tory gentlemen had formed the class of all others fitted to win the war—their John Bullish self-complacency, their stolid incapacity for taking broad views or seeing anything but the task in hand, had excellently fitted them for doing the one thing needful, which was to maintain a bulldog grip on the enemy's throat until he dropped dead from exhaustion. But the bulldog is conspicuously lacking in those gifts of intellect and imagination requisite for the task of social reconstruction.

It would be ungenerous to record the failure of my

lords and gentlemen to deal with a situation so utterly
beyond precedent, without recognising to how large an
extent, in the past, they had justified their existence. If
their wealth was derived from the soil, soil that only too
frequently comprised the recently enclosed common
lands of the peasantry, they had at least worked hard
and scientifically to make that soil bear fruit. They had
mobilised the land as the new employers had mobilised
industry. From King George III, whose most lasting
title to fame is his prefix "Farmer," and who transformed
his Windsor estate from a wilderness into smiling arable
and pasturage, from the fifth Duke of Bedford, whose
agricultural gatherings at Woburn were on a scale of
princely magnificence, and Coke of Norfolk, who worked
in a smock frock and bequeathed the Norfolk rotation
of crops, down to such small gentleman farmers as Miss
Austen's—and Emma's—Mr. Knightly, with his weighty
confabulations with his bailiff, the landed gentry had
united in the task of making the land fruitful. If they
enclosed, it was at least in order that they might substitute a scientific husbandry for obsolete methods consecrated by tradition. It does not justify the methods by
which that enclosure was effected, if we acknowledge
that if an agricultural revolution had not accompanied
the first stages of that in industry, England would have
inevitably have succumbed, amid all the horrors of
famine, to the power of Napoleon. One has only to
compare the respective functions of the English squires
and French *noblesse* of the old régime, to understand the
difference in their fates.

The landowners were something more than mere

farmers. If they were often tyrants, they were not ab-
sentee rent-drawers, like the courtiers of Versailles, but
lived and worked—even the greatest and most selfish of
them—among their people. "The Duke of Rutland,"
writes Greville in 1838, "is as selfish a man as any of his
class—that is, he never does what he does not like, and
spends his life in a round of such pleasures as suit his
taste, but he is neither a foolish nor a bad man, and partly
from a sense of duty, and partly from inclination, he
devotes time and labour to the interest and welfare of
the people who live and labour on his estate. He is a
guardian of a very large Union, and he not only attends
the meetings of Poor Law Guardians every week or
fortnight, and takes an active part in their proceedings,
but he visits those paupers who receive out-of-door relief,
sits and converses with them, and tells them that he is
not only their friend, but their representative at the assembly of Guardians, and it is his duty to see that they
are nourished and protected."

No wonder then that, after witnessing a Gargantuan
banquet given by the Duke to celebrate his own birthday—the cook had had to provide for nearly four hundred retainers and others in the castle—and after hearing
Mr. Tapps, the head coachman, and "a man of great
abdominal dignity," wax eloquent in ducal panegyric,
Greville would have liked to have seen the Radical who
"sneers and snarls at the selfish aristocracy who have
no sympathies with the people."

Nor did the landowners stop short at living and working among their people. The frequently superior interest
of the English temperament in questions of sport over

those of social betterment is no doubt the despair of reformers, but it must be taken into account by the historian. With all their faults, the gentry provided splendid
entertainment. No doubt the sport of shooting, protected
as it was by savage game laws and infernal machines in
the shape of mantraps and spring guns, had little to be
said for it from the poor man's standpoint, except that
it must have provided a good deal of employment to
gamekeepers and beaters. But a fox or hare hunt was
an event in which everybody was in some degree interested, the farmers and yeomen with horses to ride, the
"happy domestics" who, we are told, caught up the
choruses that were wafted from the dining hall on the
conclusion of a day's run, the yokels who saw what they
could on foot and perhaps had the ecstatic privilege of
holloaing hounds on to the tracks of "Mr. Reynolds"—
finally the smaller squires, who were often sumptuously
and even riotously entertained by their more important
neighbours.

There is an account of one such gathering, towards the
end of the eighteenth century, at the Duke of Dorset's
seat at Knole, where, after the conclusion of something
like a thirty-mile run with the Lullingstone pack, "The
Duke took the head, as befitting his rank," but where,
under the auspices of a mightier potentate, Bacchus, distinctions of rank were soon gloriously forgotten." *

There were also the extremely popular sports of racing
and boxing, at which the gentry provided the horses and
put up the purses, but in which all were equally inter-

* The account of both the run and the dinner were reprinted—
I think some twenty years ago—in the *Kent Messenger.*

ested. In the crowds that watched these prodigiously long fights with bare fists, bucks and Johnny Raws rubbed shoulders, and were not unknown to have joined in breaking the ring. Indeed, it was a point of pride for the buck to be a man of his fists, and he did not disdain to offer the privilege of bodily combat to any bargee or butcher rash enough to insult him.

If we look at old prints of that time of brutal amusements, we shall see how the audiences at bear baitings, bull baitings, cock-fights, and even dog-fights, comprised the finest of gentlemen along with the lowest of roughs. And those two consummate young men of fashion, Pierce Egan's Corinthian Tom and Jerry, were at least anything but exclusive in their choice of amusement. They were as much at home swilling blue ruin in disreputable "sluiceries," or joining in the revels of "lascars, blacks, jack tars, coalheavers, dustmen, women of colour, old and young, and a sprinkling of the remnants of once fine girls, etc.," all jigging together at "All-Max," in the East End, as they were when footing a stately quadrille on the polished floor of the real Almack's.

If this upper class failed to maintain its ascendency in the years following Waterloo, it certainly was not owing to any lack of energy. A superabundance of vital spirits is what strikes us at once as its dominant trait. There was no epithet so popular or so coveted among its members as "manly." The manly man was a hard fighter, a hard rider, a hard liver, a hard drinker, a hard swearer and a hard lover. He was full blooded to an extent difficult to realise in an age whose stock of manliness tends to be lessened in individuals owing to the necessity of partitioning it equally between the sexes.

And except where the Evangelical leaven was beginning to work, there was a lack of self-consciousness about this outpouring of vital energy that gives it a sort of inverted innocence. Mr. Max Beerbohm's description of the youthful George IV charging about like a bull in pursuit of pleasure, applies to him equally in his latter years, and to that brilliant and bizarre circle of which he was the centre. To realise how perfectly lacking in conviction of sin was the cult of genteel pleasure-seeking, we can cite—as among the least unpublishable of similar contemporary effusions—this, from *Life in London:*

> But fornication every man enjoys—
> A smart anchovy sandwich—that ne'er cloys—
> A *bonne bouche* men are ready to *devour*—
> Swallowing a neat half-dozen in an hour.
> "Wedlock," they cry, "is a hard-pinching boot,
> But fornication is an easy shoe—
>   The first won't suit;
>   It won't do."

There were many outlets for energy besides that provided by sexual incontinence, and the heart of the governing class was less in the West End than in the countryside, to which so many of its members remained happily rooted from year's end to year's end. It was an age of great sporting characters, men who would back themselves extravagantly to perform the most unheard-of feats of physical or equestrian prowess. It was only such an age that could have witnessed the almost incredible

career of John Mytton, a Shropshire squire who, before
he had run through a fortune and shattered an iron
constitution, left an imperishable name as a man without
fear and one utterly regardless of the ordinary limitations
of nature.

He would deliberately smash the gig he was driving
against a bank, or gallop a tandem at a turnpike gate;
he would go duck-shooting in the snow with nothing on
but a night-shirt; he would ride into his drawing-room
mounted upon a bear; he would cure himself of the hic-
cups by setting his shirt on fire, a feat that all but cost
him his life and did cost him his reason. He drank at
least six bottles of port a day, besides immense quantities
of brandy. His notions of fun comprised his slyly in-
serting a red-hot coal into the pocket of some too loqua-
cious companion, laying up his private chaplain for
several weeks by knocking him over some rails, throwing
his wife's lap-dog half way to the drawing-room ceiling,
pushing the poor lady now into the lake, now into the
kennel among his pack of hounds. "Nothing," his
biographer tells us, "is impossible with God; nothing is
improbable of the late John Mytton."

His was no doubt an extreme type, but it was only such
an age that could have run to such extremities or accorded
them a sort of hero-worship. Stories of old Jack Mytton
are still rife in his native Shropshire. And there were
other characters scarcely less famous in their day, Captain
Ross, the owner of "Clinker," and hero of a partridge
shooting match, from sunrise to sunset, for £1,000 a
side—the match was drawn; the eccentric General Char-

retie * who, trespassing on Lord Salisbury's grounds and having had his dog shot by the keeper, promptly shot the keeper's pony, threatened to do as much for the keeper, and sent a challenge to the Marquis; there was Lord George Bentinck, not yet heard of as a politician, but more heard of than trusted as a sportsman; there was, finally, the great, little George Osbaldiston, never known as anything but the Squire, equally an adept with the bat, the gun, the pistol, and the reins.

These old country gentlemen, whose individual memories have now faded like that typical epitaph on their tombstones—"He lived respected and he died lamented" —did at least drain to the dregs their cup of life, as crude and intoxicating a draught as the punch into which— horrible to relate—the sweet essences of that day's fox's brush had been piously squeezed. Nay, one noble duke even went so far as to eat Reynard's head, devilled! They appear to have been perpetually quarrelling with, and not infrequently challenging one another. They made one another the victims of the crudest practical jokes. Their manners to inferiors were of brutal roughness—not necessarily felt as a humiliation in that rough time. We have John Mytton giving one of his "horse kicks" to a groom —a dishonest one certainly, but repentant—and that celebrated M.F.H., Mr. Musters, answering, quite as a matter of course, a yokel, who had informed him, correctly, that an earth was empty: "What can you know about it, you clodhopper?"

Perhaps nothing re-creates the atmosphere of this time so vividly as a shooting story I heard told, by an old Vic-

* See *Echoes Old and New* by Ralph Nevill, pp. 257-61.

torian gentleman, of the Duke of Wellington. It appears that some unfortunate sportsman had managed to pepper His Grace's gaiters through a hedge. Prompt in action as ever, the now aged victor of Waterloo rasped out— "Who shot that bird? Hold up his hand!" and as soon as the hand was displayed, put a charge of shot through it.

What might surprise us most, if we could take a journey in reverse gear on Mr. Wells's time machine, with an entrée to upper class society, would be its extraordinary grossness. Even though England was giving an unquestioned lead to the rest of Europe in the matter of cleanliness, baths, an Anglo-Indian importation, were few and far between, and the diminutive washstands tell their own tale. Sanitary arrangements were both primitive and noisome, though one certainly does read, in a letter to her mother from a young lady on a town visit, a rapturous account of her hostess's newly installed water closet. Even more conspicuous was the grossness of mind and conversation. One has only to delve into the more obscure literature of the time to realise how crudely Rabelaisian was the tone of male society. Caricaturists delighted in making human beings as disgusting as a brilliant pencil could. Jutting lips, enormous buttocks, bulbous bosoms, were what illustrators appeared to revel in. Nothing is spared—men being sick, women belching into each other's eyes, and episodes of an even cruder nature. Rabelaisian toasts were a feature of masculine conviviality, until Lord Melbourne, on the young Queen's accession, pressed for their discontinuance.*

There is a different tale to tell regarding female upper class society. The coarse sports and amusements of the

* Ralph Nevill, *op. cit.,* p. 228.

male gentry were not supposed to be shared by their women folk, who thus filled an important function as guardians of the refinements and amenities of life. Not a few of them, however, had their full share of the robust and defiant individualism so characteristic of the time: such a one for instance as Lady Hester Stanhope, whose career surpasses, in daring originality, that of the most famous lady explorers of our own day, travelling, as she did, under the escort of only a cowardly doctor and a terrified maid, into the wildest spots and among the most ferocious sheikhs of the untamed Near East.

One is struck by the independence of upper class women at this time. The confidences of Byron to Lady Melbourne shed a strangely modern light on the private lives of his numerous fair, and aristocratic, adorers. His position as host was decidedly embarrassing when Lady Frances Webster openly announced at the dinner table that she would not share a room with her husband when at Newstead; he also found the husband's confidences rather embarrassing to the effect that Frances declined to bear him more children. Mary Chaworth, who married the sporting Mr. Musters to whom we have already referred, left him on account of his addiction to vulgar mistresses. And which of our bright young things can surpass the Lady Caroline Ponsonby, who married the future Lord Melbourne, who used to disguise herself as a page in order to obtain admittance to Byron's rooms, who forged his hand in order to get his portrait from Murray's, and who, finally, entertained her friends by burning her too unresponsive lover in miniature, to the accompaniment of Sabbatical incantations?

But the typical lady of the squire class, in the twenties,

appears to have lived a life not very different from that described by Jane Austen, except that as the eighteenth century receded into the past, the quality Miss Austen so much prized, that of urbane reasonableness or "sense," was more and more being displaced by the new, romantic "sensibility."

Even in the country, social intercourse was crowded with gaiety. Reading old diaries of that time, one is struck by the incessant round of amusement trodden by the average young woman in what we should now know as the county set. The circle in which she moved was rigidly circumscribed, but within that circle the amenities must have been very delightful, after what we should now consider a rather simple fashion. There were perpetual balls, dinners, parties, and tea-drinkings, the last taking place in the late evening, subsequently to dinner, which would be served somewhere round about 6. The assembly rooms at the nearest market town were a great centre of entertainment, and on the whole a young lady, living in county society during the eighteen twenties, must have found it a good deal less dull than her counterpart nowadays.

As for town society, it was the Court that set the tone, and George IV—who surely had unrivalled opportunities for knowing—had declared, when Prince of Wales, that he knew only two honest women in London. Since then the growing vogue of romantic sensibility had encouraged susceptible charmers to consider all bonds, including that of the marriage vow, well snapped for love. Such characters as the Lady Wanton of *Life in London* must have been pretty common, even within the jealously guarded portals of Almack's.

A feature of the time is the stress laid upon accomplishments. References in diaries are continually being made to performing upon the harp, trying the new pianoforte, or studying Italian. In the entourage of Tom and Jerry the very "Cyprians" of a superior order make a point of their Accomplishments, with a big A, not the least of these being the modish execution of "that lascivious dance," the waltz. In comparison with their Victorian successors, ladies seem to have done little work with their hands, except for the strangely popular pursuit of netting purses—and one wonders what can have become of all the immense output of this industry, or how far the demand was kept up by the activities of Artful Dodgers!

A *grande dame,* Lady Ailesbury, writing in 1810, thus delivers herself:

"I . . . abominate the modern education of females. The drift of it is to make them artists and nothing else, which, if they were to earn their bread, might be useful. The mind and morals are never thought about, the head is cramfull of rubbish. My eldest granddaughter is said to be fourteen; there can be no doubt she is, for she was sixteen last birthday. She is not a fool, but in mind and manners a baby, but not young, none of the cordiality and candour of youth, very cold manners, and the only specimen of being like a woman is a propensity to quiz: a kind of nondescript being.*

The modern girl seems to get more modern the further she recedes in time.

* *Gleanings from an Old Portfolio,* Vol. III, p. 270.

CHAPTER III

A PHYSICAL CULTURE

Now that we have seen something of the upper class life in the generation preceding the Reform Bill, we shall be less astonished at the failure of the landed gentry to maintain that virtual monopoly of political power that, at the time of Waterloo, seemed unassailable. These squires and noblemen had certainly enough and to spare of vital energy; they fulfilled their own ideal of being thoroughly and robustly manly. But a wealth of energy, without a corresponding wealth of intellect, runs to waste in unprofitable channels—the pursuit of pleasure in town, the pursuit of sport in the country, are carried on with no less concentrated earnestness than had sufficed for the classical Renaissance in the fifteenth century or the young Church of the first century.

Nobody can study the records of this time, without realising how rapidly the old, eighteenth century culture was running to seed. There was certainly a great deal of literary lion hunting, and the enormous success of Byron's Oriental poems show that there was still an upper class demand for good work, of a rather obvious kind. There were also intellectual centres like Holland House, with its brilliant Whig circle, but even here the brightest scintillations were struck from representatives of the middle class, men like Macaulay, Wilkie and Mackintosh. Certainly the mightiest and the most ethereal poetry of the time came, respectively, from a peer, and a youth, who—to the confusion of modern critics—somehow failed to be a Celt, and issued from a family of South-country squires. But their own class showed their appreciation of Byron and Shelley by making England too hot to hold the one and ignoring the other. And they found no successors.

The two principal organs of Tory culture, *The Quarterly* and *Blackwood's,* constituted themselves into a veritable inquisition for the suppression of budding genius. Whether or not one of them performed the feat of killing John Keats may be open to question, that they did their generous best—*The Quarterly* by trying to annihilate a poem of which its reviewer admitted having read no more than the first few lines, and *Blackwood's* by the vilest personal abuse—there can be no question whatever. In all the records of Philistinism, naked and triumphant, there is nothing capable of vying with *The Quarterly's* effort to dispose of the *Prometheus Unbound,* in which one of the sublimest passages in English poetry is printed as prose, and left, as sure and final evidence of Shelley's damn-worthiness, for the perusal of *The Quarterly's* readers. These effusions, whose enormous pomposity must have demanded a certain skill, of a kind, were seldom the work of gentlemen born, but more often of their jackals, such hacks as Gifford, such converted revolutionaries as Southey.

No doubt, as compared with that of our own day, the standard of upper class culture will appear high—perhaps even highbrow. A certain distinction—even if it were a pompous distinction—of speech and writing was required of every gentleman, and was exacted by him from the writers who catered for his needs. His very slang was ordered by rules as elaborated as those that had governed the composition of his "construe" at Eton. Here is a specimen of the sort of conversation that was expected from a young man about town, the funny man of the Tom and Jerry saga, Bob Logic, "the Oxonian":

"So say I, and you may travel from Dan to Beersheba and cry 'all is barren.' But I am not one of that description. I am for life and a curricle, and as it is the *opinion* of a noble Law Lord, given without a *fee,* a man of the most distinguished talents and eloquence, *that a little* MIRTH *in this* MELANCHOLY LIFE is a *good thing,* I mean to act upon it. The *unmasking* at the supper table, my dear boy, you will enjoy, as it is often a great source of laughter and surprise, when it discovers the faces of numerous acquaintances who have been playing off their wit and raillery against each other all the evening, under their various disguises. A MASQUERADE is an *unsorted* class of society, I readily admit, but . . . if you keep *aloof* from mankind on that account, you may soon become a crying philosopher, afraid to stir from your own fireside, in order to prevent *contamination,* and be devoured by hypochondriacism the remainder of your days. It principally depends, in my humble opinion, on the strength of mind possessed by the persons themselves."

At this point, we are told, Logic, who was already well primed with liquor, was interrupted by their arrival at Covent Garden for the night's orgie. It would be an interesting exercise to translate his harangue into modern Oxonian. This extraordinarily florid habit of genteel speech and writing is characteristic of the time, and Surtees's Pomponius Ego is so closely modelled on the renowned sporting critic, "Nimrod," as hardly to be a caricature. A perusal of surviving correspondence, or of the columns of Hansard, is enough proof that to express oneself like a gentleman demanded at least a veneer of acquaintance with the classics, and a reasonable proficiency in the sort of drill by which English prose had been redeemed from its seventeenth century indiscipline and made to keep time by correct Johnsonian measure.

But this upper class culture, though it might masquerade in the forms of the eighteenth century, retained little of its spirit. There was no scope in the twenties for the urbane magnificence of a Chesterfield or Horace Walpole's inexhaustible capacity for elegant trifling. Such a life as Gibbon's, such steady concentration of purpose on one intellectual end, such serene elevation above the insular and the provincial, had no counterpart after Waterloo, nor is it easy to conceive of one of the friends of George IV's last years plunging, like Charles Fox, into Euripides, to console himself for the loss of a fortune at the tables.

It is not only in speech and writing that the decline of upper class culture, since the eighteenth century, is apparent. The great gentlemen of that age of knee-breeches and ruffles may have shamefacedly exploited their monopoly of political power, they may have led selfish and scandalous lives, but they did at least impose a standard of good taste on those who ministered to their well-being. They built for themselves suitably imposing mansions, they surrounded themselves with lovely furniture, they had themselves painted by masters, they filled their libraries with beautifully bound copies of all purchasable English and foreign classics; their dress, their deportment, elegant without ostentation, proclaimed them artists of life.

All this gradually altered with the coming of the nineteenth century. The demand for beauty is no longer insistent or discriminating enough to call forth supply on anything like the old scale. The great age of furniture ends with Sheraton, and though the decline to the Early Victorian is not as steep or catastrophic as people, who have not studied the matter for themselves, are wont to believe, only affectation could pretend that there can be any comparison of nineteenth with eighteenth century furniture. It is the same with the manufacture of porcelain, despite the stimulus that this had obtained from the improved processes that were a by-product of the Industrial Revolution. But beauty is born of the soul and not of the machine, and all the wheels and chimneys of the Black Country could not give birth to one little china shepherdess of the lost exquisiteness, or perpetuate the secret of Wedgwood.

The mansions that were put up to house the great landowners, and to express their dignity, show a similar falling off from eighteenth century standards. They ceased, in fact, to be dignified, and became merely pretentious. This was not from lack of means to carry on the old tradition. The early nineteenth century was a time of high rents and lavish expenditure, and many of the finest houses in the kingdom were built, or drastically reconstructed, during this time. During the Regency, the classic tradition was enjoying a St. Martin's summer in the stucco and plaster architecture of Nash, but in the country the Gothic fashion had set in, and nothing would suffice our county magnates but to surround themselves with the trappings of feudalism, in the style of a Walter Scott novel. The typical eighteenth century mansion, with its foursquare honesty of construction and its not inharmonious classical portico, did at least express with perfect sincerity its owner's ideal of intellectual elegance. But now the mansion had turned into a castle, sprouting wholly useless battlements and bristling with towers that served no purpose either of defence or convenience. If it expressed anything, it was the desire of a rather stupid person to impress everybody in view with his own importance.

This architecture of shams was capable of the most ridiculous extravagances. It was not without reason that its most conspicuous efforts have been christened "follies," the prototype of them all having been Beckford's monkless Abbey of Fonthill, which cost half a million pounds to put up, and soon tumbled down like a card-house, being unprovided with foundations. The newly castellated strongholds of feudal baronage in top boots, if less palpably unsound, were far less interesting than Beckford's expensive toy. They were, at best, dull, the type of building described in guide-books as "handsome and imposing." At worst they were monuments of vulgarity. I have in mind one noble mansion, which had perhaps better be nameless, in which almost every available bit of surface was used for the display of coronets and coats of arms, and in which, according to a contemporary pic-

ture, one of the machicolated turrets was actually surmounted by a gigantic coronet.

Even in dress—at least so far as men's dress is concerned—and manners, there is a marked decline from the
standard of taste that had prevailed before the Revolution.
It was unfortunate that George IV and his brothers, who
were the natural leaders of polite society, and whose influence might have kept alive the tradition of Versailles,
were essentially vulgarians, whose German ancestry was
displayed in a certain full-blooded grossness, and a heavi-
ness of touch, but who were wholly lacking in German
depth and soulfulness. The society of the Pavilion and
Carlton House, with its monotony of drinking, drabbing,
and damning, might have made Charles II turn in his
grave!

The eighteenth century had been the heyday of elegance
in dress, especially male dress, as the heavy wigs and
clothes of the Pudding Age gave way to the more graceful
fashions that prevailed during the first half of George III's
reign. The Revolution here, as elsewhere, had its influence in upsetting standards of aristocratic taste. The one
definite gift we accepted from the Jacobins was the top
hat, of portentous import. It was a harmless, even a
pretty thing, in its infancy, shaped like an inverted
flower-pot; but the flower-pot was father to the cylinder,
that funereal extinguisher of the old finery and *joie-de-
vivre*.

For a time there was an over-emphasis on dress, a
sartorial self-consciousness, that was the sure prelude of
decadence. The Regency, in particular, was a time of
dandies, men like Beau Brummell, whose whole energies

were concentrated and whose fortunes squandered on their personal adornment. Even about the great Beau himself, with his perpetual, self-assertive insolence, there is a certain element of what a later age would have describe as the bounder. But in dress, he was an artist of an almost classic restraint; his aim was the self-satisfaction that comes from perfect achievement; he was above the vulgarity of soliciting attention to himself by consciousness of attire. Lord Byron—no mean judge—declared that there was nothing remarkable about his dress except a certain exquisite propriety. This, however, could not have been said of the generation of dandies that flourished in the later twenties, and included the young Disraeli, with his oiled locks and bejewelled fingers—Disraeli, who scandalised the Governor of Malta by paying his respects in Andalusian garb—least of all could it have been said of that French leader of English fashion, Lady Blessington's enamoured Count d'Orsay, whose costume and appearance constituted a masterpiece of flaunting self-advertisement. And beyond d'Orsay lay the sombre wilderness of utilitarian respectability, and the Victorian top hat, grown into a monstrous extinguisher, put out the last lights of Georgian dandyism.

The French Revolution, which had swept the aristocracy of Versailles to exile and the guillotine, had affected the English upper class in a more subtle, but, in the long run, hardly less injurious way. For that class was now cut off from its most fruitful source of inspiration and thrown back upon its own insular resources. *"La brutalité anglaise"*—as its vaunted "manliness" was called South of the Channel—luxuriated unchecked. The

Horace Walpoles, the Chesterfields, and the Gibbons, left no successors, unless we are to count that ineffable young novelist, who wore stays and poured out his romantic soul in highly artificial but quite inexhaustible prose—Bulwer-Lytton. The breed of Squire Western had prevailed as surely as the pretty red squirrels, in our own time, have been driven out by their stronger and less attractive grey cousins. What wonder that the Upper Class Tories could not retain the leadership of the nation, when their own ranks could no longer furnish leaders for themselves, but had perforce to submit to the thoroughly bourgeois Peel, and, after him, to a hated and despised Jewish parvenu, who happened not only to have been born in a library—for that matter any great country seat would probably have been found to contain as fine a collection of books as the house of old Isaac Disraeli—but to have used it for the enrichment of his brains. Where the treasure is—whether in the library or the hunting field—there will the brain also thrive or run to seed.

CHAPTER IV

MECHANISATION

W<small>HILE</small> the people who enjoyed, in so unstinted a measure, the blessings of leisure and vital energy, were thus squandering both in muscular debauches or in the satisfaction of their cruder instincts, beyond their park walls and stucco frontages a revolution was taking place more momentous in its consequences than that of Jacobin France, only in England the aristocrats had not the sharp reminder of the *Place de la Révolution* to bring home to them the realities of the situation. Rather did they resemble those Olympians of Lucretius, who, secure in their adamantine palaces, dreamed and banqueted in sublime indifference to whatever might be the fate of the teeming hordes of men below.

When the 10th. Hussars, in which Beau Brummell had condescended to hold a commission, were ordered to Manchester, in 1798, this distinguished cavalry officer promptly left the service. "I really could not go," he explained to his friend, the Prince of Wales. "Think, your Royal Highness, Manchester!" This—in the year of the Second Coalition, the Nile, and the great Irish Rebellion —certainly does give food for thought:

This is not the place to detail the history of the Industrial Revolution. We are gradually, and only gradually, beginning to view that tremendous process in sober perspective. Appreciation of it has passed through four phases, which are distinct enough, though it would be hard to say where any one of them begins or ends. During the first of these, no great account was made of the Industrial Revolution. Just as soldiers of the old school were unwilling to soil their uniforms by dabbling with the products of science, so the old type of historian felt that the dignity of his prose was better sustained by wars and genteel politics than the wages of cotton-spinners and the woes of chimney sweeps. Accordingly the History of England is vastly concerned as to whether a vulgar Queen had or had not added the embraces of a menial Italian to those of a priapic monarch, it waxes epical over the drowning and shelling to death of a number of Turks at Navarino, and it is never tired of unravelling the political combinations that preceded the Reform Bill, and subsequently exhausted the talents of those large men in stocks and whiskers, who used to impress one's boyish imagination so much in the pre-fire Madame Tussaud's.

Gradually, as the Victorian head expanded in harmony with the Victorian stomach, it began to be realised that something important really had taken place, that could be comprehended neither under the heading of slaughter nor that of intrigue. Progress had been at work, a Deity more inevitably beneficent in his mysterious workings than any of those worshipped in temples made with hands. He was a veritable god from the machine, machinery that got better with every passing day. The improving Sunday book was reinforced by the weekday horror that strove to interest the young mind in the exploits of George Stephenson and the inventors of jennys and power looms. The Industrial Revolution was a time when villas had replaced cottages, and such lovely cities as Salford and Sheffield had expanded out of insignificance, to bask under a pillar of perpetual cloud by day. The Industrial Revolution had, in fact, been the time when John Bull, like certain carp at Versailles, had developed the capacity of getting fatter and fatter through an indefinite period of time—perhaps for ever. And what more could any worshipper of Progress demand from his god?

With the dawning of a new century Progress began to go out of fashion. The condition of the People began to be talked about, and Class War, and the gospel of Karl Marx. Earnest researchers began to look a little more closely into this business of an Industrial Revolution, and, like the apostles of Progress before them, discovered exactly what they had come to look for. The suffering, the cruelty, the squalid horror involved in the process of mechanising England, were set out in the dry light of statistics and established by the evidence of long-forgotten documents. Pity and indignation were enlisted in the support of preconceived theory. The Revolutionary stage was set for a melodrama, whose villains consisted of common-enclosing landlords and skinflint factory owners. The whole of the possessing classes would appear to have been leagued in heartless conspiracy to appropriate the fruits of toil from their simple and pathetic producers. This was a story that lost nothing in the telling by earnest propagandists.

But melodrama is a crude form of entertainment, and less interested research is beginning to show that the Industrial Revolution was, in the profoundest sense, a tragedy, in which "no villain need be." The fevered imagination of a Shelley might cast the heads of the State for the parts of embodied Murder, Hypocrisy and Fraud, but take them for all in all, the landowners and employers of England appear to have been neither heartless nor predatory, and indeed the principal fault with which they are to be charged is that, when they were confronted simultaneously with the most formidable military opponent we had ever faced and a social transformation unprecedented in history, their thoughts moved in the old grooves and were incapable of devising more than hand-to-mouth expedients for tiding over an immediate crisis.

Even the enclosure of the commons turns out to have been a device on the part of genuinely improving landlords for ending an intolerable system and making two blades of corn grow where one had grown before. It can fairly be claimed that if the land of the country had not been mobilised in this way, Napoleon would have starved us out. The hardship of the scheme consisted in the fact that the big man could afford to enclose and the small man could not, so that something more than a formal equality was required in the distribution of burdens. To such heights of imaginative generosity the governing class failed to soar, and the formal justice that they generally sought and ensued turned out to be ruinously unjust in practice. Villains were they none, but human beings, with an all too human bias in adjudicating on cases to which they themselves were parties.

Nor were the horrors of the early factory system—dire as they undoubtedly were—due to any special wickedness on the part of employers or governments.

Inhuman conditions of employment, long hours, and low wages, were rife long before the Industrial Revolution. The most crying scandal of all, that of the boy chimney sweeps, stunted, terrorised, half-starved little wretches, was a heritage of the polite century, and had nothing whatever to do with the new inventions. It does not appear, according to the weighty authority of Dr. Clapham, that the standard of living of the average workman was in any way depressed by the advent of machinery. Its tendency was in fact to rise. And the enormous increase of population turns out to have been due principally to the fact, not that the birth-rate had increased, but that the death-rate had, since 1740, been steadily going down, owing to improved sanitation and the advance of medical science.

The real tragedy of the Industrial Revolution lay in the fact that it demanded an utterly different type of mind to effect the necessary adjustment of life to its new conditions, than had sufficed for the requirements of eighteenth century civilisation. The idea that the new centres of population might be made as beautiful as any Florence or Nuremberg, would have struck that hard-headed generation as excellent fooling. Not even the most advanced politicians of the eighteenth century had envisaged what we should now call social reform as an essential part of statesmanship. And during those all-important years when the social problem was beginning to clamour for solution, their wills were almost entirely bent to the purpose of beating the foreign enemy.

Such a statesman as the younger Pitt, whose prudent administration of the national finances had raised the country, in a few years, from the depths of depression following a disastrous war to something like her former prestige and affluence, might conceivably have been great enough to have comprehended and mastered the new situation, had he been free to give it his undivided attention. But Pitt was lifted up in the nation's eyes as the man who could save England from an immediate and crying peril. He was the pilot who weathered the storm. And a pilot in a storm has no time to undertake an overhaul of the vessel.

As an expedient for tiding over the crisis, it is probable that the magisterial socialism by which wages were supplemented out of rates and some sort of employment provided for all, was about as humane and effective as any that could have been devised. Its bad effects, particularly in increasing the pauper population, seem to have been exaggerated. No doubt, as a permanent solution of the problem, a measure that at one time placed about a quarter of the population on the rates was demoralising to the last degree. But it enabled the country to carry on during the war, and to make some sort of provision for the population that Napoleon was trying to starve out.

The measure that made combinations among workmen illegal ought to be regarded as one of martial law, and we can only understand the motives of its authors by putting ourselves into their position, with the spectacle of triumphant revolution before their eyes, and the exaggerated but very understandable fear in their hearts of secret societies or combinations that might harbour the germ of Jacobinism. Above all, it was necessary to keep the wheels of industry going without friction. It was cotton that beat Napoleon.

After the war, the habits of mind ingrained in the Tory rulers were too strong to be eradicated. Napoleon had gone to Saint Helena, but the Jacobin menace was ever before their eyes. A revolutionary spirit, they felt, was abroad; the least pandering to democratic ideals might open the floodgates of revolution. They had come to worship the Constitution as if it were something perfect and unchangeable—a panacea against every sort of evil. The very idea of a reorganisation of society would have filled most of them with terror, though some of the intellectuals among them, like Coleridge, Wordsworth and Southey, were putting out cautious feelers in the direction of social reform. But even with their Whig opponents, reform seldom meant much more than reforming the franchise.

But while those in authority averted their eyes from reality and allowed things to take their course, the greatest of all revolutions was gathering momentum. Steam power had come to reinforce machinery, and now the railway and the steamboat were beginning to revolutionise transport. A new England was springing up in the North and Midlands, that not the wildest stretch of imagination could have described as "merrie." Squalid and smoke-begrimed towns grew with mushroom rapidity, providing some sort of shelter for enormous herds of human beings, worked to the limit of endurance and cut off from all the beauties and amenities of civilisation. It was a spectacle that caused such a heart as Macaulay's to rejoice greatly. God—if we are allowed to assume His existence—may perhaps have wept.

CHAPTER V

THE BOURGEOIS REVOLUTION

As the war, and the French menace, receded into the past, it became more and more apparent that some sort of adjustment of the social order to its rapidly changing circumstances had got to be made. Crusted reactionaries, like the Lord Chancellor Eldon, were becoming more and more of an anachronism—to the young Disraeli he was "Lord Past Century." It was something like a forlorn hope when the Iron Duke assumed the premiership in a supreme effort to arrest the forces making for change, as he had held up Masséna before Lisbon, and Napoleon before Brussels. But now he found himself helpless to maintain discipline among his own headquarters staff, and the choice of Talavera and Burgos was repeated, between retreat and annihilation. The saviour of his country could not preserve his own window panes, and was once in no small danger of being murdered in the streets—and on Waterloo day! The victor of a hundred fights had become a figure of fun, an old woman with a mop trying to hold up the tide.

But assuming that a change was to come, from what quarter were its direction and driving impulse to be looked for? Not, evidently, from the class entrenched in power by the existing Constitution. Genius like that of Thomas Smith, whose system of casting hounds is a model to such modern masters as may chance not only to ride but to read, might have been capable of equally enduring achievement in the planning of towns or in raising the conditions of the people.   If all the talent and energy spent in avenging the rape of hen-roosts and compassing the downfall of partridges, had been mobilised for the things that really mattered, the gentlemen of England might indeed have loosened their hold on the rotten boroughs, but established it for generations upon the affections and support of the people in all Europe most loyally disposed towards leaders they can respect.   What, in the Young England movement, was only a romantic dream, might have become a reality, though whether in the long run to be wished for or deplored is a matter in which opinions may differ.

But if the upper class—that of the landed gentry— was thus tried and found wanting, still less was salvation to be looked for at the other end of the social scale. From the country labourers, the Johnny Raws and Chawbacons, whom the loss of their commons had sunk into a condition of wage-slavery and wholesale pauperisation, the utmost that could be expected was such blind and futile resentment as broke out in the Swing Riots, when threshing machines were broken up and the night sky flickered with the reflection of rick-fires.   As for the new industrial districts, the masses of overworked men, cut off, for the most part, from any environment or influence that could possibly make for civilisation, could hardly be expected to rise above the brutality and brutishness of the gin-sodden, eighteenth century mob that had burned down Newgate in the cause of true religion, and a scientist's library in that of patriotism.   There was indeed an aristocracy of labour already beginning to form, skilled and often highly paid mechanics and engineers, striving for the improvement of their minds in institutes, but this was as yet too small a leaven to affect the whole lump. The brutalities and defeats of early trades unionism, the pricking of the great Chartist bubble, were proof enough that the hour for the working class had not yet struck. It needed many years of education and experience in self-help, before it would be able to come forward with a practical policy of its own, and leaders capable of executing it.

So that, whatever the need might be of reform, in a wider sense than that understood by the politicians, it is certain that neither among the upper nor the lower ranks of society was there the mind or the will to undertake it. By a process of exhaustion, this task, if it was to be undertaken at all, must devolve upon a middle class, already more important in England than in any other country, and whose power was continually growing. There is no need to split hairs over the definition of what, for all practical purposes, is well enough understood. In the twenties, the boundary between upper and middle was recognised on both sides, and was that which, at the county ball, separated the gentry, who danced at the top end of the room, from their humble admirers and imitators who occupied the rest of it. It was a boundary none the less respected from the fact that individuals were not infrequently permitted to pass over. Between middle and lower, the exact frontier may have been a little harder to trace—it would have run somewhere between the Cratchit and the Weller families—but on which side should we put Mr. Bumble?

It has been the strength of English society, that though it had its class distinctions, it never had anything like the caste exclusiveness that was the ruin of the French *noblesse*. English history moreover resembles a fairy tale, in which the most important rôle is that of the younger son, who goes out into the world to seek his fortune. Those hordes of sons and daughters, stiffly huddled on their knees, one behind the other, at the foot of parental monuments, had their way to make, by work or by marriage, and followed the main chance with little enough regard for the restrictions that would have bound a Frenchman of noble blood to the service of Christ or of Mars. Many of them ventured overseas, in every sort of capacity from planter to pirate; some of them entered the ranks of honourable trade at home, thinking it no scorn even to be bound as apprentices.

On the other side, prosperous burghers and substantial yeomen, who formed the middle class in Stuart times, and who had been the backbone of the Great Rebellion, were by no means disposed to truckle unduly to the prestige that comes by blood. Your alderman, whose profits in trade suffice for his commemoration in Church, will stick out his marble stomach as portentously or engrave his tablet as pompously as the finest gentleman ever enclosed in lead. And this was no new thing, for as far back as the Middle Ages, royalty itself had not been ashamed to sit at the board of a Bristol shipowner or to connect itself by marriage with a family of Hull merchants.

It is probable that the eighteenth century saw an actual widening of the social gulf between birth and trade. The court of Versailles set the standard of upper class civilisation all over Western Europe, and the formal dignity that hedged those gentlemen with powdered hair and knee breeches, who trifle so elegantly in engravings like those of Woollett, made them probably more unapproachable than the rough and ready cavaliers from whom they were descended. Quite at the beginning of the century *The Spectator* has an amusing picture, drawn from a known model, of a certain ironmaster, one Jack Anvil, who so throve that he became Sir John Enville, and married Lady Mary Oddly, a step he lived to repent, as he found himself treated with open contempt in his own house, and only recognised by his "in-laws" for purposes of sponging.

Nevertheless, money continued to talk, and to talk with increasing loudness towards the end of the century, as the opportunities for making it multiplied. A class of *nouveaux riches* began to force their way into the upper strata of society under the significant name of Nabobs, men who had squeezed fortunes out of the sweat and misery of John Company's wretched subjects in the Ganges valley. Others exploited the labour of black slaves in West Indian sugar plantations. And the Industrial Revolution was beginning to provide unprecedented opportunities for quick affluence or ruin.

At the time of which we are writing, that between Waterloo and the Reform Bill, there was probably as much formal exclusiveness hedging the charmed circle of London and county "society," as at any time since the

Reformation, and the young gentleman of the period would probably have been much more chary of soiling his hands with trade than his ancestor in the sixteen twenties. But money is power, and in a society like the English, where the whole stock of blue blood is exhausted after the first male birth, social prestige will tend, slowly but irresistibly, to express itself in terms of bank balances. Money was a commodity too urgently in demand not to be bartered—after however prolonged and discreet a chaffering—for recognition or dignity. That very businesslike champion of Toryism, Mr. Pitt, fully understood with what fuel the furnaces of party machinery are stoked, and Mr. Pitt controlled the fountain of honour. It would have been a pity to let those golden and expensive waters run to waste in fertilising unremunerative merit. Corruption in politics was of course no new thing, but the old methods of Walpole and Newcastle were behind the times. The essence of eighteenth century corruption was the purchase of votes by money. The nineteenth century specialised more and more in the purchase of money by what was, with unconscious irony, known as honour. This was the outward and visible sign of the preponderance of monetary power having shifted from land, and therefore from birth, to business.

It is significant that when Pierce Egan wanted to depict the *ne plus ultra* of dashing gentility in his Corinthian Tom, he should have made that hero the son of a self-made man.

The invisible barriers stood, but they could be, and

were, scaled by individuals who climbed to the top on their own money bags. The law had always provided a ladder for humble merit to climb by, and even medicine, though the ordinary doctor was still treated as not much better than the old-fashioned apothecary, was not without its prizes. The Prime Minister Addington, afterwards Lord Sidmouth, whose charming and pious exterior masked an abysmal mental vacuum, was the son of a fashionable physician, and on this account was saddled with the contemptuous nickname of "Doctor." The effect of the Industrial Revolution may be seen in the rise of the Peel family, originally of yeoman stock. The father of the great Sir Robert had made a fortune out of the new cotton-spinning machinery, and been duly rewarded, by Mr. Pitt, with a baronetcy. The son, whose talents eventually enabled him to take over, from the politically bankrupt Wellington, the leadership of the Tory party, brought a mind and manner typically bourgeois to its refashioning.

But those members of the middle class who achieved gentility, or affluence, were after all a very small minority. For the immense majority life was a drab struggle for existence, under the stress of merciless competition. Scant leisure was theirs, and few amenities. But this very struggle, whose intensity grew as life itself was speeded up to keep pace with its attendant machinery, acted as a forcing house of character. The middle class was as grimly in earnest in the pursuit of the main chance, as the leisured gentry in that of the fox. The great Industrial Revolution, that was transforming Western Civilisation, was, so far as it can be said to have been controlled at all, under middle class leadership and direction. From that class emanated most of the genius and nearly all of the formative ideas and ideals. Mr. Chesterton was profound as well as brilliant in talking of an age of inspired office boys.

CHAPTER VI

THE NEW RULING CLASS

W<small>HEN</small> we speak of the middle class at the opening
of the Victorian Age, we feel that we have entered
an atmosphere thoroughly familiar to us. When we
transport ourselves, in imagination, to one of those old
county balls, we have to confess that our friends are all
among the worthy people who are excluded from the
genteel reservation of the upper end of the room. Here,
in the ruck, we shall jostle shoulders with Mr. John Jorrocks and Mr. Caudle, Mr. Titus Ledbury and Mr. Pickwick—perhaps young Mr. Dickens himself. But if we
presume to pass that invisible barrier, we shall at once
feel ourselves outsiders. What point of spiritual contact have we with John Mytton—or Corinthian Tom,
with Count d'Orsay or Pomponius Ego? We have
passed from a familiar to an almost incredible atmosphere, and have no right to complain of the cold shoulder with which we shall be received.

There is an even deeper sense in which this atmosphere
of the middle class, at the dawn of the Victorian Age, is
familiar to us. For it is what many of us, born in the
latter years of the Queen Empress, and imbued with their
philosophy, were taught to believe in as pervading the
universe. It was not love that moved the sun and the
other stars, but merciless competition, red in tooth and
claw, with the devil perpetually taking the hindmost and

the fittest surviving, the fittest, that is to say, to survive in a universal Black Hole of Calcutta, where God's creatures fight without truce and trample one another to death for a breath at the solitary window.

It was what struck the sensitive soul of the young Heine, when he came to London, and stood amid the roar and bustle of Cheapside. "Send no poet to London," he pleads. The dreamy Teuton, who delights to stare at print and jeweller's shops, will find himself hustled from all sides, or bowled over with a mild *"God damn! God Damn!"* For John Bull, with his enormous expenses and enormous debts, has got to be racking his brains night and day to discover new machines, to be balancing ledgers with the sweat of his brow, to be ever violently on the move looking neither to right nor left, from the Docks to the Exchange, from the Exchange to the Strand. The day-long rush of humanity up and down Cheapside reminds Heine of that most dreadful of all episodes in the retreat from Moscow, the passage of the Beresina Bridge, whereon every one struggled madly forward to preserve his scrap of existence, where friends trod callously over each other's corpses, where thousands clung vainly to the planks before slipping into the ice-cold waters, and where to fall was to be lost forever.

This was what the Industrial Revolution had come to mean, when translated into terms of everyday life. Not only machinery, but life itself, had been speeded up to an extent undreamed of in the stolid days of Hogarth and Walpole. Nor was it practicable to call a halt and return to the old order of things. An English Tolstoy or Gandhi could only have effected a return—even at this early stage—to the old domestic handicrafts and common field agriculture, by passing a death sentence on millions. Machines and enclosures had brought England victoriously through the war; still more machinery and protected agriculture were what kept the population somehow alive between the starving teens and the hungry forties; after that, machinery unlimited and imported corn ushered in the piping or hooting times of the Victorian heyday.

For it gives an entirely false impression of the situation, to imagine that during the thirty years after the war, British industry was achieving anything like a rapid or easy conquest of the world's markets. The declared official value of the produce and manufactures exported from the United Kingdom was, in the year of Waterloo, about five and a half million pounds. During the whole of the twenties, without exception, the figure was well below forty millions, and it was only four years later after the Reform Bill that the fifty million mark was touched again. As late as 1842, the figure was barely forty-seven millions. Even allowing for the difference in money values caused by the return to cash payments, this tells no very flattering tale of industrial progress. The enormous, the sensational advance, when figures doubled and quadrupled—and attained to such fantastic proportions that John Bull was able to proclaim himself the world's shopkeeper, banker and paragon of success —these were to come in the generation following the repeal of the Corn Laws. During the twenties and thirties, English industry was fighting a dour and bitter struggle to adapt the new conditions to the attainment of honest livelihood.

In order to understand the social system of these decades, we must remember that it was based upon the existence of a privileged and leisured upper class, who alone were able to evade the unremitting toil and cut-throat competition that were the lot of those outside the pale. They alone had the leisure to live well, according to their ideals. But what ideals? Their opposite to work was play, their alternative to thinking of the main chance was to think as little as possible. And so they ceased to lead—almost ceased to count—in the shaping of whatever new order was to be born of the chaos below.

The middle class man had the advantage that he was at least in contact with reality, though a hard and sordid reality. If he worked for a salary, he was more often than not compelled to put up with such sweating as a Scrooge might exact from his clerk or a Squeers from his usher. If he were in business of his own, let him work never so hard, the spectre of ruin was continually dogging his footsteps. Even if, like Hudson the railway king, he soared to fabulous wealth, his fall might be equally sudden and sensational. The advance of trade was no steady progress, but proceeded by a series of violent convulsions. Hectic booms would alternate with panics, when bankruptcy among the masters was translated into unemployment among the hands, and misery stalked the land. There was no such thing in those days as limited liability. If a concern failed, all connected with it, even the shareholders, became liable for its debts. A far greater proportion of savings than at present was invested in local banks, which not infrequently defaulted. What this might mean to some helpless widow, or maiden lady, who might wake up to find her little income vanished into thin air, is told in *Cranford*.

In the literature of the time we are continually being reminded of that grotesque limbo, the debtors' jail. It was to this that the losers in the struggle for survival were consigned, out of sight and mind, and to many of them Dante's inscription might well have applied—"All hope abandon, ye that enter here!" It was a system that cut both ways, for while it frequently doomed the honest but unfortunate to eke out an existence of hopeless misery, it allowed many a really fraudulent debtor to live securely within the "rules" and snap his fingers at his creditors.

The field was, in fact, set for such a struggle of all against all as certain ultra-Darwinians have imagined to be the order of the universe and the sole condition of progress. Business was in those days a more individual affair than it is now. Fortunes like those of the Peels were built up by real factory owners, and not by the paid representatives of shareholders. The master may have been a sweater or a tyrant, but he was really the master, with a body to kick and a soul to damn, and the difference between a good and a bad master was a vital one for the employés. It was by no means unknown for a master to stand in a relation almost paternal to those who toiled for him, but most of them were new men, without traditions, and themselves driven on, by stress of competition, to extract every penny, by almost any means. Humanity was among the many luxuries that these stern and laborious men had to deny themselves. Business, with them, was emphatically business.

Among such a class, one can expect to find few of the amenities of life. It is highly improbable that courtesies were exchanged during the passage of the Beresina, and the roar of Cheapside must have drowned more "God Damns" than "By your leaves," on the part of colliding pedestrians. In the North and Midlands, the self-made capitalists spoke a language strange to genteel drawing-rooms, and their manners had by no means adjusted themselves to their incomes. What a small country town could be like, we can judge by Surtees's description of Handley Cross, the watering place to which Mr. John Jorrocks, that *épicier* Falstaff, was called to assume the duties of M.F.H. The humour of the description cannot detract from the unspeakable sordidness of the atmosphere, drunkenness, coarseness, and petty swindling being the only qualities that the observant Surtees seems capable of detecting in the mostly middle class society of the Spa. The natural end to a hunt dinner is a free fight; a presentation to a huntsman, who falls dead drunk on receiving it, takes the form of a watch previously stolen from his master; when the Master arrives late for a meet, the field amuse themselves by making the same huntsman drunk and incapable; the fashionable doctor of the Spa turns out to be an unctuous quack, without any degrees or qualifications; the hero himself is a gross-minded and foul-mouthed old ruffian, who cannot visit a country house, in the absence of its owner, without impersonating an expected guest and seducing the housekeeper—and his retort to the barber's wife, when she remarked that "Old Fatty's been on his back," amateurs of Victorian propriety must look up for themselves.

But London had not yet ceased to be the spiritual as well as the commercial metropolis, and it is in London that the British bourgeois is seen in all his glory, as the cockney, a word that denotes something several degrees cruder than the subsequent " 'Arry." The cockney was not only an English, but a European terror. He was primed with all the energy and self-confidence proper to a merciless struggle for survival, but as delicacy and culture had no survival value, he was almost wholly lacking in both. "He is the genius of labour," says Douglas Jerrold, "the willing slave to those worse than Egyptian taskmasters, '£. s. d.' . . . a creature expressly fashioned to toil for shillings, and for nothing more . . . His every thought, like every omnibus, runs to the Bank."

The cockney, then, was by no means lacking in good qualities of a sort, the qualities his age most prized. Like the rest of the great middle class, he was working, with heroic concentration of purpose, to make England the workshop of the world. It was only when he got away from the desk or the counter—and his chances of enjoying himself must have been scanty enough—that the blatantly aggressive side of his nature had scope. Unlike the office worker of to-day, he had no safety valve for his energies through the medium of organised games. The nearest he got to it was hiring a horse, which he had no idea of how to ride, thereby affording endless amusement to rude boys and cartoonists. On Blackheath, at Hampstead, at Sadler's Wells, on any open space easy of access on a Saturday or Sunday afternoon, he was seen in all his glory. He drank heavily. He delighted in knocking off hats, playing leapfrog, practical joking, and all the cruder forms of rowdyism. He was, particularly when in his cups, ready to use his fists on the slightest provocation. When middle age had somewhat damped his ardours, he preferred to spend his Sundays "in tavern bower or humble tea-garden," puffing his pipe and solemnly absorbing an immense quantity of very black brandy and water, after which he would return home, a little unsteadily, congratulating himself that Englishmen were very different from Papistical foreigners in their manner of honouring the Lord's day.

When he got abroad the middle class Englishman had the opportunity of impressing his English superiority on foreigners. His self-confidence increased with every mile he put between himself and his native shore. He would be aggressively manly—manliness being a monopoly of the English race—and as the bearer of a superior civilisation, he took an honest pride in flaunting his English ways and prejudices on all possible occasions. Albert Smith describes a fine specimen of his type in the Jack Johnson of his novel *Mr. Ledbury,* a sort of middle class Tom to Mr. Ledbury's Jerry. This gentleman, when he goes into Rouen Cathedral, amuses himself by blowing out the altar candles, and making faces at an aged female caretaker. In Paris, he purloins a lodging house placard and hangs it on an equestrian statue of Louis XIV. When he meets an elderly Englishwoman he starts quizzing her in a manner so brutally obvious as to arouse her indignant protest. He is, in short, what would nowadays pass for an unbelievable bounder, though in his

creator's eyes he is obviously all that can be desired of a
jolly, manly young Englishman.

It is to the womenfolk that we must look for such of
the amenities of life as could be preserved in the cock-
pit of Mammon that constituted British middle class society. But the hand of necessity was heavy on them too.
Salaries were small, and even with the low wages that
were paid to servants, the average middle class woman
was either without, or with quite inadequate, domestic
assistance, for the heavy housework that kept her nose
to the grindstone. Housework was far heavier than it
is in these labour-saving days. The home was usually
its own laundry, its own jam and preserve factory. And
the task of bearing and rearing children was exacted
with a pious and pitiless rigour.

Small wonder then, if the wives and daughters of the
bourgeoisie, with such scant leisure for broadening or
improving their minds, became narrow, and stupid, and
conventional. The wonder is that, labouring under such
disadvantages, they were able to maintain such a standard of refinement as they did. For narrow as their ideas
of good breeding necessarily were, they clung to them
with an admirable determination. It was a fiction that
was tacitly adopted in social intercourse, that a lady is
exempt from the necessity of menial employment. Accordingly, when a caller arrived, all traces of work were
hastily put away. If we may judge from one of the early
Punches, the contrast between the smiling gentility of
the evening party with the frantic labour of its prepara-
tion must have been astounding. But it is all to the
credit of these much-enduring womenfolk that they did

manage to make their parlours and drawing-rooms sacrosanct from the grossness of masculine intercourse. These performed a similar function to that of the monasteries in the Dark Ages, little islands of civilisation, however primitive, in a sea of barbarism.

That smoking was considered ungenteel in the presence of ladies, that contact between the drawing-room carpet and the sole of a boot violated a taboo, that gentlemen could be induced to patronise a dull ritual, as well as strong drink, on the Sabbath—these and similar conventions, however ridiculous in themselves, did at least impose a standard of conduct on the office worker or business man, that was not dictated by the necessity for filling his pockets and satisfying his carnal affections. It must not be forgotten that the desire to pose as ladies and gentlemen resulted in an imitation of upper-class manners which still, whatever their defects, were as yet of a much higher order than those of the middle class that was establishing its claim to rule the national roost.

Not all the results of the struggle for existence are to be entered on the debit side. If, on the one hand, it engendered grasping selfishness, and a contempt for all those things that cannot be appraised in terms of the currency, it did produce an independence and initiative, that after all are the first requisites of creative genius in any department of life. The struggle of every one against all the rest must needs—given the English temperament —foster a breed of mighty individuals; it provided the middle class with a vast store of personal energy seeking an outlet, energy that, however engendered, might find an outlet in other than merely economic channels.

And not the least important feature of the struggle was the fact that a small minority did actually succeed in coming by enough wealth to retire from the arena in affluence and comparative security. Such men were seldom of the stuff of which artists or thinkers are made —their energies had been too hopelessly specialised in one direction. But their children started with a clean sheet, and often a sufficient backing of capital to enable them to employ their inherited energy in any field, however unremunerative, that might happen to suit their talents. Such was the parentage of Ruskin and the Brownings, of Peel and Gladstone.

CHAPTER VII

THE DEITY

WHAT was the spiritual orientation of this class from which proceeded most of the leadership and creative energy at the opening of the Victorian age? We would say religion, but this word has become the property of the theologians, and our concern is with life. It is the weakness of theology that its basic terms, however hard we try to pin them down by definitions, are constantly and subtly changing their meaning, the most Protean of all being the central term, God. Most of us find our God in a mirror, not undistorted. And one true history of English Gods would form a more illuminating study than all the many of English kings at present on the market.

Certain it is that the God of eighteenth century theologians, like Bishops Butler and Berkeley, differed from the addressee of Victorian family prayers not less than Victoria herself differed from George II. A favourite Victorian text used to be: "As for me and my house, we will serve the Lord." One of those urbane and excellent gentlemen, who officiated as bishops in the Walpole era, might have preferred to put it, "as for me and my class, we will postulate the moral governorship of the Deity." And the transition from upper to middle class supremacy coincides more or less with a theistic evolution of the Lord out of the Deity.

The intuition of the artist is sometimes more illuminating than whole volumes of exposition, and perhaps the most sincere rendering of eighteenth century religion was that of a German sculptor who, with the direct earnestness of his race, represented the Founder of Christianity in a wig. Such a figure must be admitted to have been more in harmony with the spirit of the age than that of a carpenter turned preacher, inciting what Burke would have called the swinish multitude against their betters, blaspheming wealth, and brimming over with that very quality most feared and despised by men of polite breeding—namely, enthusiasm. It was plainly indecent that embodied omnipotence should be allowed to appear in public with the naked locks of a clodhopper. If there were not a wigged Deity, it was necessary to create him.

The Church of England was not capable of going to these extremes of frankness, but the Deity of its worship was a very gentlemanly person, or partnership—for there was some little difficulty in deciding whether, and to what extent, He was to remain triune. He was to be sought, not with ardours of mysticism nor tears of repentance, but by a cautious balancing of analogies or calculation of advantages. And the type of character engendered by the Deity cult—though certainly more conformable to Pilate's standards than those of his Prisoner —is, at its best, by no means to be sneered at. The eighteenth century, in England, produced a good deal of solid and commonsense virtue. There were never two more amiable characters than the philosophic bishops, Butler and Berkeley, and surely few human beings more loveable, and beloved, than Dr. Johnson. It was an age, for all its hardness, of active and increasing philanthropy. Had it been given to the ungentlemanly practice of looking its problems in the face, it might have claimed that its sober cult of the Deity was a decided improvement, for workaday purposes, on that of the Nazarene enthusiast. It was at least harmless.

But was it so harmless after all? Could so negative a faith harbour the germs of positive—even of mortal danger? Perhaps the very danger lay in the fact that the Deity was less of a *dieu fainéant* than might have appeared at first blush. If He had little of the fatherlike intimacy that comforted even in the Valley of the Shadow, or the dreadful malignancy that made torture by fire an act of faith, he was, as Bishop Butler described Him, the moral governor of the universe, and though, like that of a Hanoverian sovereign, His action was ill-defined, He did, to a certain extent, govern as well as reign.

Conformably to the political ideals of the time, this Deity was a thoroughly benevolent despot, though gifted with an unobtrusive tact that was sadly lacking in His earthly understudies. Instead of constantly interfering, He contented himself with gently tilting the scales in favour of virtue, and contrived so to manage things from behind the scenes that the cosmic drama swept forward, not without vicissitudes, towards a happy ending. Pope had announced His gospel by stating that whatever is is right, and the great Doctor Pangloss, that Voltairean Coué, expanded it into the text that all is for the best in the best of all possible worlds. Writers of fiction,

which was to all intents and purposes a new art, flew
in the face of experience and morality by contriving—
like so many deities harmonising their special creations
—that virtue should be rewarded and vice punished.
There had been a man in the land of Uz who could have
taught them better. Philosophers, like Adam Smith, depicted the Deity as acting the part of a good general,
whose strategy it is to contrive the maximum amount
of happiness at any given time in His universe.

All of which might have been no worse than harm-
lessly silly, were it not that it might exercise a fatally
paralysing influence on human effort. For a situation
was rapidly developing in which civilised man would be
faced with the task of overhauling his civilisation. Unless the Industrial Revolution were accompanied by a
social and spiritual reconstruction, the result might be
chaos or suicide. But if an omnipotent Deity happened
to be so obliging as to take the supreme control of human
affairs into His own hands, it was reasonable to suppose
that He would guide matters to some desirable end, without any revolutionary effort on the part of His creatures.
It is significant that the very Adam Smith, who was so
certain of a divinely contrived moral harmony, was also
the father of *laissez faire,* or the belief that no contrivance of statesmanship could achieve such beneficent
results as might be trusted to emerge from a witch's brew
of conflicting egotisms. Leave things alone and something—the phrase was to be that of a more splendid optimist even than Doctor Pangloss—would turn up. God's
in His Heaven—or if not God, at least something equivalent—the moral government of the universe is in safe

hands, progress in human affairs, unlike that of rivers, is inevitably upwards, in short, whatever turns up is pretty sure to be right in the best of all possible worlds. Or as the Prime Minister, Lord Melbourne, one of the last survivors into the new age of the old eighteenth century school, used to say of any proposal to better human affairs by human action: "Why can't they leave it alone?"

But the Deity was an out and out eighteenth century product, and might have been expected to pass away with the aristocratic paganism of that age. And, indeed, the urbane moral governor does fade out of the picture. Not even a nineteenth century German would depict his God in a top hat—the contemporary equivalent of a wig. The Deity, as we shall see, was being forced to yield precedence to a more formidable potentate, the King Stork of the Universe, who preferred the title of Lord. But the Deity, if He usually went about incognito, was still a power to be reckoned with. His prophets were none the less influential, because many of them imagined they had ruled a God of any sort out of the universe.

Though the form might change, the function of the Deity remained constant. It was His method to eschew overt interference with the workings of nature or the order of society, but in some subtle and usually unexplained way, He did manage to harmonise and direct them, or, to put it in another way, He sat quietly on his throne to watch the great game played out between the powers of light and darkness, having previously queered the pitch against the Devil.

His names are legion. Sometimes, indeed, He retains

His old God title, as when, through the mouth of Tennyson, He foreshadows a far off divine event as the result of His activities; He is "a power not ourselves making for righteousness"; He is a "life force"; He is the spirit of progress, the world spirit, the Unknowable, Evolution, "an increasing purpose," but always with the same amiable capacity of contriving that

> "somehow good
> Shall be the final goal of ill."

Just in that "somehow" resides the whole essence, and danger, of the Deity cult. Somehow, sometime, something will in some way turn up, and Mr. Everyman Micawber will be justified in the far-off divine event. Somehow. . . .

CHAPTER VIII

At no time, even during the eighteenth century, did the Deity, as conceived of by Anglican bishops, have the field all to Himself. He was eminently a God for gentlemen and their dependents, and there were many outside the pale, who demanded something more intimate, or exciting, for the satisfaction of their pious instincts. Not so long ago Britain had owned the omnipotence of another, very different Being, a God of Hosts and Man of War—the Lord was His name. Not urbane was He, but a consuming fire to His enemies, not remote, in the cloud-land of analogy and speculation, but a very present help to His saints in trouble. Therefore He had gone forth before His armies and prevailed, so that England had served Him for fourteen years, until she could endure it no longer, and had risen in a frenzy of joy to put the saints under the milder yoke of the sinners.

After that, for a long time in England, very little was heard of this Lord of Sinai and Geneva in upper-class circles. Charles II, who had probably had ample time for reflection on the subject while yawning under the thunder of Scottish divines, had decided that Dissent was no religion for gentlemen. Accordingly the servants of the Lord were subjected, in their turn, to very considerable persecution, and throve on it sufficiently to produce a *Paradise Lost* and a *Pilgrim's Progress*. For the Lord, despite His social eclipse, was yet a force to be reckoned with, and even succeeded in returning a *quid pro quo* for the Clarendon Code by saddling the Church of England with a modified version of the Presbyterian Sabbath.

In the early eighteenth century, the cult of the Lord was about as strong in the mercantile and shopkeeping classes, as that of the Deity in the Court and country mansions. The Whig party, which ruled supreme under the first two Georges, drew a large part of its strength from the Dissenting interest. And, of course, in Calvinist Scotland the Kirk maintained her iron grip on the affection of the people, though with a certain slackening of zeal in the torture of old women. It is Dr. Watts, who flourished in the first half of the century, who forms the most visible, connecting link between the faith of the Ironsides and that of the Dissenting and Evangelical revival that reached its height at the opening of the Victorian Age. Dr. Watts's Lord was of a terrific and unrelenting sternness, and His Hell worthy of an age notable for the increased dimensions and heat of its blast furnaces. Through the medium of his hymns, the good Doctor made the divine name more terrible to successive generations of children than that of "Boney" was ever destined to become.

I used to have an old Victorian edition of this dreadful book, in which the illustrator had actually contrived to improve upon the spirit of the author. It was not enough for Dr. Watts to have written:

> " 'Tis dangerous to provoke a God!
>   His power and vengeance none can tell;

> One stroke of his Almighty rod
> Shall send young sinners quick to Hell.
>
> Then 'twill forever be in vain
> To cry for pardon or for grace . . ."

but the artist must needs emphasise the moral by a wood-cut of a tiny tombstone, "In Memory of Annie, aged 4," leaving one to imagine poor little Annie screaming now, and through all future ages, in the most exquisite tortures, and the Lord, whose unappeasable wrath is probably exacerbated by such importunity, ordering His agent, the Devil, to see if he can stoke up one or two degrees extra. It is significant that in the hymn on Heaven and Hell, three verses are principally concerned with the latter, as compared to one with the former:

> "Can such a wretch as I
> Escape this cursed end?"

a quotation to which the answer is obviously, as the Latin grammars say, expected in the negative. It is no wonder that in the unpublished autobiography of a Victorian clergyman, I find it recorded that his first remembered experience was that of being whipped by his earthly father for burning Dr. Watts's Hymns. It is a comfort to think that some children, at least, may have had the spirit to show that vengeance by fire is a game that two can play.

In the great Methodist revival, headed by the brothers Wesley, the worship of the Lord enters upon a new phase. It takes on a feminine element that the old Puritans had lacked. The believer no longer girds on his armour against spiritual and temporal wickedness in high places; he runs, like a frightened child, to hide himself in his Mother's bosom. Being a Protestant, he dares not do this openly, the divine mother must take the form of a Saviour, even if that Saviour's name has to be feminised into "Jesu," and the grand old Hebrew battle songs supplemented by a steadily increasing collection of hymns.

In these the yearning to be mothered is a constantly recurring motive:

"Let me to Thy bosom fly," "Let me hide myself in Thee," or as the Anglican, Cowper (who elsewhere refers to "Jesu" as his husband) puts it:

> "Can a woman's tender care
> Cease towards the child she bare?
> Yes, she may forgetful be,
> Yet will I remember thee."

A marked cleavage now appears, between the entirely masculine Lord, and the partially feminine Saviour. For whatever lip homage it might be prudent to accord Him, the real emotion that the Lord aroused in His creatures was one of abject and unmitigated terror. Whitefield, the most eloquent preacher of the new movement, could throw audiences into convulsions by simply vociferating, "Oh, the wrath to come! The wrath to come!" For wrath, and that of the most malignant and implacable virulence, was the quality of the Lord that seems most to have impressed His evangelists. And to this perpetual explosiveness was added a hatred of any sort of joy or happiness on the part of His creatures, that did not directly arise out of His worship. Not only play or holidays for children (which John Wesley would have absolutely denied the poor little wretches who fell into his power), not only such hideous practices as dancing, and theatregoing, but even the drinking of that Chinese decoction called tea, were discovered to be sinful.

It was natural that the worshippers of the Lord, within or without the Anglican fold, should have been chary of expressing their real feelings about that formidable personage. Even Mr. Squeers had been able to raise a cheer from his trembling pupils on his return to Dotheboys Hall, and the expressions of love for a Being who was able instantly to consign any defaulter to eternal torment, must be taken for what they are worth.* Fear is the sentiment more often associated with Him, and though it is usually qualified by the explanation that it only means respect, it is pretty evident that it means fear, pure and simple. How could it possibly be otherwise, when for all their lip homage, His ministers are never tired of saddling the Lord with the most diabolical attributes? The Rev. William Romaine, writing after the fearful earthquake of Lisbon in 1755, treats it as a kind of divine practical joke.

"They did not imagine that God was going to destroy them that morning . . . while they were speaking peace, peace unto themselves, they were called and hurried in a moment to judgment. . . . One with an oath in his mouth was calling for damnation on his soul and it came,

* With the passing of the old militant Puritanism, the God of Battles, who went before the armies of his elect and scattered their enemies, ceases to be in demand—one of his last appearances is in Dr. Watts's magnificent hymn—the free translation of a psalm: "O God our help in ages past!"

while the words were in his mouth, and down he sunk into the pit of Hell."

But the simple evangelist, in his desire to make the most of this feat of Omnipotence, incautiously contrives to give away the real state of the case as between the Lord and His creatures. "Careless sinners," he says, "may flatter themselves with their notions of safety but . . . while the Almighty is their enemy they can have no peace." Here we have the Lord in His true colours as the sinners' enemy, in direct opposition to the sinners' friend, as represented by "Jesu." And we must remember that by Romaine's account, and that of his fellow evangelists, to say sinner is practically to say man. "This is our condition," he cries from the pulpit, "we are all unrighteous: and we are without strength to attain any righteousness of our own." The Lord, it would seem to follow from these premises, is therefore to be viewed as the supreme enemy of mankind, supreme because the Devil obviously functions only as His minister, "a revenger to execute wrath upon him that doeth evil." *Qui facit per alium, facit per se.*

Therefore the salvation that the Lord's evangelists proclaim is that of mankind from the wrath, or vindictiveness, of the Saviour's Father, a wrath rendered universal and unappeasable by a crime committed when only two members of the doomed race were alive, and a vindictiveness characterised, with unconscious humour, as just. So illogical is human nature, that this inhuman theory was capable of inciting to humane conduct. Most of the leading evangelists were men of exemplary, if singularly narrow and colourless lives. Their influence was always exerted in the direction of kindness to the poor and freedom to the slave, and they did much towards softening the brutality of English life, during and after the polite century. It was to the Son, rather than to the Father, that they looked for their examplar, but none the less, the Paternal wrath and enmity to joy cast a hardening and depressing influence over the Victorian Age.

But the chief effect of this latest version of the Protestant faith was to revive and intensify the concentrated moral earnestness that was the heritage of Puritanism. It was this quality that had made such a peculiar appeal to the men of trade and business among whom the strength of Puritanism lay.* To mortify the flesh and renounce all earthly joys may or may not have been the best way of getting to heaven, but it was a most efficient discipline for those who wanted to get on in the service of Mammon. Those hard-faced hustlers in whiskers, who swirled down Cheapside and God-damned poor Heine out of their way, had probably, most of them, worked their apprenticeship in the service of a jealous God and learnt to sharpen their energies to one fine point of individual salvation, whether from Hell in the next world or the Fleet Prison in this.

During the century following the first Wesleyan revival, the Lord's sphere of influence was continually expanding. Certainly He never ceased to be in essence—what He had started by being almost exclusively—a

---

* But the connection between Puritanism and capitalism has, I think, been made too much of in recent years. The enclosure of the commons, after all, was by a class the very reverse of Puritan.

middle-class product. But the Wesleys had made their most moving appeal to the lowest of the populace—in fact the more simple and less educated the audience, the more likely it was to be carried away by such direct appeals to the emotions as those of Whitefield. A more striking triumph was the capture of the upper class, or a preponderant part of it, by the Evangelical movement that was the counterpart of Methodism in the Church of England. This was largely due to panic caused by the spectacle of the French Revolution. Infidelity, which had formerly been quite *à la mode* in fashionable circles, was now displayed as the moving spirit of Jacobinism. Priests and aristocrats went in the same tumbrils to the guillotine, the same hands that had fired the châteaux, profaned the Host, and rent the seamless vesture of the Chartres Madonna. Religion became a matter of social as well as individual salvation. Rich gentlemen like Wilberforce began to abase themselves before the Lord and fly to the Saviour's bosom. The wives of the enclosers of commons blossomed into Lady Bountifuls. Earnest young parsons, of the type of Edmund Bertram, of Mansfield Park, began to discover other possible fields of activity than the hunting of foxes and the reading of an occasional sermon. Family pews began to fill up at service time. And the servants were subjected to the anti-democratic inoculation of daily family prayers.

Even that shrewdest of observers, Charles II, had been proved wrong in this event. Puritanism with its claws out, had become a religion fit for gentlemen. The Lord was no longer a God of Battles, except in the sense that war—as Romaine explicitly points out—was, like the plague, one of His devices for pursuing His vendetta against the House of Adam.* Out of the dawn mists by the sea at Dunbar, the Ironside squadrons had called on Him, not in vain, to arise and scatter their enemies. But the message of the Wesleyans and Evangelicals was that it is better to endure all things in this world, in the hope of that which eye hath not seen, nor ear heard, nor heart understood. The Red Flag and Internationale might arise in the future from the throats of the proletariat, but not the old psalm bidding God to arise and let the bosses be scattered.

Dr. Watts, who passed the last 26 years of his life as pensioner in the luxurious home of Sir Thomas and Lady Abney, set the social tone of the new Puritanism with his comforting assurance,

> "Though I am but poor and mean,
>   I will move the rich to love me,
> If I'm modest, neat and clean,
>   And submit when they reprove me."

and the conclusion of the whole matter was that of the Victorian hymn:

> "The rich man in his castle,
>   The poor man at his gate,
> God made them, high or lowly,
>   And ordered their estate."

* "My Christian Brother—God has declared that when a land has sinned against him by trespassing grievously, then he will stretch out his hand upon it, and visit it with his four sore judgments—the sword, the famine, the noisome beast and the pestilence. These he sends to punish the land for its grievous trespasses." Romaine, *Works*, p. 866.

By the time of the Reform Bill, the old, urbane, remote Deity had gone quite out of favour as an object of ostensible worship, though as an unacknowledged influence He was very much alive. The triumph of the Lord was complete, and coincided more or less, as might have been expected, with the triumph of His own bourgeoisie in whose image He had been made. Wesleyanism had become quite humdrum and conventional, and even the Evangelicals, now that so many of them were in fat livings, had lost some of their first, proselytising enthusiasm, and were becoming, as Dean Church assures us, on quite good terms with the world. Charles Dickens was shortly to express the normal person's dislike of the petty nonconforming "shepherd," in the same spirit as Chaucer had pilloried the begging Franciscans of his own time. The "Sims," or followers of Charles Simeon at Cambridge, were, for long after their founder's death, to focus upon themselves the dislike that even Victorian undergraduates, in the mass, were capable of evincing for aggressive piety in their own ranks. But such reactions were not in the nature of persecution, but rather the sporadic and ineffectual protests of

> "Those who were bored
> With praising the Lord"

against a social tyranny that no one seriously dreamed of defying.

If we want to know what the cult of the Lord meant for the generation that was to form the manhood and womanhood of the early Victorian Age, we can sample the literature that was forming its character during the years of childhood. As a type of its lighter manifestations, take Mrs. Turner's *Cautionary Stories,* which, though prim and priggish to the last degree, are so naïve, as to be quite delightful. Who could quarrel with the Mother who, when asked by some toddling Jacobin the pertinent question why all the choicest pleasures of the table are monopolised by the grown-ups, replies,

"Because, my dear, it is not right
To spoil the youthful appetite."

but we realise the strength of Puritan austerity, when we find even kindly Mrs. Turner commenting on the incident of a tiny boy, who steals a ride on a pony, and, of course is lamed for life, with,

"Who shall pity? Who's to blame?"

Who indeed, when a just and loving Father would have thought nothing of torturing him eternally for less than that? We remember "Annie, aged 4."

But if we want to realise the spiritual pabulum on which the Victorians were reared, we should do best of all to study Mrs. Sherwood's once famous *Fairchild Family,* a book that ran into fourteen editions between its appearance in 1818, and that of a second part in 1842. Most upper and middle class children must have been subjected to its influence, either directly, or through imitations, during this time. The fact that they were not rendered nervous wrecks for life speaks a lot for the toughness of our great-grandparents' constitutions.

Mr. Fairchild, the paterfamilias of this book, after the genial manner of parents at that time, not only models himself on the Lord, but actually borrows the divine attributes so far as his own family is concerned. That this is no exaggeration will be evident from the title of one of the chapters:

"Second story of the Misery of those who are under the Anger of God. Exemplified by the unhappiness of a Child under the Anger of his Father."

Mr. Fairchild is perfectly explicit on the subject. Henry, aged six, has played with a hare instead of learning Latin grammar, he has even had the unheard-of temerity to say that he does not want to learn Latin.

"But it is my pleasure that you should," thunders Mr. Fairchild, and then rising to the height of his divine majesty:

"I stand in the place of God to you whilst you are a child . . . therefore if you cast aside my authority and will not obey me, I shall not treat you as I do my other children. From this time forward, Henry, I have nothing to do with you: I will speak to you no more, neither will your mamma, or sister, or John, or Betty. Betty will be allowed to give you bread to eat and water to drink: and I shall not hinder you from going to your own bed to sleep at night; but I will have nothing more to do with you: so go out of my study immediately."

No wonder the poor infant, who has already been held by the manservant while his father flogs him with a horse-whip, "looked surprised and frightened" at this harangue, but Mr. Fairchild is not the man to permit his programme of divine vengeance to be thrown out of gear by an inopportune repentance. Forgetting apparently, that it is Henry who has been ordered out of the study, "Mr. Fairchild walked away with a terrible look," to arrange the boycott with the servants and other children, leaving Henry "wishing he had not been so obstinate." He has good reason to wish it during the next two days, during which the work of starving and terrifying him into submission is carried on with a thoroughness that under present day conditions would certainly lead to Mr. Fairchild being boycotted himself, if not prosecuted by the R.S.P.C.C.

But Mr. Fairchild is capable of surpassing even this performance. On one occasion, in the course of eavesdropping outside the parlour door, he hears a somewhat heated dispute about the use of a doll. The mills of parental wrath are at once put into motion. First of all the children's hands are impartially whipped, till, as the authoress records with sadistic glee, "they smarted again." Next they are deprived of all food during the morning, stood in the corner, treated to extracts from Dr. Watts's hymns, "and what was worse, their papa and mamma looked very gravely at them." But Mr. Fairchild has not yet shot his bolt. That afternoon he forces them all to accompany him to a gloomy wood, in which stands a gibbet, and "the face of the corpse was shocking." While Mr. Fairchild is just warming to the improving theme of hanging, and its varieties, "the wind blew and shook the body on the gibbet, rattling the chains," and the terrified children implore to be taken away. But Mr. Fairchild is not to be moved. Instead, he assembles them beneath the gibbet, nor will he let them go till he has delivered a long account of the murder, drawn the appropriate moral, and flopped down on the grass to deliver a prayer to his God, whom it is our nature to hate, as Mr. Fairchild somewhat naïvely admits, beseeching Him for brotherly love, "and above all, make us love our dear father and mother, and everybody who teaches us any good thing."

We must be just to Mr. Fairchild. Though he may perhaps pass for the most detestable character in all fiction—his most obvious competitor, Squeers, being a less nauseating humbug, and displaying a certain affection for his own offspring—he falls far short of the Lord, whose attributes he assumes, as a tormentor of children. Mr. Fairchild is capable of relenting after a couple of days, and even he would hardly have tortured Henry, aged 6, for an hour, as "Annie, aged 4," was and is presumably roasted alive to all eternity. And perhaps many of the parents who ostensibly modelled their family discipline on Fairchild lines, mollified it a bit when it came to practice. But one can understand the atmosphere in which the future Victorians grew up, when we realise that for so many of them, during their most impressionable years, the Lord was above, and papa, if not listening at the door, somewhere below, and lower still, a not improbable Hell.

CHAPTER IX

HAPPINESS BY THE UNIT

From what we have seen of the middle class, in its faith and works, we might be led to expect that its triumph, borne to power as it was on the crest of the Industrial Revolution, would have been one of hopeless materialism. In the later twenties, the Muses seemed to be on the point of forsaking England. The period between the death of Byron, and the rise of the first Victorian giants, is one of no great achievement or obvious promise in the realms of literature, nor did the other arts seem likely to survive the substitution of the new earnestness for the old lightness of touch. In religion, between the cooling of the first Evangelical fervour and the coming of the Tractarians, there is a similar tale to tell; while in statesmanship, except for the uninspiring figure of Peel, there arise no equal successors to the men formed in the school of Pitt and Fox.

The slate is, in fact, being wiped clean of the old aristocratic culture, and after a pause, the new lords of civilisation will scrawl it over with whatever is in their souls to express. Dominating these years of transition is the urge to get on at all costs, to accumulate, every man for himself, as much happiness as possible, and, as a means to happiness, money. The middle class was beginning to add a philosophy to its religion, nor was there so much difference between the two as might have appeared on the surface.

There was a sprightly and rather loveable old gentleman, as active as ever in spite of his fourscore years, who adored pigs and mice and all four-footed things, who christened his teapot "Dick," and might be seen trotting about at stated times with the stick he called Dapple, and this old gentleman had got a reputation, not only English but world-wide, of being the more than philosopher, who had swept the cobwebs of old-fashioned metaphysics into the dustbin, and was now offering mankind a simple panacea for all its ills, called "the greatest happiness of the greatest number." The old gentleman's name was Jeremy Bentham, and you can see all there is left of him, embalmed in his habit as he lived, by getting leave from the authorities of University College.

The previous century had been one, pre-eminently, of mathematical solutions. It was dominated by the prestige of Newton. In the calculus a key had been found to unlock the mysteries of the heavens. Why not have another calculus to solve social problems? Give Archimedes a fulcrum, and he would lift the world. Give your social reformer a unit, and the adjustment of life to environment would be a matter of simple calculation. What better unit could you have than a given quantity of the thing called happiness? So at least thought old Mr. Bentham. He was perfectly convinced that it was only the quantity of happiness that counted. Any fool could tell how many joys made five. The happiness to be derived from a game called push-pin, and that to be derived from poetry, were of exactly equal value, per unit, for purposes of calculation. After this, we shall not be surprised to hear that Bentham's notion of poetry was as simple as his notion of happiness:

"Prose is when all the lines except the last go on to the margin. Poetry is when some of them fall short of it."

We cannot help suspecting that the old gentleman would have accumulated considerably more units of his favourite commodity in the course of a sternly contested bout of push-pin, than during a reading of the *Epipsychidion*.

Only such a man as Bentham, who must have had any germ of humour effectually sterilised by devouring Rapin's history, in the original, at the age of three, could not only have taken his wonderful calculus perfectly seriously, but spent a long and voluminous lifetime in working it out to the most insignificant detail. In compensation for his lost childhood, Bentham remained something of a big, loveable baby to his life's end. Even in his old age, he tried to tame mice in a room haunted by cats. In a similar spirit he had spent a great part of his energies, and much of his private fortune, on a scheme for a new kind of prison in which, he confidently believed, you could turn criminals into respectable citizens as easily as, in modern Chicago, you turn pigs into sausages. He was also ready to supply a detailed constitution, at short notice, to any nation that happened to want one. And he actually found takers!

I suppose that, except in academic circles, where anything bearing so portentous a name as utilitarianism is assured of the respect its syllables demand, there is nobody nowadays incapable of seeing the absurdity of treating your happiness, and mine, and every one else's, as if they could all be valued, and tabulated, and assessed like so many incomes. Hard-headed was the epithet that used to be applied to the disciples of Bentham. If we were to judge them by their philosophy alone, we should be tempted to substitute "muddle-headed."

But it is never safe to take any philosophy or religion at its face value. The fact that it is no more possible to make a calculus of happiness than it is to fill your cellar with bottled moonshine, is no reason for laughing the utilitarian case out of court. What Bentham and his followers most wanted to do was to cut every sort of cackle, and get on with the business of reforming society from the base upwards. That they should have cackled interminably themselves about their greatest happiness principle, is only human. And certainly few Englishmen will be found to regret that they confined themselves to this comparatively harmless form of eyewash, instead of borrowing a few leaves out of contemporary German books of philosophy, finding thereby that Being is identical with Not-Being and that the result of both is Becoming, or that everything is profoundly for the worst in the worst of all possible worlds.

It was something that the middle class, that was now to have its chance of controlling the nation's destinies, should have produced a group of thinkers with a definite policy of social reconstruction. The Benthamites were nothing if not courageous. If their first principles were not too clearly thought out, they knew exactly what they wanted in practice. They would make a clean sweep of the past, with its worships and traditions. Nothing—not even the sacred Constitution, much less what Burke had called the decent drapery of life—should stand in the way of a brand new order of society, in which everything should be ordered by reason, and the output of happiness be multiplied like that of Lancashire cotton goods.

But men who have only half thought out their conscious faith, may chance to be impelled by motives that lie beneath the surface. The greatest happiness principle might mean anything or nothing—what the utilitarians meant was that the old governing class had muddled on long enough, and that it was time for the bourgeoisie to substitute its own solid virtues and go-ahead energy for the leisured elegance of the past. Perukes and swords had had their day, tall hats and chimneys—the taller and blacker the better—were to symbolise the new civilisation.

In all this, the difference between the followers of Bentham and those of the Lord was less one of faith than of temperament. Both would have heartily concurred in Dr. Watts's scorn of the sluggard, who

"told me his dreams."

Both had the same contempt for vanities, and it is unlikely that an Evangelical Recording Angel would have distinguished more nicely than Bentham between the merits of poetry (exclusive of hymns) and those of pushpin. In spite of their talk of happiness, the utilitarians were the last people to make an art of its pursuit. They were as plain living and hard working as the most devout of the elect. And they were possessed of the same grim and unsmiling earnestness of moral purpose.

They had even, among their leaders, a very colourable imitation of Mr. Fairchild, in the shape of James Mill, the son of a Forfarshire shoemaker, trained for the ministry, and combining all the aggressive self-confidence of the self-made Lowlander with the spiritual pride of a Calvinist Holy Willy. A not unsympathetic biographer, Sir Leslie Stephen, describes him as "a curious example of a man who, while resolutely discharging every duty, somehow made even his virtues unamiable." His standard of morals is described by his even more famous son, John Stuart, as utilitarian, "taking as the exclusive test of right and wrong, the tendency of actions to produce pleasure or pain. But," adds John Stuart, "he had . . . scarcely any belief in pleasure. . . . He thought human life a poor thing at best, after the freshness of youth and of unsatisfied curiosity had gone by."

Like Mr. Fairchild, James Mill must needs undertake the education of his children. His modest purpose, as regards his firstborn, was defined in a letter to Bentham, as being "to leave a successor worthy of both of us." He probably did not realise how truly he was working to this end when he subjected the poor little fellow to a course of intensive cram, beginning with long lists of Greek words at the age of three, and including, at the mature age of seven, Herodotus, Xenophon, Diogenes Laërtius, part—only part!—of Lucian, and Isocrates Ad Demonicum and Ad Nicoclem, not to speak of six dialogues of Plato, including the Theætetus, "which last dialogue," reflects John Stuart in his old age, "I venture to think, would have been better omitted, as it was totally impossible I should understand it."

Mr. Mill must be admitted to have fallen a good deal short of Mr. Fairchild as a child-queller, though his children, with the exception of the eldest, certainly seem to have suffered in health under his ministrations, and Mr. Fairchild could hardly have improved upon Mr. Mill's precedent of starving his children, as he did one day, till six o'clock in the evening, because John, aged eight, in teaching his little sisters, had passed their work as correct when there had been a fault of one word. A visitor remarks of Mill that "no fault, however trivial, escapes his notice; none goes without reprehension or punishment of some kind," and the children are heard to cry when scolded or cuffed over their lessons. Like Wesley, Mill would never hear of holidays, for fear of encouraging habits of idleness. But he was incapable of keeping to such an heroic level of brutality as the hero of Mrs. Sherwood. His principal terrors were a cutting tongue and an uncontrollable temper. But he frankly disbelieved in the Lord, and hated the idea of Him, and therefore had not the example to follow nor the attributes to assume of that Father of Jealousy.

The uncompromising earnestness and drab virtues of the English middle-class were thus common to its utilitarian intelligentsia and its Lord-fearing rank and file. But the utilitarians had nothing corresponding to Jesu worship. It answered to no need in their temperaments. Such a contented old bachelor as Jeremy Bentham had probably never felt an acute need of flying to any one's bosom, and as for James Mill, we have the word of his son, that "for passionate emotions of all sorts, and everything that has been said or written in exaltation of them, he professed the greatest contempt. He regarded them as a form of madness." Neither conviction of sin nor the peace that passeth all understanding could possibly find an entrance into the experience of such men. They were what William James would have described as once-born. Happiness, as they conceived of it, was a very plain-sailing affair.

It is not, therefore, greatly to be wondered at, that the calculus of happiness should have tended to develop, in practice, into a calculus of egotism. In spite of an enormous amount of verbiage about such things as eulogistic, dyslogistic and neutral qualities, the followers of Bentham had hardly the faintest notion of any science of psychology, beyond what analytical cobwebs could be spun out of their own brains. But if Experience finds the front door closed against her, she will usually contrive to enter unperceived by the back. The class from which the utilitarians had sprung consisted mainly of individuals engaged in a merciless economic struggle of all against all. It was not, therefore, altogether to be wondered at, that they should have tended to simplify their study of social problems by proceeding upon the assumption that men, in the mass, were so many jarring atoms of selfishness. That assumption was never nearer the truth than among the English middle class at the opening of the Victorian era.

It was upon such a basis that a number of theorists built up the system of political economy which was known as classical and held sway during the period of middle-class rule. Its tendency was to accept the struggle for survival as a good thing in itself, and to allow every individual the utmost possible freedom to pursue its own interests, in the faith that all things would work together for good —or at any rate for the best attainable—to those who loved the main chance. No doubt these economists were not quite such inhuman doctrinaires as they were sometimes painted, but that they well earned their unpopularity among every class but their own can hardly be denied. To the wage-earners, they represented that any attempt to better their condition at the expense of their employers was foredoomed to failure, because such action could never increase the fund of capital out of which wages are paid. As against the landowners, a Jewish banker called Ricardo first propounded a theory whose revolutionary implications he and his fellow economists quite failed to realise. They put in a separate category the form of unearned increment that comes from the rent of land, and thus contrived to pillory the landlord as the villain in the social drama, who sits still and battens on the labour of the community. It only needed another even more logical Jew, with a different class bias, to prove that exactly the same case can be made against any kind of capitalist whatsoever. Where Ricardo had planted, Karl Marx watered, and Lenin garnered the increase.

And no doubt it was the accumulation of capital that had made the Industrial Revolution possible, and its continued accumulation that determined the rate of mechanical progress. Those who held the mystic faith—rapidly spreading from the middle class to the rest of the community—that such progress must be a good thing in itself, would naturally want to see everything done to encourage the capitalist. But was that progress so very good after all? A friend of Ricardo, himself one of the new economists, Parson Malthus, touched upon an even more momentous issue than that of capital and its function in the social system, by claiming that multiplication of wealth is more than counterbalanced by the multiplication of men. Population, he discovered, is continually pressing upon the means of subsistence, and unless the human species can find means of limiting its own increase, it is doomed—no matter what its mechanical achievements—to the perpetual predicament of having more mouths to feed than meals to go round. The hope of a better time coming is therefore a mirage—the poor and the wage slave ye have with you always. This worthy minister of Christ would even abolish the poor law, and leave the helpless veteran and superfluous infant to find charity or die in the nearest ditch. He is a little perturbed, though, at the thought of charity. Unless "the hand of benevolence" is restrained, idleness and improvidence will thrive.

If Malthus had been less ambitious, and confined himself to his own time and country, his law of population would have been more nearly valid. The most important fact about the Industrial Revolution in England was that every year the population was more and more outrunning any means of subsistence that the island could furnish. At the beginning of George III's reign it could have lived fairly comfortably, if it had been cut off from the world. During the nineteenth century, a steadily increasing proportion of Englishmen was becoming absolutely dependent on what they could induce the foreigner to send them in exchange for their goods. There could no longer be any question of retarding the new tempo of life —they must produce or starve. They had staked their life on maintaining the industrial lead that had made them the workshop of the world. Future generations might find that lead slipping away.

Somewhere in his essays, Jerome K. Jerome has a story of a mechanical dancing partner, with which a certain lady was highly delighted, until something went wrong with the works, and the thing started careering round the room, clutching her in its embrace, blandly repeating its stock of ballroom platitudes, and dashing out her life against the walls.

This was a nightmare, and the hard-headed fraternity were less given to dreaming nightmares than to realising them. Mr. Bumble's workhouse was solid and conspicuous, to the extent of ruining the landscape. So were the new towns. Facts—as Mr. Bounderby, and Carlyle, used to say—and no dreams at all.

CHAPTER X

I<small>F</small> the hard-headed Benthamites and Puritan Killjoys had entirely dominated the middle-class mind at the time of the Reform Bill, we should have expected the Victorian Age to have been the most colourless and unspiritual in our history, instead of the heyday it was of idealism and imaginative genius. No doubt Puritan discipline, under the auspices of the Lord and Mr. Fairchild, fostered the concentration that is the element most needful to any work of permanent value. The utilitarians may have played a part in stimulating the aggressive individualism that renders the Victorians, with all their faults, so intensely interesting. But for the colour and sweetness of that age we are indebted neither to its philosophy nor its religion, but to that deliberate stimulation of the emotions that is summed up in the term "romance."

The Romantic Movement—so far as it can be said to have had a beginning at all—was quite a century old at the opening of the Victorian Age. Indeed, there was no time when romance in England had been quite dead. Dick Steele might have passed for a typical romantic in real life, just as Sir Roger de Coverley was a thoroughly romantic rendering of the old English squire. During the time of the most enormous wigs and stiffest brocades, Chaucer was honoured and edited, Shakespeare's influence was undiminished, Milton and Spenser were not without honour. Our national temperament has ever fought shy of extremes. Even our own age of jazz and disillusionment can find a place in its heart for Walter de la Mare.

And just as the English Augustan age was never half as correct and formal as that of Louis XIV so the emotional reaction against all that correctness and formality never ran to the extremes it did abroad. The high-souled ladies who were ready, on the slightest excuse, to immolate duty, honour, and the marriage vow, on the altar of love's young dream, were never so common, or at any rate so open about it, in England, as they were at the height of the romantic moontide on the Continent. England never had any outburst of literary anarchy corresponding to the *Sturm und Drang* in Germany, nor was the English stage capable of rising to such a curtain as when the hero of Goethe's *Stella,* and two heroines, mingle in one triple and sublime embrace!

John Wesley is the figure most nearly corresponding to that of Rousseau in eighteenth century England, and as an emotional revivalist, his influence in the long run was perhaps as great. And yet, as the immortal old lady might have said on reading *The Confessions,* "How different from the family life of dear Mr. Wesley!" Certainly the latter was much more respectable. But if our old lady, being better informed on the subject than so pious an old lady was likely to be, had realised that the Evangelist's rich widow, unlike Rousseau's penniless slut (both were ex-servant girls), had been so little appreciative of her consort's virtues as to leave him, then she might have substituted the eminently safe name of Mr.

Wordsworth. Even in *The Prelude,* that most intimate revelation of a poet's soul, there is no revelation of the poet's French daughter.

It was only when it penetrated the upper ranks of English society that the Emotional Revival blossomed into anything like the extravagance of its Continental manifestations. There is, indeed, a delightful story about Blake and his wife having been discovered naked in a summerhouse, and blandly explaining that they were Adam and Eve. But the latest biographers have vindicated the poet's decency, and it would ill-become us to question so proper a verdict. But there is unhappily no doubt that the son of Sir Timothy Shelley did make a rather embarrassed passage, nude and dripping from a bathe in the Mediterranean, through a room where a mixed party of guests was dining.* And as for Lord Byron, not even the hardiest biographer has undertaken more than a very partial vindication of his respectability.

Extravagance was the very hallmark of upper-class Romanticism, in the days when that class still governed the country and could do what it would in the face of all the world. Lord Frederick North, who displayed his love for Greece by calling himself Plato and going about in classical garb, was only a Regency dandy transplanted. Beau Brummell and Jack Mytton were, each in his chosen sphere, magnificent eccentrics, though Mytton displays the tendency of upper-class extravagance to degenerate into the merely physical. The expression "drunk as a lord" probably dates from the time when a lord was no

---

* By Trelawney's account Shelley's embarrassment does not appear to have been due so much to his nakedness as to his dislike of meeting company under any circumstances.

more ashamed of flaunting his drunkenness than the Son of Jesse.

The death of Byron may be said to mark, as nearly as possible, the end of the second phase of romantic ardour in England, a phase whose character was largely determined by the influence of, or reaction against, the French Revolution. And this phase, in its ideals, if not altogether in its personnel, was mainly aristocratic. The two outstanding figures—whose influence played no unimportant part in shaping the destinies and culture of Europe—were those of Byron and Scott, and Scott, who claimed descent from a line of Border lairds, was a thorough aristocrat in spirit—a fact that proved his eventual ruin. The Lake Poets, who started as revolutionaries, were caught by a wave of patriotic reaction, and, as Byron put it, "turned out Tory at last." Landor, if a democrat by profession, was more of a Roman senator in spirit. Keats, indeed, was not only a Liberal but a tradesman, a fact which *Blackwood* made the excuse for doing its gentlemanly best to hound him into the grave. And the long neglect from which Blake suffered may be partly due to the fact that he—far more than any of his poetic English contemporaries—was robustly and unashamedly middle class, without any veneer of gentility whatsoever.

After a period of transition, during which the romantic impulse seemed to have exhausted itself, there was another great emotional quickening at the beginning of the thirties, and this time romance may fairly be said to have swept the country. It had ceased to be on the defensive— the high and dry critics of the eighteenth century tradition were no longer lying in wait to bludgeon out any sparks of sensibility. Sense, as Miss Austen would have called it, was quite out of fashion.

But now it was the middle class that took up the running. The year 1830 was one not only of political but of spiritual revolution. It was in Paris that the fire was kindled, a Paris taught by experience, and determined to show that even revolution might be conducted on lines unexceptionally bourgeois. The political revolution threw up the least kingly of all the sons of Saint Louis, whose appearance was suggestive of Fagin, and whose habits were deliberately and ostentatiously those of the prosperous bourgeois. Much more inspiring was the other, spiritual revolution whose leaders were men like de Musset and Victor Hugo, and whose battle was fought not in the streets, but in the theatre, where *Hernani* was being performed before audiences of romantics, jubilant to the point of hysteria, and of conservatives disgruntled to that almost of murder.

The English do not push their art, or their politics, to quite these stormy extremes. But they too had their bourgeois revolution, closely following on, and partly stimulated by, that across the Channel, and with them, too, there was a spiritual revolution, less sudden and dramatic, but scarcely less important than its French counterpart. In both countries it was the middle class taking romance to its own bosom and wedding it to its own ideals. In France, the new sensibility had been enlisted on the side of royalty and the Church, until 1830, when it deserted to Liberalism. In England the emotional overflow was guided into safe channels by Puritan-Evangelical discipline. The typical romantic could now, with Pomponius

Ego, say of himself, that he "never in his moments of deepest hilarity forgot what was due to beauty and moral worth."

How then are we to define the Romantic movement? Romance has no philosophy or dogma by which it may be known. A Wesley and a Rousseau, a Wordsworth and a Byron, may blossom on its stem. It may equally thrive amid the gallantries of Montmartre and the eloquence of Oxford pulpits. Its spirit flies to the pomp and chivalry of a highly recoloured Middle Ages, but returns to a bowl of punch in the company of Mr. Pickwick and Mr. Jingle.

Romance is, in fact, an attitude of soul. To put it psychologically, it is a way of reacting to impressions. The old, aristocratic, eighteenth century ideal had been that a man should be so completely the master of his impressions as to receive and classify them without any overmastering desire to translate them into action. In a different sense from that of the Psalmist, his prayer was that he should never be moved. He ordered his conduct by an elaborate ceremonial, because he did not wish to have it dictated by the mood of the moment. He had a polite smile for everything. Louis XV, when he saw the funeral cortege of his Pompadour, merely remarked that madame had a wet day for her journey. Even piety was only acceptable—as more than one epitaph testifies—if it was without enthusiasm. As for virtue, the highest praise is that recorded on a tablet in Bristol Cathedral,

"No spot of vice his polished manners stained."

The eighteenth century was artificial, not because, as Carlyle said, it was a swindler century, but because it deliberately aimed at making of the human spirit a well-ordered sanctuary, against whose walls the storm of impressions from the outer world might beat in vain.

To the romantic, such an attitude was unnatural, inhuman, moribund. He wished to be stimulated to action by every impression that came to him. The purest romantic of all, Blake, illustrated this responsiveness in a series of such terrific couplets as,

> "Each outcry of the hunted hare
> A fibre from the brain doth tear."

and

> "The soldier, armed with sword and gun
> Palsied strikes the summer sun."

and—to sum up the whole matter in two lines:

> "Can I see another's woe,
> And not be in sorrow too?"

or, as Coleridge has it,

> "He prayeth best who loveth best
> All things both great and small."

As the movement gathers strength, the romantics begin to turn, with furious contempt, upon the urbane detachment of the past. A man justified by the traditions of Versailles or the precepts of Lord Chesterfield, would be to Wordsworth,

> "One who would peep and botanise,
> Upon his mother's grave."

and as for the Butlers and Berkeleys, the Humes and Gibbons, we have the verdict of Keats:

"Do not all charms fly
At the mere touch of cold philosophy?
There was an awful rainbow once in heaven:
We know her woof, her texture; she is given
In the dull catalogue of common things.
Philosophy will clip an Angel's wings,
Conquer all mysteries by rule and line,
Empty the haunted air and gnomed mine—
Unweave a rainbow."

It was with that ill-fated trio, Byron, Keats and Shelley, that the reaction of impressions became most intense even to the point of violence. Shelley was constantly panting, shrieking, dissolving, weeping, expiring, while the transports of Keats' desire for the "mercy—pity—love!—aye, love!" of that rather coarse-grained young woman, Fanny Brawne—with love's appurtenances of shape, hands, eyes, kiss, soul, and "warm, white, lucent million-pleasured breast"—are so unrestrained as to amount almost to raving. But this very unrestraint was crowned by a glory of concentrated passion scarcely to be equalled, of its kind, in the whole of literature; such lines as,

"As on the jag of a mountain crag
Which an earthquake rocks and swings,
An eagle alit one moment may sit
In the light of its golden wings,"

or Byron's throne-shaking defiance

"of every despotism in every nation."

Such intensity of emotion was too great for flesh and blood to house. It is by no caprice of destiny that such spirits should burn themselves out in youth. Who could conceive of an old Shelley?

The difference between the Victorian and the pre-Victorian conceptions of romance is hinted at by the fact that one finds it a little difficult, mentally, to deprive Tennyson of his beard and laurels, and see him as the rather uncouth and broad-spoken undergraduate he was at Cambridge. Few of the great Victorians seem quite complete until they have mellowed; they do not, like the Lake Poets or the chestnut, burst out into one glory of May blossoms, and then settle down to a sober and blossomless maturity. They are not spendthrifts of their inspiration, squandering it all in a few ecstatic years, but they prudently conserve it, so that their personalities may have scope to develop, and make the most of the fifty or so years of active creation to which youth may reasonably aspire.

And yet romance was the very breath of the early Victorian culture. To react quickly and appropriately to every possible impression was a social duty. Even if you had not emotions, you were expected to simulate them. The minx must assume an agitated bashfulness, the harridan look up with submissive devotion into her victim's face when posing for the daguerreotype, the heaviest swell brush away a manly tear upon due occasion. Romance was, in fact, far more unquestioned in its sway than it ever had been in Georgian times, when its torchbearers were still something of rebels. It had become the fashion, almost a tyranny. But the element of unrestraint had departed from it.

For the final triumph of romance had come with the

triumph of the middle class, and the middle class had not parted with its Puritan discipline. "Thus far," said the still, small voice of the Lord and the loud, large voice of Mrs. Grundy, "shalt thou react, and no further." Mr. Tennyson would never have dared to demand his "faint smiler Adeline," or his "airy, fairy Lilian," or even his "gay young hawk, my Rosalind," in the way Keats had approached his Fanny, or Shelley his Emilia, still less with the Byronic

"I ask not, I care not, if guilt's in thy heart."

The utmost to which he ever aspired was to be the miller's daughter's necklace, and in this innocuous form to be left on át night. Even so, he was perhaps sailing a little close to the wind. For young Mr. Tennyson's propriety, like that of Miss Charlotte Brontë, was not entirely free from suspicion.

By the thirties, Romance had learnt to accommodate itself to the standards of the English drawing-room, or genteel parlour. There was its temple, and the Young Lady was its high priestess. However hard-worked and practical they might be in reality, the dream life of Flora and Caroline was passed in a world of castles and abbeys peopled by polite men in armour and saintly ecclesiastics, and haunted by well-mannered spectres. Not that Romance limited itself to a Gothic dreamland. Lord Byron had brought in a fashion for Turks and corsairs, and Scott had shown what could be done with ruffs and trunk-hose. Anything remote and fantastic would do for a *mise en scene*. The greatest as well as the least inspired poets conformed to the prevailing fashion. Tennyson's

Princess was openly and avowedly a country house party entertainment, and Browning distilled the pure essence of romantic chivalry and wildness and gloom into his *Childe Roland to the Dark Tower Came.*

But we shall get better into the romantic atmosphere by studying, not the works of outstanding genius, but the everyday and mostly forgotten manifestations of the reigning enthusiasm. Some of the most characteristic of these are to be found in young ladies' albums of the time, with the little complimentary poems, often touched with religious sentiment, in which whiskered swains, their hair reeking with bear's grease, strive to live up to the rôle assigned them of Christian knights and stainless gentlemen. Or we may peruse the numbers of *The Keepsake,* an aristocratic annual that may still be picked up in the second-hand shops, and in which the romantic spirit is exploited to the sentimental utmost.

Let us take any one of these numbers at random, say that of 1843. Here we shall find, among a distinguished list of contributors, the Countess of Blessington, the Marchioness of Hastings, the Baroness de Calabrella, the future Lord Houghton, Lord William Lennox, Lord John Manners, Sir Hesketh Fleetwood, and that autocrat of dinner tables, Bernal Osborne.* And here are the names of some of the contributions:

Servian Jealousy—The Baron's Vow—The Skeleton Hand—Lines from the Graves—Thoughts on Death—The Brother's Revenge—Death and the Child—He Told Her That He Loved Her Not—A Few Passages in the Life of Bayard.

* Then Ralph Bernal.

These titles should be sufficiently descriptive of the contents, but one quotation may suffice for a sample of the literary fare provided. It is from *The Lay of Sir Eglamour and Lady Claribel* by Charles Howard:

> "Around the portal hollyhocks are flaunting,
>   The larkspur blooms,
> The vesper wind the secret bower is haunting
>   With rich perfumes.
> What boot the fragrant tendrils that inweave it?
>   The evening shine?
> Ah! well-a-day! Sir Eglamour must leave it
>   For Palestine."

It will be seen that nothing was so dear to the romantic heart as a refined melancholy. The sensibility deplored by Jane Austen had become a part of ordinary good manners, and ladies showed their breeding by an occasional fainting fit or mild hysterical outburst.

The authoress who laid on melancholy thickest was Mrs. Hemans, who enjoyed an immense reputation as a poetess and who supplied the words for many of the most popular drawing-room songs. From the back-cover of a young lady's song book, in the forties, I have compiled the following cheerful selection of the ditties of this most popular authoress:

Better Land (The)—Bring Flowers—Brother's Dirge—Burial in the Desert—Child's First Grief (The)—England's Dead—First Grey Hair (The)—Graves of a Household—He Never Smiled Again—Hour of Death (The)—Knight's Tomb (The)—Miserere, Miserere, Pity Us Good Lord—Parting Gifts—Parting Song (The)—Passing

Away—Songs of Captivity—Those Muffled Drums—Toll for the Brave—Toll Slowly—Wild Watcher (The).

We can well believe that our Victorian Flora's stock would have risen in the matrimonial market in proportion to whatever melancholy she could contrive to impart to the rendering of these pieces, and that few eligible bachelors would have been able to resist the tears that more or less spontaneously welled to a pair of gazelle-like eyes framed in ringlets.

Her taste was certainly not "low-brow." In one typical book of bound-up songs, I find on various title pages the names of Byron, Tennyson, Mrs. Norton—Meredith's Diana, Clare, Lockhart, Schubert, and Donizetti. Mixed with their productions are others, that aspire to be even more soulful, like a certain Mrs. Crawford's *Kathleen and Dermot,* an attempt, evidently, to go one better than Tom Moore, and described as a "Balled," a Balled, I suppose, being a particularly intense form of ballad. Intense is almost too mild a word for the scene depicted on the cover—the interior of a cathedral, constructed on no known principles of architecture. Where the central aisle of the choir ought to be is a Byzantine column, supporting one side of an arch of which the other is apparently supported on air. In the nave are pointed arches reposing on Doric columns. In the foreground a Victorian young lady appears recumbent, on what seems to be a Renaissance tomb, beneath a decorated canopy, and by this tomb is seated a decrepit and disgruntled druid, trying to balance his harp on his lap and play it with one and the same hand. Here is one verse of his outpourings:

"The chambers are lonely, the hearth is neglected,
    No voice kindly welcome (sic) the pilgrim at night,
No banquet is spread, for no guest is expected,
    They slumber in death that made all things so bright.
The halls are deserted, the bard only lingers
    To pour out his griefs for the lovely and brave,
The proud battle notes that once trilled from his fingers
    Are softened and changed in a derge (sic) to the grave,
For Kathleen and Dermot, farewell! farewell!"

It is a comfort to know that for ladies whose temperaments were too obstinately cheerful, or whose noses were
too frivolously tip-tilted, for such dismal doggedness as
that of Mrs. Crawford or Mrs. Hemans, romance provided an outlet in songs about gipsies, who, we are
assured,

"Feel no care, and they dread no strife,"

or the customs of shepherds, as exemplified in the following description:

" 'Tis the shepherd's evening bell
    That o'er the vale resounds,
As homeward through the dell
    The shepherd lightly bounds;
Soon in the fold again
    Will the flock be safely stor'd,
And on the verdant plain
    Be spread the frugal board;
And when the harvest moon
    O'er the meadows throws its glance
With a happy heart he'll join

The merry village dance,
The merry village dance!"

On the whole, though, we fancy that a wise mamma
would, except in very intractable cases, train her daughters to forsake these paths of levity for the solemn and
compelling intensity of the Balled and the Derge.

CHAPTER XI

THE Victorian Era—so far as the expression has any historical value—dawned with the bourgeois revolution. The accession of the young Queen, five years later, was an event of considerable, but by no means of epoch-making importance. Even the Court had begun to take on a new respectability under the auspices of Queen Adelaide, whose work of purification her determined little niece merely continued. What dominates the whole situation is that, between 1832 and 1867, the middle class, as defined by the limit of the ten-pound householder franchise, not only ruled politically, but spiritually. In the full glow of vigour and self-confidence, it set itself to the task of straightening out the social and economic tangle caused by the Industrial Revolution.

There is no subject upon which so much unprofitable ink has been spilled as that of the first Reform Bill. The bubble of Whig eulogy has been pricked, and there is hope that not many decades hence even academic circles may cease to get excited as to the precise means by which a number of commonplace politicians succeeded in employing the mass-feeling of the populace to advance the cause of its social superiors. The mountains laboured and brought forth this sleek town mouse. As the democratic triumph for which mobs had rioted, and the beautiful Queen's Square at Bristol been wrecked, the Bill was no

doubt a colossal fraud, which even, in one or two con-
stituencies, deprived the common people of their franchise. But it could hardly at that time have been
anything else without precipitating national disaster.

The brutal, illiterate mob, without a mind of its own,
with its record of Bristol Riots, Swing Riots, Luddite
Riots, Gordon Riots, Wilkes Riots, Excise Riots, stretch-
ing back for the past century, and its recent feats of
smashing the Duke of Wellington's windows and mob-
bing him on Waterloo Day, was in no condition to take
over the government of the country. The upper class
monopoly of power had definitely broken down. The
middle class at least knew what it wanted; its top hats
covered the pick of the community's brains; it owned
most of the capital behind the new machinery; it gave
leadership to the new industrial expansion. The Reform
Bill did no more than recognise facts, by putting power
into the hands of those best fitted to exercise it. That
is its true, and only defence. It was bourgeois, not democratic, and in fact the bottom dog was soon to find, in
the new Poor Law, that the little finger of a Radical
economist could be thicker than the old squire's loins.
But even so, it might be argued, the best place for so
untrained a dog was still at the bottom.

That, however, was not realised in any quarter at the
time. All were agreed that the Reform Bill was a democratic triumph of revolutionary importance. To high
and dry Tories it seemed as if the end of the world had
come. The House of Lords, the Church, the Crown,
would be swept away in the wake of the Rotten Boroughs, the Constitution burst in pieces, and the flood-

gates of Jacobinism opened. The real democrats, who had organised runs on the banks and disaffection among the troops, were proportionately sanguine. They had roared for the Bill, the whole Bill, and nothing but the Bill, and it took them a little time to discover that what they had got was—nothing but the Bill.

The middle-class electorate was in no hurry to press home its victory. There was an overwhelming Whig majority in the new Parliament, but Whig government was no new thing, and the list of ministers was as aristocratic as any Tory combination of the old régime. The Radical element in the Commons was insignificant numerically, though its brains gave it an importance out of proportion to its numbers. A middle-class government was a thing hardly dreamed of, as yet. The ten-pound householder felt it an honour to be governed by a lord.

None the less, the popular instinct rightly divined that a new era had dawned with the passing of the Bill. The middle class might not be in office, but it was in power, and it only needed time to make that power effective. The Greys and Russells, the Melbournes and Palmerstons, owed their official existence to the ten-pound householder, and must accordingly study how to keep him in a good humour. An utterly different spirit informed the political atmosphere. The Whig government, in power by the new electorate, felt itself compelled to embark on what, for those days, was a course of heroic legislation, to satisfy its new masters. Slavery was abolished, the first effective factory law passed, the Poor Law reconstructed, and, finally, after a premature attempt on the part of His Majesty to bring the Tories back, the principle of the Reform Bill was extended to the municipal franchise. But the impulse to reform had now spent itself. Lord Grey, an upright and enormously philoprogenitive aristocrat, who had served his apprenticeship with Fox, was succeeded as Premier by Lord Melbourne, a genial cynic of the true eighteenth century tradition, whose reaction to any constructive proposal was, "Why can't they leave it alone?" But the new electorate had no use for King Log, and a few years of Whig marking time were sufficient to bring back the Tories, with an overwhelming majority, under a thoroughly middle-class leader. And it soon became apparent that a Tory government of the old sort was impossible, so, to the horror of the landed gentry, their own Premier, Peel, who had taken office for the specific purpose of supporting the agricultural interest by Protection, sold the pass, and identified himself with the middle class policy of Free Trade in Corn.

The landed gentry had thus to bow their heads eventually to the middle class yoke. But the disillusion of the manual labourers, who had expected such great things from the new franchise, was quicker in coming. The new governing class was humane, according to its lights. It was chiefly through evangelical enthusiasm that the long campaign against slavery was crowned with final success. The Factory Act of 1833 was a genuine attempt at social reform, and showed that a doctrinaire individualism was by no means the only consideration with legislators. But the West Indies were far off, and nobody seriously apprehended more than a comparatively trifling inconvenience to the factory owners from a few modest concessions.

It was a different matter when it was a question of maintaining a cheap and certain supply of labour for the all-important end of intensive production. Early in 1834, an atrocious sentence of seven years' transportation was passed upon half a dozen Dorsetshire labourers, for the crime of peacefully combining to resist a reduction of wages to six shillings a week, and it was only after endless shiftings and delays, and by dint of formidable agitation, that the men were got back from their captivity. This shows the spirit in which the ruling class was likely to act in reforming the Poor Law. Its measure of 1834 did, in fact, provide a simple solution for an admittedly difficult problem, but only by imposing a compulsion to work more formidable than the West Indian planter's lash. Those who were unable to find some employment to keep them alive on a wage, were to be kept alive indeed, but under conditions of such calculated misery that the acceptance of any offer of employment, on any terms, would be preferable to enduring them. By dint of centralised control and minute regulations, it was hoped that any possible loophole for humanity might be effectually blocked.

This very important piece of legislation, which may fairly be described as the cornerstone of the early Victorian social system, was certainly scientific. The best brains procurable had been set to the task of investigation, exhaustive evidence had been collected, and a Commission's report drawn up that most people will admit to have been a conspicuously able piece of work. The system that the new law superseded, by which the Justices of the Peace had supplemented wages out of rates, was no doubt wasteful and demoralising—though recent research tends to show that the gravest charge against it, that of stimulating a reckless increase of population, has been overstated. But this form of magisterial socialism, evolved as it was almost spontaneously as a war measure, did at least represent an attempt on the part of the county gentry to deal with their inferiors in a humane and Christian spirit. No such emotional bias marred the calculations of those who framed the new Poor Law.

Their object was simple, and was to conscript the whole labour power of the wage-earning class on the most economical terms. The effect of the new machinery had been to imbue the middle class with a blind faith in production, as an end in itself.

Progress consisted in laying up more and more treasures on earth. Capital became productive in proportion as it was laid out in producing more capital. In spite of all the talk about the greatest happiness principle, the sober citizens of the thirties thought of wealth almost exclusively as a thing to be produced, and hardly at all as a thing to be enjoyed. As in the old Puritan saga, a man, no longer in rags, but in sombre garments, broke into a lamentable cry of "What shall I do?" and a young evangelist, from the town of Ecclefechan in Scotland, gave answer: "Produce! Produce! Were it but the pitifullest infinitesimal fraction of a Product, produce it in God's name!"

In the new Puritan dispensation, there was no quarter for sin, and poverty was evidence of sin. Like the Psalmist, the respectable citizen could never believe that the righteous—which was the same thing as the productive —would come to want, or that his seed would beg their bread. If by old age or sickness a person became incapable of supporting himself, that was because he had not cultivated habits of thrift in the days of his strength. To maintain him in comfort at the public expense would not only be to encourage sin—or unproductiveness—but to plunder the righteous for the benefit of the wicked. To show mercy on his children would be to encourage the sins of the fathers by refusing to visit them in the proper quarter. In all this we see how the jargon may be that of the economists, but the voice is the authentic voice of the Lord, the God of Isaac Watts and of William Wilberforce and of Mr. Fairchild.

It was, therefore, in the full assurance of righteousness that the new Puritans provided their social system with a Hell, or rather with a number of Hells, for this was the function that the Union workhouses—which the poor flattered by the title of Bastilles—were deliberately, and scientifically calculated to serve. The spirit of these men may have been stern, but it was sternly logical. They were no more merciful to sinners, by poverty, in their own ranks. There was a debtor's jail for unsuccessful capitalists as well as a workhouse for improvident labourers. And however much you might sentimentalise over some delicate young lady in ringlets, once let her father lose his bank balance, and her lot, as governess, might well be one of brutal and completely unsentimental exploitation.* Whiskered chivalry fought shy of insolvency.

It was the new Poor Law that finally opened the eyes of those politically minded workers, who had supplied the brute force behind the Reform Bill agitation, to the true nature of their achievement. Their rage broke forth in the great and formidable Chartist agitation, that only finally collapsed in that year of revolutions, 1848. The Charter that they demanded was the really democratic measure of Reform that they had been simple enough to credit the Whig party with having provided for them. This time there should be no mistake about it—power should be transferred from the middle class to the mass of the people.

But it was one thing to put the brute force of the mob behind the brains and energy of the bourgeoisie, and quite another to expect that force to function effectually by itself. There was no means of concentrating the indignation of men so ignorant and so untrained to common action as the wage-earners of that time. They could produce no greatness or even unity of leadership from among their own ranks. Nor was superior force at their command, so long as Wellington's long-service veterans stood fast by their officers. It was enough, at the time when the Chartist menace came nearest to revolutionary action, for a general of Liberal tendencies to explain to the men's leaders by what precise military means, if it came to blows, an undisciplined mob would be torn to pieces by artillery, mowed down by musketry, and its

---

* Though not by any means always. One has heard of Victorian governesses who became honoured and permanent friends of the family. But new wealth, like new wine, goes to the head.

remnants cut to pieces by the sabres of charging squadrons.

And meanwhile, in the Bastilles, Hell, more squalid and unrelieved than anything imagined by Dante, was performing its appointed work of stimulating production. At one end of the scale little children, destined for the sweated labour market, were being inured to misery on the cheapest possible terms, at the other, Joan was being torn from Darby, lest any spark of love should mitigate the wretchedness of their declining years. The measure worked admirably. Now that it was better to be dead than a pauper, pauperism was reduced to a minimum. The waste and demoralisation of the old system were effectually checked. Production went on faster than ever.

Of course there were complaints. Even staunch Tories, like Oastler and Sadler, denounced, with unmeasured violence, what they were pleased to consider the oppression of the poor. But ears that had been roared into, week in, week out, by Cobbett, were hardened to invective. It was different when the most brilliant of a rising constellation of authors, assisted by one of the foremost black-and-white artists of his time, drew the attention of the whole nation to the spectacle of a starving child, asking for more—in vain. And then, having moved his audience to tears, this same Charles Dickens set them rocking with laughter by embodying the spirit of the new law, and the result of the Commission's labours, in the person of Mr. Bumble.

For there was romance as well as utilitarianism in Victorian England, and things whose necessity could be demonstrated by statistics, might be felt as intolerable.

CHAPTER XII

THE NEW OPTIMISM

THE most striking triumphs of the middle class were not to be registered in the field of politics. During the four mid-decades of the century, an overwhelming proportion of Victorian talent and genius was found in its ranks. Its ideals were hardly questioned, what philosophy there was emanated from its pundits, its respectability served for a moral code that not the stoutest sinner dared openly defy, its Lord was God, even of professed unbelievers. Its time of supreme power was also one of supreme opportunity. Civilisation was in the melting pot. The task of reconstruction was one for which the old governing class plainly possessed neither the imagination nor the will. The manual workers, unorganised and uneducated, might conceivably have destroyed the social system—it was wholly beyond their capacity to fashion another. But the middle class, brimming over with energy, superbly self-confident, felt itself equal to this, or any other task that might be imposed upon it. The new Pandora's box had taken the form of a top hat.

The opening of the Victorian era, which really dates from the beginning of the thirties, was one of those spring-tide periods when life seems aglow with new-born energy, and blossom all around into genius. Browning's "glad, confident morning," would serve as a description of it. The period of depression and disillusionment following the French war was definitely over. Nobody bothered any more about the Jacobin menace. Eyes were turned forward with hope, not backward with apprehension. The Reform Bill had shown that Englishmen were still as capable as ever of reconciling liberty with order, and wedding the spirit of progress to that of the Constitution. Tennyson's conception of freedom

"broadening down
From precedent to precedent,"

was no platitude to the men of his time, but stood for a national achievement more unique and startling than that of Waterloo. Burke would never have believed it possible; Wellington and the old Tories had striven against change in the belief that England, once started on the inclined plane of democracy, would go the way of revolutionary France.

This paralysing belief that any sort of reform was fraught with the peril of revolution, was finally dissipated by the success of the Reform Bill. Whatever might have been the case in France—and even France had found a way of making revolution respectable—progress in England had proved itself an eminently safe thing. Like the new steam engines, it might go forward at a speed hitherto undreamed of, but always along its appointed lines —which Tennyson visualised as grooves—and under the control of signals. The mere fact that the signals had been at danger for so long, made it all the more necessary to make up for lost time. In every department of national activity, the orders were "full steam ahead."

Among the middle class, especially, a robust optimism

had been the prevailing sentiment even before the seal was set upon it by the Reform Bill. The man in the street, no less than his intellectual leaders, seems to have been convinced that great changes were taking place, year by year, the effect of which would be to make the world, and everybody in it, unimaginably better. It was a process to which no limits could be set—the better you got, the faster you might hope to go on being better. It is about this time that the habit develops of speculating about the future, or looking back with tolerant pity on the not very remote past. The thing became a drawing-room amusement. In a young lady's album, in my possession, some young wag has imagined a gentleman of George II's time transported into the—then—present, and going for a journey on the Quicksilver coach. Even though the idea of railways does not seem to have dawned on the writer's imagination, excellent fun is made of the gentleman's abject terror, as the vehicle sways, at a headlong twelve or fifteen miles an hour, along the wonderful macadamised road. *The Keepsake,* that elegant and aristocratic annual, dips into the future, three hundred years ahead from 1830, when the journey to Edinburgh takes seven and a half hours, beggars talk Latin, doors are opened by steam porters and letters drafted by steam secretaries, pheasants are mowed down by a sort of machine gun, newspapers come out every six hours, and people talk to each other, at a distance, by means of telescopes. One passage is of ominous and prophetic import.

"I have heard," says Lady D., "that corn is rising in price: what is the reason?"

"The harvest," explains Lord A., "has failed in Tartary, and you know that the state of foreign harvests affects our prices much more than that of our own."

"I wonder," said Lady D., "we don't grow corn in England enough to feed our population."

"Enough," breaks in Mr. C., "to feed our population! My dear Lady D., we have hardly enough to feed our game!"

Tennyson's *Locksley Hall* was not published till 1842, when, though the tide of optimism was still at the flood, the poet's own philosophic honesty allowed him to entertain sombre doubts as to whether the god Progress might not after all be a devil in disguise. Here, there is the beatific vision of the heavens filled, not with angels, but with commerce, and of a war in the air, to the accompaniment of much shouting and a rain of blood, being followed by a world Parliament and, presumably, more commerce than ever. But there was that grim Malthusian threat of

"a hungry people like a lion creeping nigher,"

and Tennyson's own intuition that, though knowledge might come, wisdom might linger—in other words, that to improve machines without improving men, might lead to progress in a direction opposite to heavenward.

But Tennyson—however antipathetic his cautious and tentative philosophy may be to the cocksureness of an age that has no time to philosophise at all—could be, when the spirit moved him, one of the profoundest, as well as the most representative thinkers of his time. And his depth was in almost direct proportion to that honest doubt that he esteemed above all the creeds. It was only in his certainties—about the Crimean War, for example —that he was shallow. But doubt, honest or otherwise, troubled few of the early Victorians. If M. Coué's formula were a talisman, that would have been a golden age indeed, since—except for the disillusioned and voteless Chartists, and a dwindling clique of diehard aristocrats —there was a general and stentorian conviction that there was no country like England and no age like the present.

This conviction of righteousness had been gaining strength for some time before the seal was put upon it by the apparent success of the Reform Bill. It was an age of strenuous self-improvement, founded upon the conviction that in science, and particularly the kind of science that could be applied to commerce and industry, could be found the key to all progress and all perfection. Everywhere the effort was being made to make science popular. In 1823, Birkbeck founded the London Mechanics' Institute, and other institutes of this kind were started in the new industrial centres, attracting particularly the aristocracy of labour, such as the engineers, many of whom, both at home and abroad, were able to coin their skill into very lucrative wages. In 1825, the first steps were taken towards founding London University, an entirely middle class affair, conducted on nonsectarian lines, a formidable rival to the aristocratic and reactionary Oxford, and the only slightly more liberal Cambridge.

It was Henry Brougham who coined the phrase "the schoolmaster is abroad," though the fact that Brougham himself was abroad was even more significant of an age that honoured him as an intellectual leader. He was one of those characters in real life who would appear incredible in fiction. He was so marvellously ill-favoured as to possess some of the attractiveness of a gargoyle. He had neither dignity, nor what a Roman would have called gravity. As Lord Chancellor, he distinguished himself by belching from the Woolsack. He once put about a story of his own death, in order to get a free advertisement in the obituary columns. In his own profession of the law, despite dazzling abilities and irresistible eloquence, the diarist Greville declared that the ridicule and aversion he excited as Chancellor were universal. No colleague could work with him, and not all his brilliance, nor even the fear of his vindictiveness, could prevent the Whig government from shedding him at the first opportunity.

Nevertheless Brougham stands for the embodiment of that peculiar optimism of progress that was growing in the early thirties, though being of the Georgian tradition, he had none of the moral earnestness of the budding Victorians. Like the middle class, from which he would not admit himself to be sprung—for he had a thoroughly bourgeois capacity for detecting the blood of Norman barons in his veins—his ambitions, and confidence in his own powers, were alike boundless. "There," said Rogers the poet, as Brougham drove away, "go Solon, Lycurgus, Demosthenes, Archimedes, Sir Isaac Newton, Lord Chesterfield, and a great many more in one postchaise." He went about jingling a bunch of keys to all knowledge and all mysteries. He was a universal reformer. Being incapable of looking deeply enough into any problem to appreciate its complexities, he was also a universal provider of ready-made solutions.

It was only to be expected that such a man should place himself at the head of the movement for getting wise quick, or science without tears, that was responsible for a great mass of cheap and improving literature. Brougham was one of those who helped to found "The Society for the Diffusion of Useful Knowledge," and started it off with an essay of his own on *The Pleasures and Advantages of Science,* of which the substance, being as platitudinous as the title, ensured for it a great popular reception. The appetite for Useful Knowledge, which, to men like Brougham, meant facts without philosophy and expansion without depth, was catered for by a variety of publications that often reached a surprisingly high level of excellence, and were at least more thorough and less slapdash than many a cheap potboiler that the specialists of our own day are induced to knock off at odd moments and sweated rates.

No doubt it was an excellent thing that the schoolmaster should be abroad, and that even grown-up people should apply themselves to the improvement of their minds. Though the bubble of Brougham's reputation has long been pricked, and his most enduring title to fame, the fusty conveyance that in one's boyhood used to rumble one home from the station, is almost as forgotten as his writings, his work for the freedom of slaves, the reform of the law, and the diffusion of knowledge, should outweigh his faults in the final reckoning. But there was a danger lest, in the unprecedented crisis that confronted humanity at this time, people should be encouraged to believe that the gospel of salvation was to be found in penny encyclopædias, and that the Diffusion of Useful Knowledge was an acceptable substitute for the complete mental and spiritual readjustment to a revolutionised environment, that mankind must make or perish. There was a more ominous import than Tennyson perhaps realised in his lines:

"Let knowledge grow from more to more,
But more of reverence in us dwell,
That mind and soul, according well,
May make one music as before."

The fact is that this age, so abounding in energy, so fruitful of mechanical invention, was almost bankrupt of a philosophy. The task of enlarging the empire of man over matter, and liberalising obsolete institutions, was one that seemed to call for nothing more than practical commonsense, and it was mere waste of time to sit cogitating about the ultimate significance of the changes that were taking place. It was only practical men in a hurry who could ever have taken seriously so muddled a philosophy as that of Bentham, with his push-pin-poetry calculus. When we think that Brougham, and James Mill, and Martin Tupper passed for men of light and leading with the educated public, we can judge of the demand there was likely to be for subtle or profound thought.

But there had arisen one greater than Brougham to interpret the spirit of the age. It was in 1825 that Thomas Babington Macaulay had leapt into youthful fame with an article on Milton in *The Edinburgh Review*. It was in 1837, the year of the Queen's accession, that he made a new edition of Bacon's works the excuse for writing Bacon's life, and that, again, the excuse for proclaiming his own gospel under the guise of expounding Bacon's. Two words form its key, Utility and Progress. All else is vanity and word-spinning. The only fruitful philosophy is that which concerns itself with supplying what Macaulay himself alludes to as vulgar wants.

We do not imagine that those who are most scornful of Macaulay's Philistinism would find it too easy a task to refute him. His case is put with downright, John Bullish commonsense. The endeavour to make men perfect can do no more than "fill the world with long words and long beards." "The wise men of the Stoics would, no doubt, be a grander object than a steam-engine. But there are steam-engines. And the wise man of the Stoics is yet to be born." Or to put it still more plainly, and in a way that would have shocked even Macaulay, it is better to serve Mammon than God, because the former can reward you with treasures on Earth, whereas the latter can only give you treasures in heaven, which, to Macaulay, are about as valuable as cheques payable in moonshine. Therefore scrap philosophy, annihilate spiritual values, and get something really useful and progressive. Among various benefits to be derived from this new gospel, Macaulay includes the lengthening of human life, and the furnishing of "new arms to the warrior," for the purpose, presumably, of cutting it short. But it is all progress, so what does it matter?

Macaulay, at least, was robustly confident that progress was a good thing, and industrialised England on the high road to Utopia. He revelled in statistics of increasing population, expanding commerce, multiplying wealth. The prospect of suburban villas moved him to ecstasies. When Southey, the Poet Laureate, dared to contrast the beauty of the old cottages with the hideousness of the new manufacturing towns, Macaulay retorted with a positive bellow of indignation: "Here is wisdom. Here are the principles on which nations should be governed. Rose bushes and poor rates rather than steam-engines and independence. . . . Mr. Southey has found out a way, he tells us, in which the effects of manufactures and agriculture may be compared. And what is this way? To stand on a hill, to look at a cottage and a factory, and to see which is the prettier." You cannot make omelettes without breaking eggs, and when progress is afoot, you cannot, even by the admission of a poet like Macaulay, bother about such trifles as beauty.

The conclusion of the whole matter, so far as Macaulay and the great middle class for which he stood are concerned, is fairly summed up in the conclusion of this review, written in 1830:

"By the prudence and energy of the people . . . England has hitherto been carried forward in civilisation; and it is to the same prudence and the same energy that we now look with comfort and good hope. Our rulers will best promote the improvement of the nation by strictly confining themselves to their own legitimate duties, by leaving capital to find its most lucrative course, commodities their fair price, industry and intelligence their natural reward, idleness and folly their natural punishment, by maintaining peace, by defending property, by diminishing the price of the law, and by observing strict economy in every department of the State. Let the Government do this: the People will assuredly do the rest."

Sentiments so inspiring as this can hardly fail to be rounded off with an involuntary "Hear! hear!" No wonder that the Gospel of Progress was received with gladness from the lips of Thomases so undoubting as this! And even Macaulay falls short of the lilting finality of Browning's, or rather Pippa's

> "God's in his heaven,
> All's right with the world!"

the God in question being not unlike our old friend, the eighteenth century Deity, grown hearty, and a little vulgar, in His second childhood. However far this may have fallen short of expressing Browning's own philosophy of life, it summarises pretty fairly the robustuous optimism of the average middle class Englishman, an optimism that was steadily rising, throughout the thirties and forties, and reached its high water mark about the time of the Great Exhibition of 1851.

CHAPTER XIII

THE VICTORIAN ZENITH

WHILE men of letters were thus prodigal in spilling the ink of optimism, men of affairs were hard at work translating that of optimism into the fact of history. And English history, as the men of that time understood it, and as it was written long afterwards, constitutes a sufficiently respectable record. The fears aroused at the time of the Reform Bill were now dissipated. The throne stood; the Lords sat fast on their crimson benches; the Church seemed more solidly established than at any time in its Protestant existence. And the party game of Whig and Tory, with its atmosphere of genteel corruption, and its alternation of aristocratic Cabinets, went on to all appearance very much as before. It was the heyday of Taper and Tadpole, though they were at work behind the scenes, and did not get into the records. English History consisted of the manœuvres and contentions and policies of such substantial gentlemen as Lord John Russell and Sir Robert Peel, as Palmerston and Aberdeen and Graham and Derby, men whose very names on the directorate of the firm, John Bull and Co., constituted, in most peoples' eyes, a guarantee of permanence.

The works of these men, and the laws that they fathered, and the history that they made are recorded in volumes as substantial as themselves. The story of the Victorian Age, as the Victorians themselves understood it, is told, at length, and with dignity, by Sir Spencer Walpole.* We wonder how many modern readers have accomplished the labour of its perusal. It is not Sir Spencer's fault if such rare and arduous bibliophiles are left wondering whether these matters, that seemed so important to their grandparents, are really worth setting out in such detail. Whether or not a Whig Duchess should be Mistress of the Robes, or Palmerston should have his tit for tat with John Russell, of how many still-born Reform Bills Lord John was father, or for how many useless fortifications Pam could succeed in touching a neuro-patriotic taxpayer, on what point of national honour the British Navy consented to play the part of bailiff for a Portuguese Shylock, what horrid invasions were supposed to be meditated by Napoleon III, and before him, by the Prince de Joinville, how much murderous excitement could be worked up over what Mr. Jorrocks described as "Nicholas Rumenough's wagaries"— these and similar things that loomed so large in contemporary eyes, appear in our perspective,

> "As foolish as a fable,
> And feeble as a pointless jest."

We glean the same impression from conventional Victorian history as from all but the very best Victorian fiction, namely, that the most important part of the story is that which a decent reticence forbids. For indeed the most important thing of all, in the long run, was the least mentionable—for it consisted in the increase of the population beyond any means of subsistence that these

* He leaves off at 1880.

islands were capable of furnishing. And the ways and means of such increase were taboo.

It was, in fact, the habit of the Victorians to take for granted the broad outlines of their social system, and to busy themselves about improving the details. Even to the Radicals, whose very name committed them to getting at the root of things, it did not occur that the way to find roots is to delve below the surface. During the years of middle class rule, it would have seemed hardly sane to doubt that the results of the Industrial Revolution were good in themselves, that better machinery, and increased production, and the advance of science, must, by their very nature, lead to a beneficent progress. And if a few exceptional spirits, like Ruskin and Newman, harked wistfully back to the traditions of an earlier, simpler age, this was too much in harmony with the fashionable romantic pose to be taken very seriously by practical men.

If it was the habit of the Victorians to shirk contact with vital issues, certainly all the circumstances of the time combined to encourage them. Until well on into the seventies, England enjoyed a perilous run of good luck. The lead she had obtained in the industrial race, that enabled her to become first the workshop and afterwards the bank of the world, was well maintained during the fifties and sixties, owing to the fact that her principal prospective competitors were busy settling their internal and external differences by force of arms. The most formidable rival of all, the United States, threw herself temporarily out of the running by plunging into a long and exhausting civil war.

Yet another of England's problems, that threatened to become more immediately pressing, she was enabled, by a terrible stroke of fortune, to shelve. When within three years of their great Reform Bill, the Whigs settled down to a time of comfortable stagnation, there stepped to the front of the stage the huge figure of Daniel O'Connell, the Irish "Liberator," and Irish affairs demanded an ever-increasing share of the politicians' attention. This was because the situation created by Pitt's Act of Union with Ireland in 1801 was one that was bound, sooner or later, to become impossible. Like so many other of the legislative expedients of that period, it had been a war measure, dictated by overmastering military necessity. England could not afford a practically independent Ireland on her flank, and accordingly the Irish Parliament had to be got rid of by the only possible legal means, that of bribing its members. This golden argument was employed by those realistic patriots, Pitt and Castlereagh, with as little hesitation as that of lead and cold steel had been. Unfortunately the insane fidelity of George III to his coronation oath forbade them the only concession by which Union could have been palatable to the Irish, that of votes for Catholics. This was forced from a Tory government in 1829, for the excellent reason that they were unable to face a civil war, in which the considerable Irish part of our army might have mutinied. The lesson that John Bull will concede to fear what he will refuse to justice, was not thrown away on the Irish.

The fact is that the Act of Union had given Ireland the power, sooner or later, to make things intolerable for England. So long as the party game was played between

Whig-Liberals and Tory-Conservatives, there must always be the danger of an independent group in the House holding the balance and dictating its own conditions. Even a small and determined element in a British House of Commons, something more than indifferent to British interests, might inflict untold injury on the delicate mechanism of Parliamentary government. And finally, an Ireland, governed against her will, might constitute a liability rather than an asset to her governors.

But O'Connell, the big, loveable romantic, with his hatred of physical force and his devotion to "the darling Queen," was no Parnell, to play Ireland's cards with the cold ruthlessness of Bismarckian realism. Having by his patriotic eloquence brought her to the verge of revolution, he shrank from forcing a decision, and Peel and Wellington, in the early forties, with a solid Tory majority at their backs, were not disposed to surrender the Act of Union as easily as they had conceded the Catholic vote. The prestige of the Liberator was shattered, and the leadership of young Ireland was already passing into the hands of extremists, when a fearful disaster, that of the Black Famine, fell upon that most unhappy of all islands, reducing her population, ultimately, to about half its former numbers. To dilate on the horrors of those days is foreign to our purpose. Suffice it to say that Ireland's tragedy was England's release, and the Irish question ceased to be a serious trouble to her statesmen for another generation.

Thus the Victorians were enabled to indulge in their favourite habit of bequeathing the solution of vital problems to their heirs. Their attitude towards the Irish,

until the rise of Parnell gave them reason to change it,
may be described as one of faintly benevolent contempt.
The typical Irishman, as we see him in the pages of
Punch, might well have been designed to prepare its
readers for the reception of the Darwinian theory. The
Irishman was a Yahoo, and—what was almost worse, a
Papist, led by priests a degree more sub-human than himself. When he took to Fenianism, this confirmed John
Bull in his opinion that the most effective way of appeal-
ing to Patrick was not to his reason but to his senses.
Unfortunately, this was just what Patrick was learning
about John, and the Treaty of 1921 put the seal on his
estimate.

But if the Black Famine enabled the early Victorians
to shelve the Irish question for an indefinite period, the
even greater problem presented by the Industrial Revolution clamoured for some sort of a solution. That Revolution may be said to have consummated itself, to all
intents and purposes, in the forties. The process of mechanising industry, though rapid beyond all precedent,
had been more gradual and patchy than we are apt to
realise to-day. In the Yorkshire woollen industry, as late
as the forties, a few weavers and hand combers still carried on their work in their homes—the last survivors of
the old domestic industries.* But now the railway had
come to its own, and the process of mechanisation gathered irresistible momentum. Even Manchester—if we
may trust the evidence of Disraeli's *Coningsby*—was con-

* For this I am indebted to Mr. Gerald Foster, whose family
have so long been connected with the Bradford Wool Industry.

sidered, by go-ahead employers in places like Rochdale, behind the times in its machinery.

But even to such hardened optimists as middle class Englishmen, it was becoming evident that mechanical progress might prove a qualified blessing. The very name, "the hungry forties," that still clings to the decade, is sufficient reminder of the miserable condition into which the great majority of the working classes was plunged. The condition of the people was a question that positively forced itself upon the attention of any one with a brain to feel or a heart to think.

It was about 1841, that Elizabeth Barrett Browning, who, though an invalid and a spinster, could feel like a mother for little ones whose sufferings only reached her through the medium of print, published her "Cry of the Children":

"The young, young children, O my brothers,
    They are weeping bitterly!
    They are weeping in the playtime of the others,
    In the country of the free."

In the same year, *Punch* started on his long career as the representative, in motley, of average middle-class opinion, a *Punch* burning with indignation against social wrong, and quite innocent of the good taste that forbids even the jesters of our own time to disturb the complacency of comfortable people. In 1842, a Commission set up to enquire into the conditions of Child Labour issued the first of its reports, dealing with the mines, and this disclosed a state of things that profoundly shocked public opinion, even in those days of Ricardian economics. And it was Mr. Horne's report on the State of Workers in Coal Mines that produced, two years later, a cartoon in *Punch* concerning Capital and Labour, that would, if brought up to date, be welcomed by any Bolshevik organ of Moscow or the Clydeside. It depicts a horrible contrast between bloated luxury above ground, and something worse than slavery below. And—in case this should seem a mere eccentricity of Radicalism—the fighting champion of the Diehard Tories against their own leader produced his *Sybil,* a merciless exposure of social injustice, written up, very largely, from the bare evidence of official reports.

It was not only in the new industrial districts that distress was acute. In what was still the basic industry of agriculture, the state of the workers during these "hungry forties" beggars description, and this largely owing to the very measures of protection that were taken to keep the English farmer from being overwhelmed by foreign competition. When wages were only a few shillings a week, and the price of food was forced up to artificial levels, it was impossible for Johnny Raw and his family to absorb the amount of nourishment that their human frames required. If they could keep alive at all, and avoid the Hell of the Poor-house Bastille, they had done as well as could be expected.

Even for the middle class itself, though its members were normally exempt from the pangs of physical hunger, prospects were none too rosy. It seemed as if it were impossible to realise the blessings of progress without ruining more people than were benefited. One of the worst of the now periodical financial smashes occurred as the direct result of the revolution in transport, consummated in the first half of this hungry decade. A perfect mania of speculation seized upon the investing public, and there leapt into prominence the figure of Hudson, the Railway King, whose rise and fall would have been a fit subject for one of Balzac's novels. Hudson, however, fell on his feet, to the extent of ending his days in reasonable comfort, which is a great deal more than could be said for countless victims of his, and other speculators' megalomania.

During the forties, then, we have a growing conviction, that there was something in the condition of England that called for a remedy. But not even Dickens nor Disraeli, not the militant clique of journalists who staffed *Punch,* not more than very nebulously even Carlyle, detected a lack of adjustment of man to his environment that called for a fundamental change in human as well as mechanical civilisation. It was part of the peculiar Victorian sense of decency to avoid going to the roots of things. And the Victorians were not only decent, but eminently practical folks, which meant, that when they were faced with any difficulty, they went straight for a practical remedy. They acted in the spirit of people who, on perceiving a suspicious swelling, do not rush off to a specialist, who would probably order an operation, but contrive, by faith or some homely remedy, to keep it from hurting, and are triumphant if, at the end of a month, this policy has been successful.

The middle class, who held the reins of power, had no mind for any expedient that could be called revolutionary. The Chartist remedy, that of presenting a blank cheque, in the shape of the franchise, to an uneducated proletariat, its commonsense had ruled out as premature, though its more advanced spirits were moving cautiously in the direction of universal suffrage. Socialism, a French importation into our language, was associated in most people's minds with the kindly and somewhat nebulous schemes of Robert Owen, a true romantic, whose ideal was as different as possible from the uncompromising realism and class war subsequently preached by Karl Marx. But Socialism was not yet practical enough politics to be felt, like Chartism, as a menace to respectable society.

The advanced thinkers of the middle class had, however, hit upon a remedy of their own for the admittedly deplorable condition of the people in the hungry forties. The problem to them was a simple one, and the solution equally simple. The people were hungry because they could not afford to buy food, particularly bread, and bread prices were being maintained at artificial levels to support the old governing class of the days before the Reform Bill. Therefore let trade be free, let the price of bread find its own natural level, and the poor man's wages would enable him to keep the wolf from the door. There was also the chance, not wholly displeasing to some rich employers of labour, that the poor man's wages might be cut down to suit the diminished cost of living.

There was another way in which the matter might have been regarded, had there been any one capable of probing the controversy to its depths. What the Industrial Revolution had done for England had been to commit her to a huge gamble. Every year her own natural resources were becoming less and less adequate to maintain the ever-swelling hordes of her urban population. To an increasing extent she had to rely on the foreigner to feed her, and the foreigner would only do this in return for goods—mostly the product of her new factories. The protection of agriculture was an attempt to check this process, and—if not to make Britain self-supporting—at least to mitigate the mounting disproportion of what we ate to what we could possibly produce, or, in other words, to put some limits to the task imposed on future generations, of inducing foreigners to fill our bellies in return for the products of our mines and machines. No doubt we were in a fair way to become the workshop of the world, and the British Fleet was believed to rule the waves—but once let either of these two conditions fail to be fulfilled, at any future time, and England was doomed to a tragedy of starvation to which the horrors of the Black Famine in Ireland and the Bolshevik Revolution in Russia would seem mild by comparison. That precisely was the gamble to which the Industrial Revolution had committed, and still commits, England.

The Free Trade solution consisted in solving the difficulties of that generation by increasing the stakes for posterity. Even if the true nature of the choice had been appreciated there would have been much to be urged in favour of such boldness. The Corn Laws were at least an incomplete brake on a process that had gathered too much momentum to be more than slightly retarded. There was no hope of making England a self-sufficing nation, no hope of emptying the hives of Oldham and Huddersfield into the unspoilt countryside. And the

Corn Laws, and Import Duties generally, were doing a great deal of immediate harm, not only in raising the price of living for the workers, but in handicapping efforts to capture the world's markets. There was never a time when British Industry was in less need of artificial support. And not even a Cobden could have appreciated the full strength of the position of England on the eve of a period during which her principal competitors would be engaged in knocking themselves and each other out of the running. As for agriculture—an urban electorate could allow that to take its chance, especially as the danger from the remission of the Corn Duties was less in the present than the future. And as for the future—whatever texts a Victorian might put on the walls of his room, there was one always engraven on his heart, to the effect that the day after to-morrow might take thought for the things of itself.

The Free Trade agitation was the first serious attempt of the electorate to impose a policy of its own upon the aristocratic magnates whom it permitted to administer its affairs. It is also the first indication of the way in which power had shifted from London and the South to the industrial North and Midlands. The leaders of the movement, prosperous, self-made business men, imparted to it something of the emotional fervour of a crusade. A cynic might have remarked that it was a very convenient crusade for such leaders. Not only did it divert working-class enthusiasm into a more harmless channel than that of Chartism, but the Corn Laws provided a serviceable stick for beating the rival agricultural interest. And when philanthropic gentlemen like Lord

Shaftesbury urged the business men to put their own house in order, and even proposed to interfere with the factory-owner's freedom to impose inhuman hours and conditions on his employés, it was possible, with magnificent audacity, to retort with the accusation of cant.

"This I will tell you," were the words of Richard Cobden, "that if you would give force and grace to your professions of humanity, it must not be confined to . . . occasional visits to factories to talk sentiment over factory children—you must un-tax the people's bread."

There is no need to doubt these men's earnestness, because—as was said of another earnest Victorian—they sometimes followed their consciences as a driver follows the horse. No one can fail to detect the true ring in Cobden's beautiful words to his friend, John Bright, after the death of Bright's first wife:

"There are thousands of houses in England at this moment where wives, mothers and children are dying of hunger. Now, when the first paroxysm of your grief is past, I would advise you to come with me, and we will never rest until the Corn Law is repealed."

Such was the fervour that swayed huge audiences, and finally swept even a Tory prime minister off his feet. Sir Robert Peel, who had come into office, in 1841, supported by the votes of the landed interest, with the avowed purpose of maintaining a Protectionist policy, was one of those eminent personages who seem to have been designed by Providence for the sub-acid purposes of the modern biographer. He was rich, respectable, awkward, a little smug, and a politician. He surrendered, under pressure, the principal causes he was pledged to defend.

Moreover he was portentously earnest, as befitted his time and middle-class origin, without the least spark of humour.

Sir Robert, the sleek politician, becomes the inevitable foil for his Tory colleague, the honest soldier Wellington. And yet their guiding principle was the same, that the King's or Queen's government must, at all sacrifice of party principles, be carried on. Only Wellington, being more habituated to command than to persuade, was less fitted to make the task of government a success than Peel, whose lifelong training had rendered him a past master in the technique of statesmanship. It was Peel's great achievement, on succeeding in 1841 to a notoriously inefficient Whig administration, to have selected and trained perhaps the ablest ministerial team of modern times. If Pope's test, that the government that is best administered is best, be applied to Peel, his reputation will stand unsurpassed. But his hold upon party principles was weak, and he was not the man to take long views. The future was no concern of his; it was enough if, under his auspices from year to year, England could be godly, and quietly, and prosperously governed.

To Peel's matter-of-fact intelligence, it soon became apparent that the protection of agriculture, to which he and his party were committed, was proving thoroughly bad business. Cautiously and by gradual stages, he convinced himself that the Corn Tax would have to follow most of the other import duties to the scrap heap. The deciding factor was the Black Famine in Ireland. "Rotten potatoes," as Wellington brutally put it, "have put Peel in his damned fright." It is doubtful whether the

repeal of the Corn Laws was an effective remedy for
rotten potatoes. What an Irish Parliament would have
done, and what no English statesman would have dared
to suggest during the hungry forties, would have been
to have detained in Ireland enough Irish corn to have
sufficed to have kept her people alive when the potatoes
failed.

But there was hunger in England as well as starvation
in Ireland, and Peel, in his pedestrian fashion, believed
that it is better for principles to be discarded and pro-
grammes to suffer, than for bellies to remain unfilled.
It was easy for so brilliant a debater as Disraeli to put
political faith above political expediency, and taunt his
apostate leader in a series of scarifying phillipics. Peel
had other objects in view than that of consistency to Tory
principles. At heart he was no Tory. He had more in
common with business men like Cobden, than with the
nobility and gentry who had chosen him for their leader,
and never quite regarded him as one of themselves. And
when, after the bill repealing the Corn Laws had been
passed under his auspices, and his own infuriated Die-
hards had hurled him from office by voting against an
Irish Coercion Bill with which most of them probably
agreed, Peel closed his premiership with the simple
words:

"It may be that I shall leave a name sometimes remembered with expressions of good will by those whose lot
it is to labour and earn their daily bread by the sweat of
their brow, when they shall recruit their exhausted
strength with abundant and untaxed food, the sweeter
because it is no longer leavened with a sense of injustice."

The attitude of the still unconvinced landed gentry towards their lost leader and shattered customs barriers was certainly not determined by any more far-sighted calculations than those of Peel himself. The prospect of diminished rents affected them more than the spectacle of rotten potatoes and hungry labourers. Surtees, who understood them thoroughly, was speaking for the typical squire, through the mouth of Mr. Tom Scott of Hawbuck Grange, replying to the query of Lord Lionel Lazytongs as to whether he was a Tory.

"Dashed if I know what I am. . . . I *was* a Tory or Conservative or whatever you call it, and joined the *gobemouches* in abusing the Whigs and *hooraying* Sir Robert; but I've thrown up politics and devote myself to draining and d——ing him instead."

What Peel, for his part, thought of Mr. Scott and his like, may be judged from one of his letters to his wife at this time, in which he asks, with contemptuous exasperation, how those who pass their time in hunting, shooting and drinking can know the motives of those responsible for the public safety.

So, in 1846, the middle-class remedy for the disharmonies of the social order was applied, and England was finally committed to the alternative of perpetuating her command of the world's markets or suffering the agonies of starvation. But for a long time to come her position was assured. For the generation that followed the Repeal of the Corn Laws, Free Trade proved an overwhelming success. The hungry forties were succeeded by the prosperous fifties and—except for the Lancashire cotton famine—the even more prosperous sixties. Wealth increased by leaps and bounds. Exports doubled and redoubled. Wages rose; the cost of living fell. Chartism collapsed like a pricked bubble. The working class, as a whole, seemed to have forgotten the spirit of Captain Swing and King Lud, and had not yet learnt that of Karl Marx. Even agriculture managed to pay its way without the assistance of the Corn Laws—for the competition of the Canadian wheat fields and the Middle West was not seriously felt during the fifties and sixties. Surveying the almost incredible statistics of material progress, the man in the street could hardly fail to conclude that mechanical civilisation had been justified by its fruits, and that the Victorian social order, if not yet perfect, was every day, and in every way, getting better and better.

CHAPTER XIV

ENGLAND IN EARNEST

T HOSE who wish to understand the Victorian Age, or the Victorians themselves, will be defeating their own purpose if they start by making the valet's distinction between the hero and his achievement. The Dickens who is more concerned with Maria Beadnell than the characters of his novels, the Ruskin whose tragedy is not that of social injustice but of Rose de la Touche, are like the kings of fairyland, whose highest function it is to strut about in ermine and interview their daughters' wooers. And the fairy tale, or Hamlet-minus-the-Prince-of-Denmark biography of So-and-so "the Man," are not the most appropriate forms for the solid substance of Victorian history.

To a reader who returns one of these all too human biographies of Victorians to the library counter, it must sometimes occur that something is missing that accounts for a difference between the Victorian Age and our own. Our patronage of our grandsires, however tolerant, however understanding, is a little too reminiscent of the kind of comment that private schoolboys pass, among themselves, on old Fatty, the form-master, or even—with bated breath—on the Presence in the Study. After all, the Victorians did achieve things that make an attitude of patronage towards them seem a trifle lacking in humour. In the Crystal Palaces of some Bowdlerised Utopia, it may be that a committee of Eminent Victorians is earnestly and voluminously attempting to account for a certain dearth of Eminent Georgians. And the Georgians agree, to the extent of proclaiming that the Great Man business went out of date with the great Queen. It is human, if not very convincing, to add that there never were any great men.

And yet we, the Post-Victorians, cannot help feeling that the Victorian giants ought to be—even if they are not—the veriest pigmies in comparison with ourselves. In so many ways we have progressed beyond them. Our standards of taste and criticism are indisputably higher. The veriest tyro among us can go through their works as a schoolmaster corrects the papers shown up by his boys. If we cannot produce a Dickens, we should be ashamed to shed tears over Little Nell, and if Sir William Watson's comparison with Tennyson:

"Here was a bard shall outlive you all,"

is even more obviously applicable to the poets of our day than those of the last generation, it does not need a poet to make merry over the Idylls of the Prince Consort Arthur. In surveying the stature of these giants, we cannot help feeling as if, in Tennyson's own words:

"What should not have been, had been,"

and are ready to cheer anybody who will inform us that these awful figures, looming through the mists of time, are no more than a row of superannuated windmills.

Unless, therefore, we are to fall back upon this palpably disingenuous evasion of the whole difficulty, we are driven to seek for some element of genius which the Victorians must have possessed in abundant enough measure to compensate for their lack of its more obvious adornments. It is to the very immensity, or—if we prefer to express it so—the solidity of their achievement, that we must look for a solution. For the essential element in all genius, that which distinguishes the master from the dilettante, is nothing more nor less than the power of concentration, the ability to keep any creative idea in the mind at a steady white heat until thought is crowned by achievement. It is what Napoleon was trying to express when he defined genius as the infinite capacity for taking pains. He would have come nearer the mark had he defined it as the art of turning dreams into realities. Many of us have had a dream in which we have imagined ourselves achieving masterpieces of art or literature, with inspired ease. Sometimes we are able to capture, on waking, some fragment of bathos that was the admired product of our afflatus. That is an extreme instance of the capacity for dreaming dreams, without any concentration whatever for their realisation.

Every race is not to the swift, nor is it always the artistic temperament that fathers the greatest art. We have all of us known the youth whose lyrics or water-colours gave promise of a career that never got further than a drawing-room prettiness, while some more stolid-seeming competitor was bearing off the palm. It has been a perpetual subject of wonder that the Celtic peoples, whose very speech brims over into poetry, have yet not even been able to produce a Shelley or a Keats—let alone a Shakespeare. The deliberate and earnest Saxon excels in that faculty of concentration without which even brilliance is of no avail. And so it was with the Victorians. We laugh them to scorn on account of their earnestness, and yet it is by virtue of this very earnestness that their greatest are sitting where so few of ours can aspire to soar.

It is our custom, in making out our own case against the Victorians, to put our finger, with a gesture of triumphant finality, on the very source of their achievement. They were quite ludicrously in earnest; they took themselves with portentous seriousness. They were also moral, and not content with moralising their own conduct, they must needs do the same to their art and literature. All of which we have been taught to regard as the lowest depth of Philistinism. And no doubt our verdict is the expression of a half truth. Novels with a moral turn out, on analysis, to be profoundly immoral; buildings with a moral may offend the eye without elevating the soul; men with a moral are not infrequently of the breed of Holy Willy. And yet, when all this is taken into account, it remains profoundly true that not only human personality, but its outward expression in art, thrives in direct proportion to its morality.

For, if we consider the matter closely enough, morality turns out to be one aspect of the sovereign faculty of concentration. The moral man is he who is capable of concentrating his will invincibly on what he takes to be good. *"Tenax propositi,"* tenacious of purpose, is what best describes him. The execution of that vast design on the roof of the Sistine Chapel, the completion of the Choral Symphony, of the Divine and the Human Comedy, were, in the highest degree, moral acts. It is not only the quantity of work that counts, but its quality, its intensity, its constancy to the highest ideal. "Be ye perfect," is the first and great commandment to every artist, "even as your Father in Heaven is perfect."

Immoral, by this reckoning, will be the work that is turned out, not for its own sake, but for what it will fetch in the way of money or reputation. The smart journalese article that is dashed off to order; the sermon of conventional platitudes strung together; the review designed to do a good turn to a friend or to "dust the jacket" of a rival; the novel which, instead of developing the truth of a situation, wrenches it to point a conventional moral—these are acts, not of morality, but of prostitution, whose heinousness must be judged according to the comparative value we set on the body and the soul.

To say without qualification that the Victorians were moral, would be to imply that they fell not far short of perfection. It would, however, be true to say that—in so far as we can generalise about their dominant middle-class—it did most earnestly seek and ensue after morality, according to its lights, and that though some of these lights may have been as false as those hung out by wreckers, it is perhaps better to concentrate upon an imperfect ideal, than to have no steady ideal at all.

The whole training and circumstances of the middle class, in the early part of the nineteenth century, were calculated to create and foster the habit of concentration. The stress of a competition, fierce beyond all precedent, kept its nose to the grindstone. Leisure was a luxury only to be attained by those few of its members who were able, and willing, to retire on their fortunes. And herein the middle class differed most from those landed gentlemen whose rents lifted them above all anxiety for the future, and who sometimes gambled away their fortunes in sheer wantonness. To Matthew Arnold's sensitive, bourgeois soul, there was something actually distressing in the idea of Byron's writing with "the careless ease of a man of quality," but he glows with a genuine moral exaltation in recording the immense amount of work that Sainte-Beuve put into each of his *Causeries*. For Matthew Arnold and the self-helping Mr. Smiles were caste brothers under their skin.

Not only his environment, but his religion, provided the Ten Pound Householder with schooling in concentration. He and his Ten Pound House did most emphatically serve the Lord, and the Lord was as great a lover of work for its own sake, as He was a contemner of labour-wasting joy.

> "How doth the little busy bee
> Improve each shining hour!"

were words that every child was forced to remember, together with the jingle about the bee's unedifying foil, the sluggard, who indulged in dreams, and was tactless enough to confide them to Doctor Watts. As for Wesley, his educational theory would have been precisely summed up in the lines:

> "All work and no play
> Makes Jack a holy boy,"

which James Mill would doubtless have amended to "a perfect little utilitarian philosopher."

The cult of work soon got detached from its religious moorings, and became a gospel of its own, on both sides of the Atlantic. Emerson gave it its most uncompromising expression when he made the whole of human wisdom to culminate in the dictum that time was never lost that was spent in work. His friend, Carlyle, is never tired of proclaiming the sanctity of work, as work, almost irrespective of its quality or purpose. "All work, even cotton spinning, is noble; work is alone noble"—in such words might a master sweep have addressed his apprentice, while lighting a fire to hustle him out of the chimney; so might the sweater have retorted to the songstress of the shirt, with her

> "Work, work, work,
> And the labour never flags . . ."

"Work," he might have quoted from the Prophet, "never so Mammonish, mean, *is* in communication with Nature; the real desire to get Work done will lead one more and more to truth."—Work, and not truth, being significantly helmeted with a capital letter.

This cult and practice of work, unlovely as they might be when the object was to gather not honey, but money, all the day, did nevertheless form an effective discipline in concentration. It engendered that peculiar moral earnestness, common to all the great Victorians of the middle class heyday, with the possible exception of Disraeli. It accounts for the solidity and thoroughness of their output. It took more than twenty years of patient and obscure research to produce what is perhaps the crowning achievement of that age, *The Origin of Species*.

Herbert Spencer's *Synthetic Philosophy* was the work of a long, and invalid, lifetime. The library edition of Ruskin, in 39 huge volumes, would make the reading alone a Herculean task. But the Victorians revelled in vast undertakings. It took Carlyle fourteen years of almost unimaginable drudgery to complete his *Frederick*. It was in 1862 that Browning embarked upon the task of telling the same murder story, in twelve long blank verse poems, from twelve different points of view, and it was in 1869 that the last of his four substantial volumes issued from the press.

Sometimes the task was too vast to be comprehended in one lifetime. If Macaulay had carried out the plan of his History, at the rate it actually took him to write it, it has been calculated * that it would have taken him 150 odd years to complete it. Another similar torso is Buckle's *History of Civilisation in England*. But the marvel is not what the Victorians left unfinished, but what they actually accomplished. The itch for quick intellectual and artistic returns was an accompaniment of modern progress not seriously felt before the *fin de siècle*.

In an age so convinced of the sanctity of labour, there was little corresponding to the modern demand for economy of intellectual effort. The Victorian had a tough mental digestion, and did not expect his food to be dished up to him in highly spiced or tabloid form. He delighted in three-volume novels; in set speeches lasting for hours on end—as when Palmerston held the House spellbound from the dusk of one June day to the dawn of another; in sermons of prodigious length—and I remember one

* By Mr. Cotter Morrison.

famous old Dean who was reputed to have been good for an hour; in leaders of a deliberate and narcotic solemnity, without any vulgar exordium of headlines. Most potent, grave, and reverend signors were the statesmen, divines, editors, headmasters, employers, and persons in any sort of authority and influence in those days. But it was also, inevitably, an age of the most redoubtable bores. Those whose memory goes back far enough, can remember a type of sententious and autobiographical old gentlemen, whose orations commanded a resigned deference that would hardly be obtainable to-day. And what our grandsires had to put up with in the way of minor and perishable literature, can be vaguely realised by a purchase of some of its relics, for a few pence, in a second hand bookshop. The most popular of all forms of mental pabulum was provided by collections of sermons—and such sermons! They must be read to be appreciated, and the experiment is not likely to be repeated.

That the Victorians were moral, consciously and earnestly moral, to an extent scarcely to be paralleled before and certainly not since, will hardly be disputed. They were peculiarly rich in that faculty of concentration that is the indispensable foundation of all morality, and under the influence of a middle class Protestantism that affected those who believed in neither God nor devil this concentrated energy of will was directed to ends believed to be good.

And yet, by a curious paradox, it is just in the field of morals and religion that this age, though most voluminous, is least distinguished. With the exception of Newman, a rebel against the prevailing spirit of his time, there is hardly such a thing as a religious genius, though there is no lack of talented organisers such as Manning and Wiseman, Pusey and "Soapy Sam" Wilberforce. Even the cold and formal eighteenth century was able to produce a spiritual genius of the first rank in William Law, not to speak of Blake, whose rhymed *Everlasting Gospel* penetrates more deeply into the spirit of Christianity than any formal theological treatise of modern times. Nor is there anything in the Victorian Age comparable to the apostolic genius of the Wesleys, nor any preacher, not even Spurgeon, with the compelling force of a Whitefield. Instead, we have a phenomenal output of dreary books and dreary divines, the spirit not of Assisi or Geneva, but of Barchester Towers.

As for moralists, there is certainly Carlyle, but his grip upon the essentials of morality is so unsure that he is at last reduced to bawling at the top of his voice that might and right are the same thing, and, in a somewhat lower key, implying that the rape of Silesia and the Partition of Poland were by no means discreditable episodes in the career of a hero-king. As for Ruskin, he started as a tiny boy by preaching a sermon on the text, "People be good," and he continued to preach it for the rest of his life. But his moral trumpet, though sonorous, sounds a somewhat uncertain and inconsistent note. What moralist, of this age of morality, approaches the curious insight of Thomas Browne, or the glowing sweetness of Jeremy Taylor, or—in spite of his record—the concentrated wisdom of Bacon's *Essays?* What Victorian parallels have we to:

> "Who sweeps a floor as for thy name
> Makes that and the action fine,"

or

"He prayeth best who loveth best
All things, both great and small,"

or

"Teach me to live, that I may dread
The grave as little as my bed?"

The Victorian morality was no doubt solid and genuine, but it was somewhat lacking in inspiration. It was the exact opposite to that of Jesus Christ, with its central message that the Kingdom of Heaven is within you. The Victorian morality did not come from within, but was mainly regarded as a discipline imposed from without. The Lord, whom the Victorians worshipped, was not the Christian Father who is one with His children, but more akin to the Hebrew Jehovah, who imposes His law, and whose relations with men are regulated with the formal precision of a covenant or contract. He was no doubt a Father, but then—we know what Victorian fathers could be.

If we examine a little more closely the moral code of the average respectable citizen, we shall find that it was supported by two pillars, on which was inscribed:

(1) It pays to be good:
(2) If you must commit sins, at least don't talk about them.

The first of these flows logically from both main sources of Victorian religion. The aristocratic Deity of the eighteenth century had tactfully tilted the scales so that virtue should be rewarded and vice punished, and if the more bourgeois Lord was a little uncertain about the reward,

His explosive temper was sufficient guarantee of the punishment. Moreover the new voters of the Reformed Franchise were thoroughly imbued with the business instinct. What was the use of a virtue that did not pay? "Just," cries Martin Tupper, "is the everlasting law that hath wedded happiness to virtue!"

It is for this reason that the Victorian divines were so sensitive to any threat of closing or cooling Hell. It was not enough to do good for its own sake; there must be bribes and threats to make virtue as much the result of selfish calculation as the purchase of government stock—that was what a Divine Governor was for, as Paley, whose posthumous reputation as a moralist and theologian was at its height, had long since demonstrated. It was also the reason that such importance was attached to literature, and particularly fiction, being of an improving nature. It would never do if dog were to have his day or Devil his due. If the picture of life given in contemporary novels had passed for gospel among practical men, there is not an insurance company that would have accepted a client without the certificate not only of a doctor, but of a clergyman. Barring the few glorious exceptions, like Becky Sharp, bad characters have bad ends provided for them, and vice must never be allowed to have any agreeable or redeeming features. When Thackeray comes to treat of Her Majesty's royal and lamented Uncle George, the result is not a biography, but an awful warning.

But here arose a difficulty, for it was another dogma of Victorian morality that it was encouraging vice even to acknowledge its existence, or at any rate to present it vividly enough to form a lifelike image of it in the reader's mind. You could not be too careful in these matters. The old Marquis of Hertford, for instance, one of the last and raciest of the old Regency school of aristocrats, of whom a Gilbert might have said:

"To hide his guilt he did not plan,
But owned himself a bad old man."

What was to be done with him? He was obviously cut out for an awful example, but—original sin being what it was, and marquises and snobs and lovely houries what they were—might not a too veridical account of his proceedings prove the temptation of Saint Anthony to youths and maidens unfortified by Theban austerities? Thackeray does the job very creditably in *Vanity Fair;* the Marquis of Steyne is an unmitigatedly disgusting old villain, and though we are only allowed to guess vaguely at the conveniences incidental to his connexion with Mrs. Crawley, we have the most vivid possible presentation of the inconveniences of being flung bleeding to the ground by Major Crawley. But then Thackeray, like most of his fellow novelists, aspired to be something more than a mere story-teller. Did not Miss Charlotte Brontë—whom rumour actually credited with being the original Becky to Thackeray's Rochester—liken him to a Hebrew prophet? Though Miss Charlotte's own masterpiece was not found pure in the eyes of a Quarterly Reviewer.

The subject of Victorian prudery has, perhaps, been a little overworked. There was never a time when Englishmen had anything but ridicule for the ineffable refinement of people in Puritan America, who hid in decent drapery what they called the "limbs" of their tables. And there were successful rebels, even in literature. Surtees succeeded throughout in maintaining a rich level of coarseness and sexual frankness, without the least attempt at being improving. But then the place for the sporting novel was along with *Bell's Life* in the smoking room—if any—out of the official reach of the ladies. But Disraeli, who did write for the drawing room, and was far less the spiritual child of Abraham than of Byron, dared even to present old Lord Hertford in the not wholly unattractive colours of life. Nor did Tennyson himself shrink from exploiting a by no means edifying legend of the seduction of a doddering old magician by a competent young harlot, duly described as such.

But making all allowances, Victorian morality did, to an extent inconceivable nowadays, repose upon the ostrich-like faith that you could best conquer evil by shutting your eyes to its existence. More important than the truth itself was the purity, or rather the respectability, of family life. And the family was a rigidly closed circle, presided over by the Lord, and his deputy, the Paterfamilias, and into that circle not the least suggestion of evil, or carnal affection, or anything unrefined was allowed to penetrate. It was on exactly the same principle that the prince, in Edgar Allan Poe's story, isolated himself with all his courtiers and servants in a well-provisioned palace castle, while the Red Death was wasting the countryside. Even Shakespeare, though the recipient of unmeasured adulation, must be thoroughly scrubbed and disinfected by the Reverend Mr. Bowdler, before being allowed to pass the guard and stand in the presence of the Young Person.*

A passionate morality would never have suffered these limitations. Christ, as the Pharisees had not been slow to point out, was entirely oblivious to respectability. But the Victorian standard of righteousness approached much more nearly to that of the Pharisees than that of Christ. It was a genuine and potent discipline, but it fell just short of being passionate. "Respectable" was, in fact, the word by which it may best be described, and it was a reign of respectability that the middle class triumph imposed upon society. Not the proudest nobleman could have rebuked an insult to his order with more unforced dignity than Mr. Brownlow, in *Oliver Twist,* in venturing to enquire the name of the magistrate "who offers a gross and unprovoked insult to a respectable person." As an ideal of life, Victorian respectability, with all its limitations, must be owned, when judged by its fruits, to be at least worthy of respect.

It is easy for us, with our more accommodating standards, to see the chinks in the armour of righteousness wherewith our grandsires encased themselves. It is less easy for us to realise its strength. If the accepted moral code was imperfect, lacking in profundity, lacking in comprehensiveness, and above all, lacking in passion and spontaneity, it was at least held with undisputing faith. On this point there was no difference between Christian

* Not so Moses, whose alleged account of Judah's sons and Lot's daughters was thrust, in the Family Bible, under the most virginal noses.

and unbeliever. Tennyson's honest doubt did not apply to questions of conduct. Perplexed in faith a man might be, provided he were pure in deeds.

Even an imperfect and formal morality, with faith and zeal to back it, is capable of working miracles. And the age of middle class ascendency was whole-heartedly moral. There was never a time when men and women were so much in earnest, when they took themselves and their mission in life so seriously. It was a seriousness too often impervious to humour, and hardening into spiritual pride. But it did produce a concentration of energy that made the Victorian Age not only fruitful, but also, in a sense, heroic.

CHAPTER XV

THE CULT OF THE DOUBLE BED

I F you had chanced to broach the subject of morality in the fifties, you would probably have been informed, in no uncertain terms, that such subjects were not discussed in refined society. For then, as now, most people associated the word with that branch of conduct that is concerned with the relations of the sexes. And indeed, Victorianism itself is connected in the average mind with crinolines and Mrs. Grundy, with bread-and-butter misses and submissive wives, in short, with the sexual life of the age.

This is not quite so indefensible as it might seem at the first blush. For there is a sense in which it would be true to say that the sexual aspect of life, if not all-important, was at least the most important. The Victorian Age was distinguished by the ever-increasing quantity of the things it produced. But the historian of a future age, who can see to the close of the story, may perhaps decide that the production of men was even more revolutionary in its effects than that of things, and that the vital statistics were not those of imports and exports, but of a population mounting every year above the possibility of maintenance, except from overseas. The workshop of the world was gambling more and more recklessly on the prospect of keeping its custom for all time. No wonder that the Victorians made work into a gospel!

"Produce! produce!" was the cry, not only of its prophet Carlyle, but of the age itself. But the output of the factory was less important, in the long run, than that of the double bed.

True to their instinct of concentrating on immediate necessities, and ignoring deeper issues, the Victorians were careful to invest the marriage chamber with a taboo of absolute secrecy. Gone was the time when the bridal bed had been covered with flowers, and the guests had escorted the happy pair in triumph thither. That room was now the Holy of Holies in the vast temple of middle class domesticity. All ways led thither. Paterfamilias toiled, wages were kept down and rents screwed up, in order that an economic basis might be provided for the business of refined propagation, and the most attractive partner secured. "Mamma" toiled and intrigued, with indefatigable zeal, that she might see the last of her brood of daughters pass beyond her ken and authority into the Unmentionable. To attain this consummation, innocent Flora exposed a virginal bosom, and pinched and expanded her contour to hint at charms that nature never owned. To provide a safety valve for masculine animal instincts, that were not allowed to exist save behind those portals of silence, an outer darkness was provided, peopled by beings whose very existence it would have been unrefined for Flora to have suspected, and into which Charles and Reginald faded away at discreet intervals.

It was the same with fiction. The happy ending was the one in which the chamber door closed, for the first time, behind the hero and heroine. "Further," as Mr.

Robert Montgomery would have said, "the red and raging eye of imagination is forbidden to pry." And yet one wonders, sometimes, how beings so apparently devoid of fleshly passion as the heroes and heroines of most Victorian novels, could ever have effected the transition from courtship to parenthood. It has been asserted that the Brownings—two of the greatest lovers, in all conscience, that ever lived—never saw each other naked. Evidence on such a point must be hard to collect, and the statement itself may conceivably have originated in a deduction from an article of Victorian faith, that the Holy of Holies is as proper within as without.

By fearful sanctions was this hymeneal propriety defended. Once the goal was attained and the door closed, the destiny of Flora was regarded as finally settled. Whatever happened, there was no appeal and no escape. For a woman to divorce her husband was next door to impossible. For her to leave him was social ruin. One of the rare gleams of light on these inner mysteries is provided by a dreadful story, in Lady Cardigan's *Recollections,* about a certain Lord Ward, whose pleasure it was to gloat on the spectacle of his young wife's naked body, covered with jewels, against the background provided by a black satin-covered couch. In terror and disgust the poor girl appealed to her parents, at whose behest she had gone to the altar, and who had probably trained her to notions of the most fastidious prudery, only to be told to conform to her husband's entirely legitimate desires. The sequel is perhaps not surprising, of her betraying her marriage vows in good earnest, being publicly expelled from her husband's and rejected from her parents' house in the small hours of the morning, and dying of the consequent miscarriage. The last scene of all—as ghoulish as anything dreamed of by a Poe or a Bram Stoker—may be read in the original by those with strong enough nerves. There was a grimness, as of Hell itself, beneath the veneer of Victorian gentility.

For however gentle her manners might be, the Victorian woman had no pity either for herself or her sex when vital issues were at stake. She, who produced the men while man was producing the things, was instinctively conscious of the importance of her function. Her sphere was the home, and there was never a time when the home had played such an important part in the social system. The eighteenth century aristocracy had been inclined to see something a little vulgar in too strenuous a domesticity. But the middle class flaunted its domesticity in the light of day, and imposed its standards on the country as soon as it got into the saddle.

The cult of the home was all-pervading. It was the theme of unlimited sentimentality. No song more exactly hit off the taste of the time than *"Home, Sweet Home."* Eliza Cook defied the whole world to blame her for loving an old arm-chair. Tennyson moved countless readers to tears with the story of a marital tiff healed over a child's grave. Mrs. Hemans gave a highly coloured account of the homes of England, from the "stately homes," with their proper accompaniment of ancestral trees, deer, swans, and streams, to the cottage homes where

"Fearless . . . the lowly sleep
As the bird beneath their eaves."

It is a time when Family Prayers, Family Bibles, Family Shakespeares, Household Words, Home Chat, Home Notes, Family This, and Home That, are constantly *en evidence*. And humour, instead of running to the mock heroic, as in the previous century of classical tradition, now goes to the kitchen and the nursery for its sustenance. Even Ruskin, who was inclined to look on all humour with grave suspicion, quite purred over his Rose's nickname for him of Saint Crumpet, and Herbert Spencer's awful and solitary attempt at a joke was on the subject of chops. Thackeray was no doubt considered irresistibly funny when he described a lady's court dress as being trimmed with bouquets of Brussels sprouts, and of her mother having a muffin for a stomacher. Indeed it was a safe lead for a would-be funny man to introduce some such word as muffin, crumpet, onion, caudle, pap, warming pan or rolling pin, into his discourse, for success to be assured. Parody was largely a mechanical grind of interlarding romance, of the high-flown kind so popular in the drawing-room, with those humble, necessary terms.

To preserve the home intact, in all its purity and sanctity, was, then, an object of supreme importance in the eyes of the Victorians, and it is merely boorish to twit them with cant for accepting the logical consequences of their belief. To be fruitful and multiply, in spite of the teachings of Mr. Malthus, was a sacred duty. That was what the marriage union was originally for, and that, too, what the Holy of Holies, the marriage chamber, was for. Though it would have been violating a taboo to have said so, there was probably not a parent in the country who would not, in his or her heart of hearts, have approved

Mr. Shaw's description of marriage, as combining the maximum of temptation with the maximum of opportunity. The double bed, otherwise so obviously inconvenient, is a silent witness to its truth. By the strange inversion of propriety that reigned behind closed doors, any suggestion of substituting two beds for one would have been regarded as not very nice. There are old-fashioned people, even to-day, who have not wholly cast off this prejudice.

But the marriage union meant more to the Victorians than a mere partnership in breeding. The bond between husband and wife was held by them to be of the most inviolable and sacred intimacy, rising above fleshly passion as the flower rises above the manured earth in which it strikes its roots. It was—to adapt a phrase of Burke's— a partnership in every virtue and in all perfection. Had the Victorians been habituated to the jargon of the latest psychology, they would have said that carnal affections were meant to be sublimated. Passion was in their view necessary to life, as food is necessary, but the life is more than meat, and food, when it has left the plate, is like passion that has passed the stage of courtship, to be digested in a decent obscurity. For decency is not necessarily hypocritical. The Victorians might have pleaded that their reticence about sex was no more misplaced than the desire of the Greek dramatist to get his killing done "off." The modern flaunting of passion and sex-appeal would have struck them as not only wicked, but vulgar. To be carnally minded is death.

Nor may we plausibly tax them with cant because they

put a more serious emphasis than is fashionable nowadays upon marital constancy. Their shades might retort with a rather obvious *"tu quoque"* upon the right we are in the habit of claiming to the unconditional fulfilment of our personalities. The Victorians believed that passions ought to be under control, and that self-sacrifice is better than self-indulgence. The marriage vow was not to be lightly broken—to do so was to incur the guilt of treason. There is no more popular target for modern satire than the Arthur of Tennyson's *Guinevere*. The awful sternness with which the King rebukes his unfaithful consort, and the solemnity of his forgiveness, strike the average commentator as the pose of a priggish old cuckold. And yet to judge thus is to show a complete ignorance of the Victorian point of view.

Arthur certainly takes himself and his mission as seriously as men of Tennyson's time were accustomed to do. He was like Thomas Arnold, like Ruskin, like Lord Shaftesbury, a moral idealist, and his ideal was surely one of the noblest ever propounded, one of Christian knighthood "breaking the heathen" of truth, of honour, of service, of chastity, and of "the maiden passion for a maid," as the spur to

"High thoughts, and amiable words
 And courtliness, and the desire of fame,
 And love of truth, and all that makes a man."

It was all this that Guinevere had undermined by her surrender to that most compelling of lovers, Sir Lancelot du Lake.

"Then came thy shameful sin with Lancelot;
Then came the sin of Tristram and Isolt;
Then others. . . ."

with sin's nemesis,

"Sword and fire,
Red ruin and the breaking up of laws,
The craft of kindred and the Godless hosts
Of heathen swarming o'er the Northern Sea."

The illicit indulgence of passion was, in fact, sin, and its
wages death—death, in this instance, to the whole fabric
of Christian civilisation that the hero king had built up.
The modern point of view, that moral codes are like the
proverbial laws of Ireland, and that passion is only guilty
when repressed, may claim to be more advanced, or—
what is often the same thing—more primitive, than that
of the Victorians. But it is hard to pour scorn upon poor
Arthur for not having anticipated, or reverted to, it.

Carlyle had shown a more than Tennysonian austerity
in endorsing that of Dante towards Paolo and Francesca:

"Strange to think; Dante was the friend of this poor
Francesca's father; Francesca herself may have sat upon
the Poet's knee, as a bright innocent little child. Infinite
pity, yet also infinite rigour of law: it is so Nature is
made; it is so Dante discerned that she was made. What
a paltry notion is that of his *Divine Comedy's* being a
poor impotent terrestrial libel; putting those into Hell
upon whom he could not be avenged on earth! I suppose if ever pity, tender as a mother's, was in the heart
of any man, it was in Dante's. But a man who does not

know rigour cannot pity either. His very pity will be cowardly, egoistic—sentimentality or little better."

The Victorians could not conceive of a happy ending to vice. It might be possible, by an heroic stretch of toleration, to extend Christian pity to the fallen but repentant fair, but to suggest that forbidden fruit could produce anything but violent indigestion would have been to constitute oneself an enemy of society. If a wife left her husband, it was assumed that this could only be with a blackguard of the deepest dye and the longest Dundrearys, who would shortly abandon her, penniless, to the Thames or the schoolroom. The classic instance of this is *East Lynne*. In *Bleak House*, though Lady Dedlock is allowed to flourish for a while, it is only that the justice of the Lord and Dickens may fall on her more awfully in the end. Wherever you look, whether in fiction, or journalism, or melodrama, you find not the least shadow of doubt that punishment follows the violation of sexual taboos—at any rate by the female—as inevitably as night follows day. If you want the view of the sixties in a nutshell, it may be studied in the first series of *Echo* cartoons, one of which is called *The Husband's Friend,* in which the tragic story is depicted, starting with the innocent girl, dandling, under the approving glances of her father, a brother hardly larger than her *chignon,* and proceeding, through philandering, elopement by the "Night Mail North," and divorce, to the final scene on the parapet of the New Embankment:

> "Thus in her misery murmured one, for whom
>   The happiness of life had utter end.
> Say, to what fate would rigorous justice doom
>   Her husband's friend?"

Such was the stern side of Victorian family life, and that it could be not only stern, but ugly and cruel, is not to be denied. Poor Lady Ward was certainly not the only wife who found that the Holy of Holies was a nightly torture chamber, from which the only escape was into the outer darkness of social ruin. The bride in *Locksley Hall*, dutifully tender to a boorish husband, was probably typical of thousands. Moreover the Lord, still brooding upon the peccadillo of the first woman, was inclined to claim as His due a certain amount of suffering from all the succeeding ones. When anæsthetics first came in, there were many husbands, and even some doctors, who were as much scandalised at the idea of mitigating the agonies of childbed, as a Carthaginian priest might have been at that of painting the hands of Moloch instead of red-heating them for the reception of infants. And however romantically chivalrous a husband might be in other ways, he was the most austere taskmaster in exacting the punctual succession of children that so often overtaxed his wife's strength, and brought on premature age, or death.

But there is no reason to believe that there was any general desire on the part of women to shirk this essential of what was then conceived to be their duty. The Queen herself set the example, and there is something heroic in her submitting, amidst all the cares of state, to be the bearer of nine children. If it was improper to talk about these obligations of marriage, it would have been grossly improper to default from them, and the woman who attempted to do so would certainly have got short shrift from her sex.

But if there was austerity in the Victorian conception of the marriage bond, there was a deep and compensating tenderness. Never was there a time, in European history, when married love was held in such honour, or when it was the theme of such lofty idealism. Mixed with this idealism there was naturally a great deal of bathos and not unpleasing sentiment of the Darby and Joan order, as in the following verse, from an old *Family Economist*:

> "Though morning's early splendour
>   May rapture's thrill impart,
> The vesper hour, more tender,
>   Sinks deeper in the heart. . . .
> E'en age's weary weather
>   Inspires no thought of gloom,
> In hearts that share together
>   Hopes of bliss beyond the tomb."

To pass from the sentimental to the sublime, there was never a more splendid pæan of Love triumphant over Death than Browning's line to his dead wife, beginning:

> "O lyric Love, half angel, and half bird,
>   And all a wonder and a wild desire!"

A more serene and philosophic note is struck by Coventry Patmore's

> "Why, having won her, do I woo?"

and his contrast of wedded love with other human affections, that cloy with satiety:

> "But truly my delight was more
>   In her to whom I'm bound for aye
> Yesterday than the day before
>   And more to-day than yesterday."

No less lofty analogy will suffice Patmore for wedded love, than that of Christ for the Church.

He was, in fact, the very high priest of the Victorian Hymen, and Mr. Max Beerbohm is hardly caricaturing him when he represents him on one knee before the Rossettis, vehemently preaching that "a teapot is not worshipful for its form and colour, but as a sublime symbol of domesticity." With an earnestness, humourless even for his age, he was almost capable of doing so, and certainly the sermon could hardly have been more funny than large portions of his poetry, in which he is so imbued with the sanctity of the domestic commonplace that he does not recoil from such lyric heights as:

> "I rode to see
> The church-restorings; lounged awhile,
>   And met the Dean; was asked to tea,
> And found their cousin, Frederick Graham,
>   At Honor's side,"

and a modern reader may be more inclined to laugh than to cry over the delightful idyll—Patmore's own favourite —describing an engaged couple's idea of a perfect afternoon's enjoyment:

> "To-day, the mother gave
> To urgent pleas, and promise to behave
> As she were there, her long-besought consent
> To trust Amelia with me to the grave
> Where lay my once-betrothed, Millicent,"

an idyll that is punctuated by the penetrating, but unexpectedly cynical observation:

"For dear to maidens are their rivals dead."

We must dig deep and sift patiently for the gold amid the churchyard soil of Patmore's poems, and it is not wholly inappropriate that the philosopher bard of Victorian love should also be the producer of so much Victorian bathos, for the two are not infrequently found in conjunction.

To most people the proof of the pudding will not be the menu, but the eating, and it can hardly be denied that the married lives of Victorians were, in an extraordinary number of instances, crowned with a happiness that no dreams of romance could have surpassed. We have already referred to the Brownings, who lived an even greater poem than any they wrote. Whatever differences there were between Gladstone and Disraeli, there was none in the unruffled harmony of their domestic relations. Disraeli had married an elderly, eccentric, and monied widow, but—supreme Romantic as he was—he achieved his supreme romance in that union. "If he had the chance again," the old lady proudly replied to some impertinent suggestion that her Dizzy had done so for her money, "he would do it for love." And where is there a more charming spectacle than that of the two aged Gladstones, when they happened to be feeling specially happy, waltzing round the room chorusing:

"A ragamuffin husband and a rantipoling wife,
    We'll fiddle it and scrape it through the ups and
        downs of life!"

Sir Robert Peel may be classed among the first genuine Victorians by nothing more certainly than his home life. Awkward and ungenial as he appeared to the world, he had no reserves with his Julia, as his many affectionate letters to her bear witness. On the morning that he met with his fatal accident, he was just about to mount his horse, when he called her to him, and said: "Julia, you are not going without wishing me good-bye, or saying those sweet words 'God bless you.'" * So, all unknowing, she pronounced the closing benediction on their love.

John Stuart Mill, who might well have had the last spark of human feeling crushed out of him by his fearful education, and who was so coolly logical to outward seeming, could yet rise almost to poetry in recording his too brief union with the widow of his friend Taylor. "For seven and a half years that blessing was mine; for seven and a half only! I could say nothing that could describe, even in the faintest manner, what that loss was and is. But because I know she would have wished it, I endeavour to make the best of what life I have left, and to work on for her purposes with such diminished strength as can be derived from thoughts of her, and communion with her memory." †

But of all the many triumphs of married love that the Victorian Age affords, none is more conspicuous than that of Victoria herself, and her beloved Prince Albert. Most people would have augured ill from the masterful tone adopted by the young Sovereign in her engaged cor-

* *Private Letters of Sir Robert Peel*, p. 288.
† Autobiography, pp. 240-1.

respondence, but once married, she soon elected to submit herself, with queenly humility, to the influence of one who, though a foreigner, was endowed with all the high seriousness of purpose and chastity of life that the Victorians most prized. Those who can derive food for ridicule from her touching constancy to his memory throughout her long widowhood—even to the extent of having his room kept exactly as if he were alive—are not to be envied.

> "For love is strong as death. . . .
> Many waters cannot quench love,
> Neither can the floods drown it."

CHAPTER XVI

THE VICTORIAN WOMAN

MODERN discoveries, in the realm of mind and spirit, often consist in the invention of a new word to define what has been known and practised for generations. Auto-suggestion is one of these dictionary parvenus. The Victorians knew nothing of the word, but they were convinced exponents of the thing. They believed that if you wanted anything to be true, you must go on pretending that it was true. There were certain moral archetypes to which reality had got to conform.

The British soldier, for instance, of the Crimea and Mutiny, had got to stand for a hero of the most improving order, a leonine type—in the mediæval sense—with a strong infusion of Protestant Christianity. That British soldiers should ever show an unwillingness to rush into the jaws of death because "somebody" continued to blunder—though this certainly happened at the Redan —that the British soldier's drunken propensities, as more than once during the Mutiny, should threaten to bring disaster out of victory, these things were as unmentionable as the possibility that any woman might have a temperamental aversion to children. And the Victorians, to do them justice, knew just how far to go with their pretending. That the soldier was a hero was no reason for denying him the privilege of being lashed to the triangle and tortured, or for trusting him in a responsible ex-service job, and very little for improving the inhuman conditions of his daily life. The employer, the inn-keeper, the mother of any good-looking wench, might have been more inclined to echo Wellington's "scum of the earth" as a description of those heroes with whom they might be brought into personal contact. But not one of them would have seen anything incongruous in going wild with Tennysonian enthusiasm over the spectacle of a cavalry brigade gratuitously offering itself as a target for artillery, though it would have required extraordinary strength of character and skill in horsemanship for any individual soldier to have shirked his part in that act of criminal lunacy.

And yet the efficacy of such auto-suggestion is on scientific record, and it was perhaps a good thing, in the long run, that the whole nation, from the Queen downwards, should have accepted the civilian bard's rather than the Iron Duke's estimate of Thomas Atkins. The mere fact that he saw himself as a hero, and not as the rough he was, enlisted, probably, through hunger, and disciplined by fear, tended to make him behave like a hero, as he did on the Ridge of Delhi and in the fog at Inkermann. It also induced a few great-hearted souls, like Florence Nightingale and her band of nurses, to give the hero his due of service and sacrifice, and it is the amazing fact that the soldiers, to whom they ministered in the hospital at Scutari, played up, almost without exception, to the part assigned them. In the crowded wards, no less than in the drawing-rooms they had left, these ladies found themselves in the society of gentlemen.

We have taken this instance in order to make it clear

what the Victorian attitude was likely to be towards the reality, not of the barracks, but of the home. It was certainly not going to be one of disinterested observation. There was nothing, in the Victorian view, either good or bad, but thinking made it so. The nation, therefore, that would be saved, must so think of the family as to preserve the correct moral archetypes. As there was a military fiction, so there must be an elaborate and sacred family fiction, which faith would crown with reality.

Accordingly the Victorians got to work with the strenuous evocation of types. We know these types only too well. We have probably seen them in a purer form on the stage, and in the mirror held up to the past by present-day journalism, than the Victorians ever saw them in real life. In fact, if it were not irreverent, we might even suspect the Victorians of having accomplished the highly improper feat of pulling their posterity's legs. There is that portentous figure of the Paterfamilias, the tyrant and terror of his family, whom our fancy naturally endows with a submissive and henlike wife; there is the even more submissive daughter, with her tendency to faint and her virginal simplicity, a type invariably contrasted, by no means to its advantage, with another—scarcely to be described as moral—labelled "the modern girl."

And, in passing, we may be permitted to express our surprise that, even accepting these types as genuine, that drawn of the modern girl should be so much in favour. A girl devoid of tenderness or any unselfish trait, whose solitary intellectual interest is in sex-problems, who is brutally rude to her parents and indecently frank in her intercourse with men, who ruins her constitution with gin and her complexion with cosmetics, whose plastered lips are foul with oaths, and who has probably parted with her virginity in a week-end cottage at the age of eighteen—this journalese paragon would seem, in many ways, a questionable improvement even on poor, silly Flora. Let me hasten to add that so many modern girls seem to have got into the novels and newspapers, that there are hardly enough left over to stock a small and self-advertising coterie of plutocrats. But one trembles to think what would happen to any contributor to a society journal, who let it out that there are houses in Mayfair entirely innocent of cocktails, and that in an even greater number of old-fashioned country houses the cult of feminine gin-swigging is thought to be more than a little vulgar.

This digression has a very real bearing on the question of the Victorian woman. For if we grant that there is every prospect of our hoaxing our grandchildren, it will be easier to believe that our grandparents have played the same trick on us. We can imagine, somewhere about the end of this century, the prize essay, fat with footnotes, proving that such a thing as a gentle or sober young woman was not to be found for at least twenty years after the War, and perhaps the Georgian girl will then be displayed reeling before the footlights—to the accompaniment of such expletives as can be got past the censor —from one man's arms to another. A preposterous caricature, we cry, forgetful that it was we who set the example by first drawing it. And it was the Victorians themselves, with their determination to force truth into the mould of their proprieties, who started the Victorian woman of our imagining.

Still we must admit that there is just that element of truth in the portrait, that is more misleading than falsehood. For the Victorian girl, at least, knew the part that she was expected to play in the social drama, knew too that her matrimonial chances would very largely depend upon her success in impersonating the prescribed type. If the aggressively manly man of that time happened to prefer a correspondingly womanly woman, the ring was not too dearly bought at the price of playing up to his protective instincts. There would be time enough, once the partnership was sealed, for Charles, as well as Flora, to make trial of whatever difference there might be between polite fiction and reality.

Those of our contemporaries who repeat so blandly the commonplaces about the Victorian woman, are perhaps too much biased subconsciously by a version so favourable to modern self-esteem, to test their theory very severely. If they did, it is possible that they might find a certain difficulty in making all the facts hang together. We are, for instance, perpetually having it drummed in upon us that the Victorian woman, compared with the modern variety, was hopelessly inferior physically and intellectually, her status relatively servile, and her usefulness bounded by such futilities as working cross-stitch— though even this, one would imagine, was no less productive an occupation than the cutting of divots. How does this square with the fact that the mid years of the nineteenth century in England were graced by the most brilliant galaxy of feminine genius that has adorned any

age or country? Where, even beneath the beams of the
Roi Soleil or amid the glitter of the Quattrocento, will
you find such a conjunction as that of Elizabeth Barrett
Browning, the two great Brontës, George Eliot, Mrs.
Gaskell, Christina Rossetti, Florence Nightingale, Octavia Hill and—many would be inclined to add—the
Queen herself? Would any candid apologist for modern femininity, with its votes and emancipation, undertake
to produce a contemporary list to compare with it? To
put one down in black and white would be so cruel as
to fall not far short of libel on the selected champions.

And then, again, are not we apt to fix our attention,
a little too exclusively, on those darlings in poke bonnets
and crinolines, who look so charming in the drawings
of Leech? Flora we know—or, like Flora's Charles, flatter ourselves we know—but how about Flora's mamma?
She is an equally conspicuous figure in the cartoons and
literature of the time, and a great deal harder to square
with our notions of Victorian womanhood. And behind
that formidable figure looms one more formidable still,
that of Mamma-in-law, before whom the doughtiest husband must perforce bow his crest.

There is nothing in the fact or fiction of the time to
suggest that the usual pose of the wife in the daguerreotype, looking down with an expression of meek devotion into the face of her seated lord, is more than an
ironic travesty. At Barchester Palace, there is probably
preserved a portrait of Bishop Proudie and his wife in
just that attitude. But, if we may trust the pages of
Punch, or almost any novel of the time, husbands were
more inclined to be henpecked than tyrannous. There

was, of course, a good deal of give and take, according to temperament. The Victorian marriage chamber must often have been a battle ground, in which dire woe was the lot of the vanquished. The Reverend Theobald Pontifex, in *The Way of All Flesh,* did, we know, "kill his cat" on the first evening of the honeymoon, and even Mr. Caudle himself, when, on the death of his redoubtable first consort, he married Miss Prettyman, contrived to set up as a domestic bully, though he proved a much less accomplished and convincing nagger than his at last silent Margaret. And we have, in real life, one or two classic upholders of the Fairchild tradition—The Reverend Patrick Brontë, for example, and Mr. Barrett, who became, in his own despite, father-in-law to Robert Browning. Both these champions of masculinity were fortified by intimate association with the Lord, and Mrs. Brontë was as feeble-bodied as Mrs. Barrett seems to have been feeble-spirited.

The methods of the female tyrant are more subtle, and less likely to pass into record. She does not fire off blunderbusses at doors, like Mr. Brontë—it is part of her ironical technique, as exemplified by the great Margaret Caudle, to maintain her pose of the poor defenceless woman. No shorthand reporter has ever been invited to be present at a curtain lecture, that unremitting, persistent, process of will-breaking that must have made the double bed a veritable nightly rack to many a lord and master. But as from the dungeons of the Inquisition, so from that double bed of respectability, no cry is permitted to penetrate to the outer world. The victor does not blazon forth her triumph nor the vanquished protest his shame. So that we have admittedly only indirect evidence to go upon.

That supplied by fiction is overwhelming. One would imagine that the interpreters of daily life would have been naturally biassed—especially those of them who were of the male sex—in favour of so eminently proper an accompaniment of marriage as the subjection of woman. But the facts were evidently too strong. You can hardly find a *Punch* without some joke about the henpecked husband. That Bishop Proudie was not unique in his domestic status is evident from an incident, depicted by Leech, of the awful prelate demanding of the "buttons,"

"Wretched boy, who is it that sees everything that we do, and before whom even I am but as a crushed worm?"

and receiving the reply,

"The missus, my lord."

The Caudles have their successors in the Naggletons.

Dickens has left us a veritable portrait gallery of masterful wives. Mrs. Wilfer, Mrs. Mantalini, Mrs. Joe Gargery, Mrs. Squeers, Mrs. Bumble, Mrs. McStinger, are hardly the types one would take of poor defenceless creatures. Thackeray has contributed "The Campaigner" and Mrs. Rawdon Crawley, and Disraeli his gentle, but all-managing, Duchess of Bellamont. Meredith may have pleaded for the emancipation of women, but we should like to have seen the tyrant hardy enough to have got much change out of one of his average female characters—Diana, for example, or Mrs. Mountstuart Jenkinson. Indeed we are positively moved to sympathy by the fate of that ill-starred egotist, Sir Willoughby Patterne, tossed contemptuously by Miss Durham into the arms of Clara, and by Clara precipitated grovelling at the feet of Letitia Dale.

The sheikh type of lover had to wait upon female emancipation for his emergence. No Victorian lady would have condescended to that charming appeal,

"Treat me rough, kid, treat me rough!"

The sheikh's solitary predecessors are the creation of two maiden sisters. But then we cannot help suspecting that Mr. Rochester, like Mr. Caudle, was working off on a convenient victim an inferiority complex, implanted by that Creole wife of his in the days of her sanity. As for Heathcliff, some critics have seen in him the mirror of Emily Brontë's own tameless soul, and, in any case, he had his peer in the first Catherine. If Emily had lived, and married, we do not think, to put it mildly, that the gentleman in question would have succeeded in coming the Heathcliff over her.

But it is not only on fiction that we have to rely in exposing the myth about the Victorian woman being a poor downtrodden thing. There are still many of us whose memory goes back to the nineties, and beyond. They will remember, clearly enough, the generation of old people who were young in the forties, and children at the time of the Queen's accession. They will remember, surely, those majestic and bonneted old ladies, whose very kindness could be more terrifying than the wrath of those who now fill their arm-chairs. I challenge any one to come forward and declare that he saw in any one of these old ladies the least sign of that submissiveness that is supposed to be the hallmark of Victorian womanhood. Very much the reverse! It was, in fact, far more often the old lady than the old gentleman who had the appearance of ruling the roost. As the bailiff of a certain large estate is said to have remarked of his employers:

"I can always get over Charlie, but I can't do nothing with Carrie."

The supreme representative of this order of Victorian old ladies was the Queen herself, with her innate though not unkindly dignity. Though the remark is generally misunderstood, as applying to some harmless joke, I have good reason for believing that her famous "we are not amused," was really an annihilating snub of an excursion into the *risqué* at her dinner table. It is impossible to believe that anybody can ever have dared to take a liberty with her. But then, with which of those Victorian old ladies would the brightest young person, or even the most pompous old husband, have dared to overstep the line?

There comes back to me, out of those now remote nineties, the memory of a certain dinner party, annually inflicted on such of the local clergy and their wives as were above the suspicion of ritualistic leanings. On this particular occasion the monotony of the subsequent round game was broken by a distinguished legal luminary, who happened to be staying in the house, uttering a loud gasp, and falling back in his chair with the announcement, "This is the beginning of the end!" But the resultant consternation was allayed as quickly as it had arisen, by the great man's wife, who was engaged in an elderly rubber, calmly commanding, without rising from her chair:

"Pray do not take any notice of him. He has only overeaten himself."

That was the Victorian old lady of real life, self-contained, not to say self-important, to an extent hardly conceivable to-day. And remember, Flora, of the forties—clinging, submissive little Flora—was one and the same person as Great-aunt Florrie, of pious but formidable memory. Even the most inveterate believer in the Victorian legend must sometimes ask himself how this startling transition was ever effected, how the Victorian girl, as we visualise her, ever turned into the Victorian old lady, as we knew her—an evolution far less credible than any associated with name of Darwin, who never expected the leopard to change his spots in the course of one lifetime. And how, for that matter, did the Victorian daughter effect the even more abrupt transition into the Victorian mamma? Can it be that we have been grossly deceived in Flora, and that the darling creature was, in fact, a romantic fiction?

And we have to account for yet another transition—that of the Victorian girl child into Flora. By every account that has come down to us, Victorian children, not excluding girls, were of a rougher and tougher breed than children to-day. The unhappy governess could—and, when her name was Brontë, did—a tale unfold of what we should consider veritable little devils, who delighted in tormenting the governess, or any other inferior animal they could get hold of. From personal accounts one gleans the same impression. I have heard of children in country houses who used to run, with delight, to watch a pig being killed, and of certain little boys and girls whose strange pastime it was to pay visits to the cottage of the public hangman, a fatherly old gentleman who would fit round their little necks the ropes with which celebrated criminals had been disposed of—and who perhaps could not have been expected to foresee that the young ladies and gentlemen would end by all but hanging their youngest brother. One old lady used to relate how she and her sisters would stand round wasps' nests, and fight the wasps with sticks, considering themselves quite disgraced if they came home unstung. Are we to believe that Flora succeeded in putting off her nature when she put up her hair?

To this extent she changed—that she put away childish things and entered upon the responsibilities of womanhood. And we ought to realise how grave, in the eyes of the Victorians, these responsibilities were. For in an age that would otherwise have run wholly to materialism, women were the guardians of the refinements and graces of life. We have already compared their position with that of the monks and nuns in the Dark Ages. Their standards were formal and imperfect, and their refinement lent itself, not infrequently, to such satire as that embodied in Dickens's Mrs. General, with her recipe for giving a correct, aristocratic form to the lips by the words, "Papa, potatoes, poultry, prunes and prisms." But it was better that there should be even that standard of refinement than none at all.

The young lady appears to have been fully conscious

of her dignity, and her tone towards her brothers was
less inclined to be submissive than censorious, the ironical "sir" being employed a good deal in rebuking their
supposed lapses from good-breeding. Even speech had
to be carefully pruned, long words being preferred to
short—thus governesses were reputed to prescribe "nar-
rative" as an obligatory substitute for "tale." At the same
time Flora was expected to be skilled in as many kinds
of "accomplishments" as her parents could afford to get
her taught.

Victorian accomplishments are seldom mentioned nowadays, except in a tone of pitying or amused contempt.
This pose is singularly disingenuous on the part of those
whose business it is to extol the glorious freedom of the
modern young woman, whose accomplishments—by their
account, at any rate,—lie more in the direction of terror-
ising pedestrians on the high road and compounding sym-
phonies on the theme of gin. Indeed the Joy Flapper-
ton or Miss Mai Fair in the newspapers are distinguished
by nothing so much as their flaunting contempt of brains.
If one of them is told of a famous conductor, she will
ask what tram he is on. If she visits a solicitor—an extremely probable contingency—she will twit him with
the dulness of his library, and suggest an Edgar Wallace
or two. Poor Flora, with her music, her water-colours,
her fancy needlework, her fretwork carpentry and poker
work, may surely claim to have been as attractive, and
even as useful a member of society.

But we are always being told that these accomplishments were quite trivial, and resulted in nothing good.

Even if they had merely led to the infusion of some prettiness and harmony into the drab materialism of the Victorian struggle for the main chance, one would have thought that their existence was sufficiently justified. But the legend that the Victorian woman was a mere trifler had never the least warrant, except in the modern prejudice that a deliberately womanly woman must needs be a fool. Those ladies in crinolines were, in fact, as hard and earnest workers as the gentlemen in frock coats, and apart from its extraordinary outcrop of feminine genius, the age was adorned by countless women of distinguished culture and rich attainments, women like Mrs. Haldane, the mother of the statesman, Lady Dorothy Nevill, Jane Welsh Carlyle, Mrs. Potter, mother of Mrs. Beatrice Webb —but one could go on prolonging the list for pages.

We must not forget the time and energy that Victorian women put into what were known as "good works." Some of them, no doubt, became rampant busybodies, of the type satirised by Dickens in Mrs. Jellyby, with her overwhelming interest in the affairs of Borrioboola Gha. But there were others, like Mary Carpenter, Josephine Butler, "Sister Dora," and Octavia Hill, who must have exercised an untold influence for good. And in every parish there were those who devoted themselves, with unostentatious zeal, to ameliorating, according to their lights, the hard lot of the poor. No Victorian would have dreamed of frowning on such womanly activities as these. Florence Nightingale was one of many Victorian women with the instinct for social service—she was only peculiar by virtue of her genius and opportunity.

And she had no difficulty in finding, among the delicate ladies of her class, recruits for the heroic adventure of the Black Sea hospitals.

Of what the Victorian woman was capable will best be illustrated by one concrete instance, of three ladies who in no way aspired to intellectual distinction or moved in intellectual circles, but held to the strictest tradition of Victorian, Low-church domesticity. I refer to the three daughters of the Earl of Abergavenny, father of the first Marquis. The extent and skill of their craftsmanship must have been amazing, to judge by its results. In Birling Church, in Kent, there is a tall and elaborate font cover, which must often have been mistaken for fifteenth century carving, but which—as an old photograph remains to testify—was the work of their hands. They also succeeded in designing a stained-glass window, with their mother depicted in the not inappropriate rôle of Dorcas, and the effect is at least more pleasing than that of the ordinary glass of the period. There seems to have been scarcely any sort of ornamental furniture that they were incapable of constructing. Marquetrie, poker-work, inlay, woodcarving, held no mysteries for them. A particularly fine specimen of their handiwork is an ebony cabinet, set with stones, which would probably now command a respectable price, in spite of its unfashionable period. All were competent painters, and one of them, Lady Augusta, a portraitist of real distinction in oils. They were, besides, fearless horsewomen, and the eldest of them, by great courage and presence of mind, once averted what looked like being a fatal carriage accident. They were untiring women of affairs, and the seaside resort of Llandudno is a monument to the foresight and enterprise of Lady Augusta, who, when left a young widow, with the fortunes of an infant heir in her keeping, saw and realised the possibilities of what was then the haunt not of trippers, but of snipe. The last survivor of the trio, Lady Isabel, retained all her faculties and power of work at the age of 84, sitting bolt upright all the morning at her desk transacting the business of her estate and writing innumerable letters, until the week of her death.

I cite this example, which I believe that many readers will be able to parallel from their own experience, not as a case of outstanding genius, but as typical of what the real Victorian woman was and did. The supreme instance of all is furnished by the Queen herself, the most untiring worker in that age of work, and, if not the most considerable, certainly the most representative of its personalities.

We must glance, in passing, at another count in the modern indictment of Victorian womanhood, that of chronic unhealthiness. To a certain extent, no doubt, this accusation would lie equally at the door of either sex, in an age so devoid of modern notions of hygiene. And Flora was no doubt not only a homekeeper, but a window-shutter, and considered that an appearance of ill-health conferred a positive *cachet* upon her. "Mamma," said a little girl somewhere about the middle of the century, "I wish I had rosy cheeks like the little girl we have just passed." "That, my dear," was the reply, "would be extremely unrefined"—this incident is vouched for by the little girl's nephew. And Flora also indulged in ferocious tightlacing, though probably this was no more harmful than her great-granddaughter's practice of starving herself, in order to plane down any protuberance suggestive of femininity—let alone cigarette-smoking unlimited, and such gin-poisoning of the tissues as journalese mass-suggestion may have caused her to indulge in.

But Flora, though she did not make sport the fetish it is to the modern girl, got a good deal of fun, in an informal way, out of doors. Archery was a great amusement of the time, and a very frivolous and unscientific croquet. For those who could afford it, there was riding —though not often, or seriously, to hounds. And—still in an informal way—there were more strenuous pursuits. Even football had its amazons. This I once heard vouched for by one of them, an old lady of the strictest Victorian school, though how she managed it in crinolines I was not curious enough, at the time, to enquire. There was cricket, with brothers, and skating, and also a forerunner of the paper-chase, known as hare and hounds.

And, with all her errors, the Victorian woman appears to have succeeded admirably in what she, at any rate, regarded as the most important function of womanhood. It was she who bore that generation of robust children whom Du Maurier was so fond of drawing, and whom we still see around us as the hale and evergreen old people of to-day. Whether golf prices and speed records are an adequate substitute for the kind of goods that Flora delivered, raises a controversy that dates, in principle, as far back as the Mother of the Gracchi.

To judge fairly of the Victorian woman, we have to make whatever effort is required to appreciate a standpoint so different from that which has since become fashionable. It was only a very small minority of advanced spirits that desired to see women of the middle or upper classes—for it was a different matter with the factory workers—enter into any sort of direct competition with men. The Queen herself was never more the supreme representative of contemporary feeling, than in her intransigeant anti-feminism. Of a lady who advocated women's rights, in the modern sense, she remarked that she ought to be whipped. And those formidable mammas, who knew so well how to maintain their authority in the home, would almost certainly have been solid behind her.

Indeed, if it had been proposed to emancipate women by giving them the right to be dragged away from their homes, and packed into jury boxes along with men, to discuss with them the most indelicate matters, it is pretty certain that Mamma would have put down her foot, and flatly refused to stand any such nonsense. She would have pleaded religion, modesty, and her own defenceless womanhood—and what is more, would have ridden roughshod over the State and its minions, as only a defenceless woman can.

If we turn to Mrs. Ellis, who had a considerable vogue in the forties as a monitress of her fellow women, we shall find it stated, with a bluntness that would hardly be tolerated nowadays, that "women, in their position in life, must be content to be inferior to men; but," she instantly goes on to explain, "as their inferiority consists chiefly in their want of power, this deficiency is abundantly made up to them by their capacity of exercising influence." Woman's strength was, in fact, to be made perfect in weakness—Mrs. Caudle would never have been such a fool as to have met Caudle with his own weapons of blustering violence. As in war, the indirect approach is the most deadly.

In direct competition with man, woman—at any rate in the opinion of most Victorians—labours under a handicap. All the more reason, therefore, for preserving the conditions that enable her to apply the influence, that is her real strength, most effectually. To quit the vantage ground of the home for the hurly-burly of business or professional competition, would, from this standpoint, have been suicidal. It was not only her own battle that she was fighting. Her influence was the most powerful of all factors making for civilisation. As Mrs. Ellis puts it, in her quaint and governess-like diction,

"I ask again whether it is not good, in these practical and busy times, that the Daughters of England should make a fresh effort to retain that high-toned spirituality of character, which has ever been the proudest distinction of their sex, in order that they may possess that influence over the minds of men, that the intellectual and refined alone are capable of maintaining?" *

We do not recognise what a battle it was that the women of England had to fight. The coarseness of male society, as it had been in the days of George IV, and as it was, outside the sphere of female influence, in the early days of Victoria, is something difficult for us to realise. The way in which the Queen, and her Aunt Adelaide

* *The Daughters of England*, p. 133.

before her, had set to work to purge their court from the taint of the Tom and Jerry days, was a labour as heroic as the cleansing of the Augean Stables. Like all drastic reformations, it was accompanied by much that was regrettable—as when innocent Lady Flora Hastings was thrown to the wolves of respectability. But the urgency of the task was great enough to excuse some incidental harshness and prudery. And the Queen's task was being undertaken by women in countless homes all over England.

In all the domestic literature of the time we are conscious of a world outside the home, where drunkenness, and crude bawdry, and a gross sort of masculine good-fellowship, flourished unchecked. It was to combat this spirit and hold it at arm's length that Flora and her Mamma made their homes into sanctuaries of such refinement as they were capable of conceiving. The old chestnut, about the husband coming home drunk from the club and receiving a wigging from his wife, typifies what must have been one of the commonest incidents in this battle for civilisation. The quaint and—to our minds—ridiculous taboo about not smoking in the presence of a lady or a clergyman, as it is formulated in a contemporary book of etiquette, is only part of an elaborate technique for keeping the home sacrosanct.

The long day's task was, in the main, crowned by success. In spite of its rampant Mammon-worship, the all-powerful middle-class was acquiring at least the veneer of civilisation, and a great improvement in manners and morals did undoubtedly take place. Drunkenness enormously diminished. Lechery no longer dared to flaunt itself in the light of day. Kindness to man and beast was slowly, but continuously, on the increase, and a spirit of social service was being developed. The love of the humanities was kept alive, in spite of deplorable, and deteriorating, standards of taste. For all this we have to thank the much-derided wearers of the poke bonnets and crinolines.

To complete even so summary a portrait, there is one touch that needs adding. No true idea of the Victorian woman can be conveyed without reference to her religion. The conjunction of women with the clergy in the cigar taboo was dictated by no arbitrary caprice. For women were the recognised torchbearers of Victorian piety. It was the piety of a hard and narrow religion, a piety so devoid of any intellectual content that Kingsley could in all seriousness perpetrate that unbelievable line,

"Be good, sweet maid, and let who will be clever,"

though most Victorian divines would have thought it equally appropriate had the addressee been "sweet youth." It was dominated less by love of the Father than fear of the Lord. But it did inculcate an ideal of self-sacrifice. A woman was supposed to find the fulfilment of her personality in living, not for herself, but for others. Even suffering, as we gather from so many pious treatises, might be fraught with the blessedness of a sacrament.

Writing in 1842, Mrs. Ellis put the contrast between what is now the feminine ideal of self-expression and the Victorian one of self-sacrifice, with an exactness that will hardly be questioned by an adherent of either.

"In one case your aim is to secure for yourself all the

advantages you can possibly enjoy, and wait for the satisfaction they produce, before you begin the great business of self-improvement. In the other, you look at your duties first, examine them well, submit yourself without reserve to their claims, and, having made them habitual, reap your reward in that happiness of which no human being can deprive you, and which no earthly event can entirely destroy.

"Is it your intention beyond this to live for yourself or for others? . . .

"Again, is it your aim to live for this world only, or for eternity?" *

* *The Daughters of England*, pp. 4, 5.

CHAPTER XVII

SPIRITUAL ORIENTATION

THE conclusion we have reached about Victorian womanhood will apply with equal force to the Victorian Age—the way to understand it is to comprehend its religious basis. But then the question arises—what do we mean by religion? If we are to mean what the Victorians meant, or what the textbook writers mean to-day, our task would be plain-sailing if rather long-winded, with so many pages for the Oxford Movement, so many for Evangelicalism, perhaps one or two for the Broad Church and Christian Socialism, ending up with something about a conflict between science and religion—about as conceivable a contingency as a twenty round set-to between somebody's eye and his soul.

We have already explained that we shall take religion in the sense of life's spiritual orientation. Or, to put it in another way, it is what, in the last resort, determines the response of man to his environment. It is the kingdom within him of whatever god or spirit or informing principle he may chance to be at one with. Being an attitude of soul, it cannot be bound up with any theory of the universe or any set of intellectual propositions. The life is more than the brain, and religion, being life's informing principle, has the two-fold property of transcending and merging individuality. The savage, being initiated into the cult of his tribal totem, and Christ, seeking to unite man by love with God and his neighbour, are both alike religious in a sense that "reverend gentlemen disputing about the width of a chasuble's hem" could hardly comprehend.

The Victorian Age was, within certain limits, conspicuously religious. That is to say, it was intensely in earnest. Of all the outstanding personalities of the time, there was scarcely one who was not gravely concerned with his own and his community's standing right with God, or—what amounts to much the same thing—in correct adjustment to reality. But what we have found of Victorian morality applies with equal force to Victorian religion—there was not the sustained white heat of passion that has burned during the great ages of faith, and there was consequently a disinclination to make a reconstruction of life from the foundations upwards, a change in man himself as revolutionary as the change in man's surroundings. The greatest religious genius of all time had warned mankind that new wine could only be put into new bottles. The Victorian way was to examine the old bottles very carefully, and patch them up wherever required. It was probably a more dangerous course than total neglect, for a well-patched old bottle may be depended upon to hold the new wine—for a time.

It is characteristic of each of the two main forms of Victorian orthodoxy, that it was concerned, not with adapting the inner life to the demands of the present, but with making it conform exactly to the standards of the past. The Evangelicals pinned their faith to the letter of the Hebrew Classics, as embodied in the two Testaments, and translated by divines of the Tudor and Jacobean periods. The new High Church party resurrected the Fathers, and tome after patristic tome dropped heavily from the press to line the shelves of clerical libraries. The wonderful doings of saints were revived and received with a credulity that would have done credit to the monks, whose meals they had once enlivened. The Evangelicals sought to trump the Tractarian ace, by printing what can fairly claim to be the dingiest and stodgiest collection of printed matter on human record, in the shape of the writings of the English Protestant Fathers. It was the extraordinary air of unreality that hung over the clerical controversies of this time that moved the wrath of Carlyle:

> "The Builder of this Universe was wise,
> He plann'd all souls, all systems, planets, particles:
> The Plan he shaped all Worlds and Æons by
> Was—Heavens!—Was thy small Nine-and-thirty
>   Articles."

The bourgeois revolution accomplished by the Reform Bill had its repercussions on the religious no less than on the secular side of national life. The Church, like the Throne and the Aristocracy, was believed to be in danger from the triumphant Liberalism of men like Brougham. A Parliament of laymen actually did proceed to lay sacrilegious hands upon her, to the extent of pruning away certain minor abuses and ensuring a slightly more equitable distribution of her funds. But if Lord Grey had been Lenin, and Lord Melbourne Trotsky, their proceedings could hardly have caused greater consternation in the common rooms of Oxford Colleges, from whose windows the prospect was viewed in a very different perspective from that of ordinary men. These common rooms contained clerical enthusiasts of curious erudition—and one of ardent genius, John Henry Newman. The situation appeared to them to be one with which the methods of the now dominant Evangelical party were powerless to cope—to come to Jesus was a means of individual salvation, but now it was the Bride of Christ that was in peril. And the leading Evangelicals—no longer outcasts but secure in comfortable benefices—seemed more and more disposed to a reasonable accommodation with the world, the port-bottle, and the Whigs.

One culminating outrage fired the train of ecclesiastical revolution. Catholic Ireland had long been saddled with a staff of Protestant Bishops, who, in the eyes of the immense majority of their flocks, were not only damned heretics, but symbols of a detested tyranny, a perpetual irritant to an open sore. Parliament proposed to reduce the number of these Bishops. This, in the eyes of the excellent Mr. Keble, famous as the author of the *Christian Year,* constituted nothing less than an act of national apostasy, and he thundered against it in impassioned terms from the University pulpit. His sermon gave the signal for a new crusade, conducted not by arms, but by tracts and wire-pulling arts of which the average don is a past master.

The new appeal was addressed not so much to the nation at large, as to the clergy. The Anglican parson had not, hitherto, been encouraged to take a very exalted view of his position. As a rule, he enjoyed a comfortable and leisured gentility, second only to that of the squire in the parish. No doubt the Evangelical impulse had tended to make him take a more serious view of his duties. But now his whole status was to be changed. He was no longer a useful adjunct to the social system, but a Priest, a person set apart and consecrated, armed with awful powers, and, in respect to his office, above all human authority. The first tract, by Newman, is a skilful appeal to that power complex that is latent in most human beings:

"A notion has gone abroad that they can take away your power. They think they have given and can take it away. . . . Enlighten them in this matter. Exalt our Holy Fathers, the Bishops, as the Representatives of the Apostles, and the Angels of the Churches; and magnify your office, as being ordained by them to take part in your ministry."

An appeal to any one to magnify his office seldom falls on deaf ears—least of all, on deaf clerical ears.

The parson was taught to discover not only a new importance, but a new interest in his office. He was invited to exchange the dull Anglican routine—and during the eighteenth century it had become unbelievably dull— for a highly attractive ritual and symbolism. The vista that slowly unfolded itself was one full of colour and variety. A new kind of clerical "shop" began to be talked —albs and chasubles and dalmatics, prevenient grace and auricular confession, became things of vital moment. The fine old mediæval sport of heresy hunting was revived, and the prayer that reverend gentlemen put up at regular intervals for deliverance from envy, hatred, malice, and all uncharitableness, was blessed with no very obvious response. It was not long before the new apostles were thoroughly enjoying themselves in moving heaven and earth in order to hound out of his office a scholarly and inoffensive Professor of Divinity, Dr. Hampden, who was supposed to have conceded a thought too much to the claims of presumptuous reason. The Oxford Evangelicals hit upon the counter offensive device of erecting a pretentious memorial to Cranmer, Ridley, and Latimer, on a site where these worthies did not happen to have been burnt, the object being to work up a case against the Tractarians by their certain refusal to subscribe. And then, in 1841, one of those events occurred whose full horror it requires a clerical mind to appreciate. The State Churches of England and Prussia combined to set up a bishopric of Jerusalem. The idea of such communion between Christ's followers, on the scene of Christ's passion, was too much for Newman. "It was one of the blows that broke me," he confessed in his *Apologia*.

Preoccupation was trivialities of this kind, when problems of vital import are clamouring for solution, must strike the unbiased observer as nothing short of tragic. For at the back of the Tractarian mind was the sense of a profound need. More and more, since the dawn of the Modern Age, the social organism had tended to become a body without a soul. It was the deliberate intention of the new, Liberal school of thought that it should be so. The State was regarded as a mere device for keeping clear the ring for the struggle of conflicting self-interests. Any collective expression of a common faith or personality, such as the Church had supplied during the Middle Ages, and as Fascism and Bolshevism are attempting, each in its fashion, to supply to-day, was anathema to thinkers like Macaulay and the Mills, to statesmen like Melbourne and Lord John Russell.

Newman, who possessed incomparably the clearest and most powerful intellect of any Victorian theologian, and who, with the "bright and beautiful" Hurrell Froude, constituted the brains of the movement, formulated the philosophy of Liberalism in a series of very lucid propositions, and his own, by implication, as the exact contrary. He held, like Mussolini and Lenin, no less than Hildebrand and the Schoolmen, that there is such a thing as a national or state conscience, and that the civil power has a positive duty to maintain religious truth, which amounts to saying that its first responsibility is for a nation's spiritual orientation. No doubt it is open to any one to hold, as the Low Church did of the Catholics, that the religion of Fascist Cæsarism or Bolshevist materialism is that of Anti-Christ, but that would merely prove that the Devil's disciples are going to work on sounder principles than those of God.

The Oxford Movement is a flat contradiction of the then dominant idea that, as Newman put it, "education, periodical literature, railroad travelling, ventilation, drainage, and the arts of life, when fully carried out, serve to make a population moral and happy," or that "utility and expedience are the measure of political duty." The Evangelicals had laid it down that a man's first duty was to get right with God. The Tractarians went a step further in applying this principle to the community. What should it profit a nation if it were to gain the whole world and lose its own soul?

It is unfortunate that, having laid these foundations, the new apostles could think of nothing to build upon them better than a mediæval edifice, guaranteed correct to style, with stained-glass saints and other theatrical properties to order. No doubt even this was better than nothing. The Church became more alive, and a great deal more attractive and interesting, as a result of the Oxford Movement. But she never even approached the ideal of providing the body of the State with a soul, or of effecting such a spiritual revolution as alone could enable civilisation to survive the results of a material revolution.

In 1845, the Oxford Movement sustained a check that crippled its activities for a generation, in the defection of its two most brilliant intellects, those of Newman and W. G. Ward, to Rome, where, as they had discovered at last, they could alone find the Church of their dreams. They were followed six years later, amongst others, by Henry Edward Manning, a born romantic, without any pretensions to an intellectual grasp like that of Newman. No better illustration of the extent of the average clerical outlook can be afforded than the incident that determined this step. The Bishop of Exeter, whose capacity for finding quarrels in straws was already notorious, hit upon the device, not altogether original, of badgering candidates for livings with inquisitorial questions on points of doctrine. A reverend botanist, of the name of Gorham, whom the Lord Chancellor had presented to a living, was, by this means, discovered to be unsound, in a fashion hardly comprehensible to the lay mind, as to the precise potency of the magic imparted by process of baptism to squalling babies. A lay court, having neither the competence nor the disposition to comprehend a divine procedure so contrary to human notions of justice as to favour one baby at the expense of another, ended the matter, after a vast amount of expense in lawyers' fees, by deciding, in effect, to consign the good prelate's list of conundrums to the waste paper basket, and allow Mr. Gorham to retire from the limelight into the obscurity of a Devonshire vicarage.

This was the last straw. The stricken Prelate wrote to Manning to the effect that he could no longer communicate *in sacris* with the Archbishop of Canterbury, on account of the latter's complicity (by complying with the law) "in this awful work," and the awfulness of it so worked on Manning's mind, that he shook the dust of Anglicanism from off his feet, and made the best of his way to Rome, in the spirit of the chicken in the fairy story, who left the farmyard to tell the King that the sky had fallen on his poor bald pate. There is nothing in Manning's record that affords us the least warrant for impugning the sincerity of so tragic a conviction.

The conversions to Rome tilted the balance of power decidedly in favour of the Low Church. Its honest Protestants were now able to point out how they had all along warned their fellow Churchmen of the real goal of the Oxford reformers. There was still a formidable amount of anti-Papal feeling, that expressed itself in Fifth of November orgies, and the song demanding a rope and a faggot for the Supreme Pontiff. There was, in fact, a regular anti-Papal scare when, in 1850, the Pope authorised the creation of a Catholic hierarchy for England, but the Whig Premier, Lord John Russell, fully imbued though he was with the Protestant traditions of his family, was too deeply committed to Whig principles of tolerance to do more than make a harmless demonstration.

Sectarian bigotry, during the generation that followed Newman's secession, reached a pitch of extraordinary bitterness. Though, as the pages of *Punch* bear witness, no insult was too crude to hurl at the Pope, the principal fury of the Evangelicals was reserved for what they regarded as Romanisers within the Anglican fold, or Ritualists, as the High Churchmen now came to be called.

"We know what Ritualism means," cried a certain Reverend George Chute. "It means the defilement of your daughters, the seduction of your wives, and all the other evils that abound on the Continent." Sometimes invective takes the form of poetry:

> "This wily, crafty Ritualist,
>   With cope and incense strong,
>   This unctuous and bearded priest,
>   With broidered vestments long. . . .

> "Your wives and daughters soon will learn
>   On him their hopes to rest,
>   And every feeling overturn
>   Unless by him expressed."

Sometimes practices that are now part of ordinary ecclesiastical routine, are singled out for special denunciation, as in the crusading appeal from which the following is an extract:

"Let us now make a grand proposition
To unite in a firm opposition,
To do all we can
To get rid of a man
Who favours the Eastward position,"

and ending on the heroic resolve:

"Though we die in the field,
We never will yield,
To this Ritualistic position."

The fact that issues of this sort could excite such passion
in clerical minds, is significant of the religious outlook
of the mid-Victorian decades. With the cessation of
Tracts for the Times, a great and deceptive calm settled
on the Church. Never had she seemed to enjoy such unruffled security. The alarm excited by the Whig triumph
had passed away; the few reforms that had been forced
upon her had served rather to strengthen her position.
Society had become respectable, and the broad-brimmed
hat of the parson ranked above the "topper" as a symbol
of respectability. A genteel infidelity was no longer *à la
mode.* The ideal of a Christian gentleman had, even in
the highest circles, superseded the polite worldliness of
a Chesterfield or Horace Walpole. The Pavilion at
Brighton, dismantled and handed over to the Town authorities, was allowed to stand as an awful monument of
predeceased naughtiness. Infidelity was in a worse case
than vice, because it stood in more need of publicity, and
the social taboo upon any tampering with the foundations
of Christianity was almost as powerful as that upon the
overt recognition of carnal passion.

The foundations of Victorian Christianity were in peculiar need of such strengthening. The Low Church theology was bound up with the letter of Holy Scripture, including that of the Old Testament legends. It was supposed to be literally true that God had created the world in seven days, that He had drowned it for forty, and that a Hebrew General had discounted the importance of the time factor in war by his ability to hold up the solar system. Christianity was made to stand, not on any spiritual support, but on all sorts of "evidences," and inferences from the supposed workings of nature. Had not Paley ransacked all that he knew of science for phenomena that could only be explained as special acts of God? Was not the very absence of any conceivable development of one species out of another sufficient proof that God must have designed and constructed at least two specimens of each type? It amounted to crediting anything that science had as yet failed to explain, to the divine account. But this, when science was explaining more and more things every day, was fraught with obvious peril. One or two outlying positions might be tacitly abandoned—but what if the scientists were to produce evidence of the world having been more than a week old at the creation of Adam, or of the gulf between species being bridgeable? The answer was that respectable scientists did not, and others must not, make such discoveries.

The clergy had no more taste than other Victorians for exploring foundations. So they were content to shut their eyes to ominous signs of the coming storm. Geology was already beginning to take dangerous liberties with the

Mosaic time-table, and in fashionable drawing-rooms they were discussing a book called *Vestiges of Creation,* which, as a young lady in Disraeli's *Tancred* put it, suggested the possibility that we had been fishes and might one day be crows.

Unfortunately, the stimulus of Tractarian opposition had done nothing to relieve the poverty of thought that had been so fatal an accompaniment of the Evangelical movement. Of the vast amount of pious prose that was produced under Low Church and Dissenting auspices during the first half of the Queen's reign, practically nothing has stood the test of time. Most of it is of a kind that the modern educated reader would find it difficult to take seriously. Where now can we find a responsible divine to write such a book as *The Church Before the Flood* by the Rev. John Cumming, D.D.—over 600 pages in length—which accounts for the acceptance of Abel's sacrifice by the discovery that Abel was a Protestant, and points the subsequent tragedy with the moral:

"Be not deceived; what Romanism has made Spain, Italy and Austria, morally and intellectually, it would make Westminster. The Cain mark is upon it."

Where now would you find a theologian to compose, or a firm to publish, so elephantine a treatise as the *Horæ Apocolypticæ* of the Rev. E. C. Elliott, in which vast labour and considerable erudition are devoted to proving the Book of Revelation to have been an anti-Papal pamphlet?

Now that family prayers have gone out of fashion, people are beginning to forget the dulness and dreariness of those interminable petitions that were read out morning and evening by Paterfamilias to the kneeling children and domestics. For the most part, they were inspired by a fear of the Lord that expressed itself in a routine of grovelling self-abasement. They must have been singularly ineffective, for as the week progressed, the household were inevitably destined to sink to depths of villainy that resulted in an appalling catalogue of sins at the stocktaking on Saturday evening, with the certainty that so long as the Family Prayer Book remained in use, the dread process of backsliding was destined to go on, week in, week out, without the faintest hope or chance of amendment.

Particular attention was devoted to the impressionable minds of children, and the output of improving literature for their benefit was enormous. The spirit of Mr. Fairchild was still abroad, though the growing humanitarianism of the age was inclined to lay somewhat less stress upon the inhuman qualities attributed to the Heavenly, even more than to the earthly Father. But a child's nerves must have been tough not to have been permanently affected by the perpetual harping on deathbeds, funerals and other accompaniments of mortality, that was supposed to be peculiarly edifying for the young mind. In juvenile literature the moralising tendency of the Victorians had full scope because—since the effective demand was created by the buyer and not by the reader—there was no incentive to aim at being anything but improving.

To give one instance of the sort of fare provided, we will take an incident from a book of Mrs. Carey Brock's, about some children every episode in whose lives is supposed to illustrate one of the journeyings of the Children of Israel. A schoolgirl is just beginning to recover from an attack of scarlet fever, and the Doctor has expressly prescribed for her light reading and cheerful talk. But the improving clergyman of the book has gathered from something let fall in her delirium that she has been committing sin—burning a school book—and at all costs he is going to worm it out. Accordingly, no sooner has he got her alone, than he produces his Bible, and after having perused it ominously for some little time, asks if he may read to her. The poor child having made the only possible answer, Mr. Somers, the clergyman in question, opens the attack with a chapter of Hosea, "making the cheek yet paler, the uneasy look yet more uneasy."

Having produced these desirable symptoms in the patient, he now proceeds to harrow her feelings with a lurid description of God's wrath and its effects, and having frightened her almost to death, rams home the moral with the words, "it has been thus with you," after which the sick and trembling child has the confession torn out of her.

But Mr. Somers has not done. "Mr. Somers prayed, but before prayer came a thanksgiving, an earnest thanksgiving," nor does the torture end even here, for the Bible is produced again, and another chapter read, and another sermon preached, "very faithfully, yet with many comforting words," about Moses, and the golden calf, and the quails in the wilderness, and sin, and the consequences of sin, until the triumphant consummation is attained, that little Gertrude, who, we are asked to believe, survived the experience, "abhorred herself and repented in dust and ashes."

That was the light in which God and His ministers were presented to little children, objects of fear, the grown-up person in his most terrifying aspect. Religion was a stern and joyless discipline, and if any element of love entered into it, it was because God would make it exceeding hot for you if you didn't love Him. It was the same with God's House, if we may judge by one of Mrs. Alexander's hymns:

> "Little children must be quiet
>   When to holy Church they go,
> They must sit with serious faces,
>   Must not play nor whisper low,
>
> "For the Church is God's own temple,
>   Where men go for praise and prayer,
> And the great God will not love them
>   Who forget His presence there."

As for God's day, everything was done to make it one of gloom and boredom for the junior members of pious families. As a shocked and saintly servant girl is made to gasp, in another of Mrs. Brock's Improvers:

> "Fun, on a Sunday!"

In many families, not only all amusements, but all books, were prohibited, except those tending directly to edification, and there is a case on record of one heroic old gentleman who used, on Sunday afternoons, when there was no service to occupy the time, to improve it by family readings, at full length, of the Church homilies. It is significant that those who made it their business to root out any sort of pleasure—even that afforded by museums and picture galleries—on the Sabbath, were usually careful to avoid the word Sunday, which had too obviously cheerful associations, and substitute "The Lord's Day." The Lord was not likely to let any day of His be enjoyable to the children of His wrath.

On one subject, at least, the Evangelicals were in agreement with the Ritualists, and indeed, with the Catholics. There could be no question of tampering with Hell. The idea that there could be any limit to the implacability of an all-loving Father was too terrible to be entertained for a moment. Even Jesus was not free from complicity with the Devil and his work of eternal torture. This is quite clearly brought out in *Peep of Day,* a book from which countless thousands of children imbibed their first ideas of religion:

"At last Jesus will sit upon a white throne, and everybody will stand round his [the small "h" is in the original, the capital being doubtless Popish] throne. He will open some books, in which he has written down all the naughty things people have done. God has seen all the naughty things you have done. He can see in the dark as well as in the light, and knows all your naughty thoughts. He will read everything out of his books before the angels that stand round. Yet God will forgive some people, because Christ died upon the cross."

Only some! And these fortunate few would have to accomplish the feat of loving that blend of Peeping Tom and the Marquis de Sade whom pious evangelists dared to cast for the divine rôle.

"This is what God will do to those who do not love him. God will bind them in chains and put them in a

lake of fire. There they will gnash their teeth and weep
and wail forever. God will put Satan in the same place
and all the devils. Satan is the father of the wicked, and
he and his children shall be tormented for ever. They
shall not have one drop of water to cool their burning
tongues."

In view of which prospect, what prudent little child
could hesitate for a moment about loving so amiable a
Father?

But all these performances are put into the shade by the
Catholic Father Furniss—a singularly appropriate name
for one whose principal title to fame is to have produced
the most super-heated and agonising Hell on imaginative record. His sadistic outpourings were for the special
benefit of children—hence his title of the Children's
Apostle—and no doubt, with the little boys, he must have
achieved considerable popularity as a specialist in torture.
Certainly no Red Indians could compete for a moment
with Father Furniss's God, Saviour, and Devil, who combine to damn a poor little child to everlasting confine-
ment, screaming, stamping, struggling, in a red-hot oven.
This is by no means the only form of torture that the
good Father is capable of devising for his little friends—
perpetually burning suits of clothes, audibly boiling blood
and brains, and one divinely neat practical joke, that of
half opening the door of a cell wherein a little girl is
agonising in eternal solitude on a red-hot floor, and then
shutting it again—forever. "Oh, that you could hear the
horrible, the fearful scream of that girl!" But why
horrible?

There was nothing that aroused orthodox divines to a

greater pitch of fury than the least attempt to put limits to the divine ferocity. Their attitude was that of the military authorities towards the torture of flogging—take away the stimulus of fear, and it would be impossible to keep the rank and file under authority. But thanks to the sturdy individualism of the age, it was impossible to prevent some of the more earnest and thoughtful spirits from using their brains or following the dictates of their hearts. One of these was Charles Kingsley, who, though in no sense a philosopher, had a fund of John Bullish common-sense, and a heart of gold. It was he who pointed out that the use of fire and worms was to set free the elements of decayed and dead matter to enter into other organisms, and that to tax God with perverting it into an instrument of torture was blasphemy. But Kingsley was looked upon as a dangerous firebrand, and his friend, F. D. Maurice, who, though he disclaimed the title of Broad Churchman, held that it was impossible to set limits to God's love, even for defunct sinners, was on that account deprived not only of a professorship of divinity, but one of history, at King's College, London, the Bishop of that diocese having threatened to decline to receive the College certificate as a qualification for examination. But, as we have already seen in the Gorham case, the last word in these matters is not with the Bishops, and it was in 1863 that Lord Chancellor Westbury put an end to a rather similar heresy hunt by "dismissing Hell with costs and taking away from orthodox members of the Church of England their last hope of eternal damnation."

Another form of activity that was gravely disapproved of by those in ecclesiastical authority, was anything tending to stir up the people. There was a tacit agreement to ignore those unfortunate passages in the Bible that tended to the disadvantage of Dives. When, after the final failure of the Chartist movement, a small group of Christian Socialists, who included Kingsley and Maurice, made a serious but abortive effort to deal with the social problem on Gospel lines, there was much fluttering of clerical dovecotes, and Kingsley's sermon on the message of the Church to labouring men drew on his head a perfect storm of abuse, and an episcopal prohibition against his preaching.

We have so far dealt with the less favourable aspect of Victorian religion, and it must be confessed that—contrary to the popular idea—it is on their religious side that the Victorians are most vulnerable. Their habit of shirking fundamental issues disqualified them from the all-important task of adapting the inner man to the revolution in the outer world. They clung, with passionate obstinacy, to the old traditions and formulas, or when they did reform,

"They fed not on the advancing hours,
Their hearts held cravings for the buried day."

What may be the ultimate consequences to civilisation of this, their great refusal, time will show. Certain it is that their position could only be maintained at the cost of an intellectual impoverishment and spiritual obtuseness, for which the Church had to pay a terrible reckoning, when she found herself committed to a devil's—or donkey's—advocacy, against truth and scientific enquiry.

But when we have allowed for all this, we can freely

pay our tribute to the work accomplished by the various religious bodies within the sphere to which they chose to restrict their activities. For all their narrowness of outlook, the Victorians did, at least, make religion—as they understood it—a leading principle of their lives, and if their religion was more that of the Pharisees than that of Christ, it can at least be added, in the light of modern enquiry, that few indeed have ever lived up to a much higher than the Pharisaic standard.

"Think," some Victorian shade might say, "of what we did for our own generation, before you tax us with the shortcomings of our posterity."

Even the cult of the Lord, as practised by the Evangelicals, grotesque and horrible as its basic principles may seem, has a large balance of practical good to its account —at least in England, for we cannot acquit it altogether of responsibility for those two great Imperial tragedies, the Dutch Exodus from the Cape, and the Indian Mutiny. The Lord, though a God of gloom and terror, was also, by a strange paradox, a patron of righteousness.

It had been the early Evangelists who had given the driving force of the enthusiasm to the anti-slavery crusade. It was one of the sternest and most kill-joy of Low Churchmen, Lord Shaftesbury, who did more than any other man of his time to promote the cause of social reform. And there were others, of the same stamp, fighting for the same cause in more restricted fields. For it is a mistake to think of the Evangelical parson as a mere unctuous bigot. Our notions of him are apt to be unconsciously formed on the pattern of Samuel Butler's hateful clergymen in *The Way of All Flesh*. Theobald Pontifex, one fancies, would have done little credit to any profession, and as a parson, he exhibits all the worst qualities that tend to flourish on an Evangelical soil. But even by Butler's account, he has the true Victorian capacity for work, and looks after his parish—providing for the material as well as the spiritual needs of his flock—in a way very few eighteenth century parsons would have dreamed of doing. And the Low Church could produce a very different type from that of Theobald. In many a parish, the Parson went about carrying his simple Gospel message into slum and hovel, wearing himself out in the service of his Master and his flock, leaving a memory of which a faint fragrance even now lingers, so long as there are old men who can remember the days—if I may be pardoned for citing names from my own district—of Mr. White of Ryarsh or Mr. Bligh of Birling.

Quite apart from the Low Church, a great change came over the clergy in the first half of the Queen's reign. In the middle of the century, people were already talking of the "old school," comfortable, leisured men of the world, often with scholarly tastes, and not infrequently with an epicurean affection for port. Even before the Queen's accession, this sort of thing was beginning to be frowned upon. In a young lady's letter of 1831, I find the following stricture of the "extremely vulgar and unclerical conversation," of a certain young clergyman, "about . . . the late king at Belvoir Castle, all drunk except some maidservants and the Archbishop of Canterbury, and he was pretty well."

The man who did the most to set a new standard for the clergy was Bishop Wilberforce, or Soapy Sam, a child in intellect—as his attempt to break a lance with Huxley proved him—but, like so many Victorians, a giant for work. "God," he said, "numbers the Bishop's idle or absent hours," and he laboured tirelessly in his diocese of Winchester to inculcate a high professional standard of clerical duty. His influence was as much felt in the Church as that of Thomas Arnold in the Public Schools. The new type of parson tended continuously to become more of a clerical specialist and less of a country gentleman.

The new High Church party greatly contributed to this growth of specialisation. A technique of saving souls was evolved, on the Catholic model, depending less on violent outbursts of spiritual excitement than that of the Evangelicals, and more on a patient and calculated discipline, under priestly supervision. The routine of a ritualist clergyman's life became complex and exacting beyond anything dreamed of in pre-Victorian times.

When all has been said about the shortcomings of Victorian religion, this at least must be acknowledged, that it did provide a discipline for character of the most potent order. To one text at least the men and women of that time may claim to have been faithful. Whatsoever their hands found to do, they did it with their might. And the many repressions—to use the fashionable modern word—to which they were subjected, did inculcate a faculty of self-denial, an ability to sacrifice the lesser end to the greater, that produced a strength, if not always a sweetness of personality. Whether they were building their house on adequate foundations, or whether it was destined one day to collapse about their children's ears, time would show. For their time it stood, stately and imposing, a landmark to the world.

CHAPTER XVIII

THE MORAL INTERIOR

I⊤ is a stock charge to bring against the Victorians that they introduced morality into their art. In other words, they failed to be artistic because they tried to make art moral. And it is perfectly true that, before Swinburne raised this standard of revolt, it would have occurred to hardly anybody to separate art from morality. But even the muse of Swinburne could scarcely have been described as morally neutral. The man was an evangelist, and even if his Gospel was that of Satan, he would doubtless have replied that Satan was in every way a more desirable master than the orthodox Lord. It was when Mr. Whistler delivered his "Ten O'clock," in 1885, that the real separation of art from life, and therefore of art from morality, was proclaimed. And Whistler himself had all the moral fervour, and even some of the fanaticism, of a prophet.

The common accusation against Victorian art misses the real point. The trouble consists not so much in its morality, as in its failure to be moral enough. As long as art remains the expression of life, so long must it continue to express that aspect of life which is called morality. To say that good art need not be moral, is to say that it need not be good. Keats divined that beauty was truth —he might have gone on to add that both were goodness. The deeper the insight brought to bear on the development of art, the more clearly it will be seen that an artist is a moralist working at a white heat of inspiration. Of Dante and Æschylus, of Giotto and Fra Angelico, of Palestrina and Bach, it will hardly be disputed that they were expressing, each through his chosen medium, the highest moral ideas of their time. But to apply our principle universally, we shall have to adopt a wider and less formal conception of morality than that in customary use, one closely akin to that which we have already taken of religion, and, in fact, hardly to be distinguished from it except by difference of emphasis. Religion we have defined as orientation of life, morality we should define as orientation of conduct, and both might be included in the one word direction—vital or spiritual direction.

Christ, in the conventional sense, can scarcely be described as a moralist, and in fact the formal moralists of his own time held him to be the exact opposite. His morality is correctly interpreted by Paul as being one not of the Law, but of the Spirit. The wind bloweth where it listeth—so is every one who is born of that Spirit. Shakespeare, again, was no formal moralist, but the gospel implicit in his work is one of passionate humanity, of pity and loving kindness and all that makes us instinctively think of him as "sweetest Shakespeare." No one, not lacking an ear or a heart, can fail to be penetrated by the moral sublimity of Beethoven's music, though no words would suffice for its translation. The prophets on the roof of the Sistine Chapel are entitled to the style of "moralities" in an even deeper sense than the mediæval guild plays. There is a morality of pure colour, as in the Five Sisters at York, and sermons in stones only become tedious when we try to put them on paper. In that Trinity, Beauty, Truth, and Goodness, none is greater or less than another, none is before or after another.

But the Victorian morality was of the Law, Pharisaic. It was a discipline of rules, imposed from the outside, and did not well up spontaneously from the depths of the soul. In spite of all his piety and Liberalism, the average Victorian had not the faintest idea of what was meant by the glorious liberty of the Sons of God. He would never have dared trust to his own inspiration, or have allowed any artist to trust to his. In his æsthetic judgments the sentence, as in Looking-glass Jurisprudence, preceded the trial. Art had got to say certain things, and the artist's only choice was in his way of saying them. A formal morality, cold and heavy as a millstone, hung round the muse's neck.

That was the besetting weakness of Victorian art—and we need hardly say that we are taking the word "art" in its widest sense, as including all forms of creative activity. But if its weakness was moral, so also was the strength it derived from the tremendous discipline of concentration and self-denial that was the true source of Victorian greatness. The gospel of work, or of self-help, was more vital to the Victorians than that of love, and this imparts a noticeable bias to their æsthetic valuations. The Victorian political economy was inclined to determine the value of commodities by the amount of work put into them, rather than their use to the consumer. And in judging of a book or a picture, the Victorian liked to feel that he was getting work for his money.

Hence arose a demand for solidity and elaboration, and

a corresponding distrust for any sort of genius that did not obviously consist in an infinite capacity for taking pains. The Victorians dearly loved a plodder. Readers of Dean Farrar's school and university stories will remember the contrasted fates and characters of the brilliant but Satanic Bruce, and that dreadfully stodgy but laborious hero, Julian Home; he will remember how the wooden-headed but pure-hearted Daubeney is allowed to over-work himself to the supreme elevation of a holy and didactic death-bed. The Dean's standards were those of his age. A picture like Frith's *Derby Day* was admired because you could see that Frith had put such a tremendous amount of work into it. It was the same with that manifesto of Pre-Raphaelite principles, Millais's *Ophelia*. Here every leaf, every reed, every flower, even the robin in the background, is painted with the same minute care as if it were intended for a separate masterpiece. Here is full measure, pressed down and running over, to justify every penny of the £798 for which the picture was sold in 1862, and even the £3,000 for which it subsequently passed to Sir Henry Tate.

It was just this question of pictorial economics that was the crux of the famous libel action of Whistler v. Ruskin in 1878. Ruskin's counsel was merely taking his stand on ground common to all good Victorians, when he demanded, concerning one of Whistler's Nocturnes,

"The labour of two days, then, is that for which you ask two hundred guineas?"
and received the annihilating reply,

"No, I ask it for the knowledge of a lifetime."

The applause that burst out in court was the death knell

of an ideal. But it was not uninfluenced by the implication that Whistler had sweated for his guineas after all.

It was the same in poetry. It was what convinced the ordinary man about Tennyson, once his fame was finally established, that here at last was something very like the *ne plus ultra* in poetry. Not only did he give you substantial fare for your money, but all the detail was so astonishingly accurate. No man of business instincts would fail to appreciate the advantages of working in a free course of natural history, geology, botany, history, and other useful and entertaining subjects, all up to date and thoroughly reliable, and all in addition to the usual benefits to be derived from the reading of poetry. Contemporary admirers of Tennyson seldom failed to make the most of these prosaic merits. But even Tennyson could not compete with Browning in the minuteness and accurate erudition of his detail.

It was in literature that the Victorians had the most favourable field for the success of their moral discipline. The spoken or written word constitutes the best medium for the expression of formal morality. At the other end of the scale stands inarticulate sound, which speaks direct to the heart, and on which there are no means of imposing formal morality. The Victorians were not able to abandon themselves whole-heartedly enough to their inspiration to make great musicians. The time before the seventies was one of extraordinary barrenness in English music, a barrenness that appears more striking in contrast with the harvest of genius in Germany and Italy. All sorts of theories have been brought forward to account for this, and poor Handel has even been blamed for having crushed English music, in the previous century, with his foreign genius. But a people whose deepest instincts forbid them ever quite to let themselves go, ever to trust unreservedly to their inspiration, will never breed musicians.

To a lesser degree this is true of Victorian painting. It would be the merest affectation to belittle the work of the greater Pre-Raphaelites, of Watts, or of that strangely neglected portrait painter, Lucas, but there is something lacking in it that in France is known as *"flair,"* and is the power of complete surrender to inspiration, a lust for form and colour that knows no limits of orthodoxy. The Pre-Raphaelites were rebels, but they were Menshevists, and their boldest flights fell short of post-impressionist Bolshevism like that of Cézanne. Such boldness would have been too obnoxious to Victorian respectability. There was a fearful hullabaloo, as it was, over the extremely proper and devout productions of the Pre-Raphaelite Brotherhood, for no better reason than that they represented a departure from academic convention. The motto even of the greatest Victorian artists might have been that of the fairy-tale,

"Be bold, be bold, but not too bold,"

and consequently their very greatness lacks something of the divine fire—it is never supremely great.

Nor was supreme greatness a quality that the Victorian public would have appreciated in, or even stood from, those who catered for its æsthetic needs. When, in spite of everything, a great decorative artist like Alfred Stevens rose among them, he found himself thwarted at every turn—the history of his Wellington Monument at St. Paul's is that of a pearl of great price, cast before swine. On the other hand, work that was pretty without being great, was sure of its reward. The blasphemously smug Christ of Holman Hunt's *Light of the World,* which is in painting what *The Lost Chord* is in music, passed for a work not only of artistic beauty, but of pious elevation. And there is a no greater tragedy in the annals of art, than the sale of Millais's soul for fame and an ultimate baronetcy. Like Lord Leighton, his predecessor in the Presidential chair of the Royal Academy, he has gone down to posterity as an artist of entire respectability, and only one or two of his early works remain to suggest what, under more encouraging circumstances, he might have become. If an age does not always get the art it deserves, it seldom gets more.

In the arts of sculpture, painting, and decoration, we become conscious of an even worse handicap than that of formal morality, one directly arising out of the conditions of a machine age, that of mass commercial production. The commercial motive, in one form or another, has indeed always had its influence on art, since even the craftsmen of the Middle Ages and the dramatists of the Elisabethan theatre were quite alive to the main chance. But there is a joy of creative achievement as well as a desire for material gain, and under the conditions of machine production the balance between the two, the spiritual and the material impulses, is tilted more and more in favour of the latter. There comes to be no more, if no less, joy, in the making of a chair or a china shepherdess, than in turning out endless quantities of cheap cloth by means of the power loom.

That is looking at the matter from the producer's standpoint. But there is no supply without a corresponding demand, and during the nineteenth century the demand for machine products expands along with the means of supply. The aristocratic civilisation of the eighteenth century had aimed at a life that should be beautiful and dignified, with comparatively little regard for comfort. A man of breeding was expected to be a man of taste, and to impose his cultured ideals not only on his surroundings, but on the very landscape. The beautiful china and furniture of that time were produced to meet the requirements of people with wealth and leisure enough to insist on living exquisitely.

The nineteenth century witnesses a marked decline in upper class taste, accompanied by the rise of a new, and all-powerful bourgeoisie, without any traditions of culture, and so busy competing for the means of life, that they had scant leisure to devote to its graces. The women, who were engaged in so heroic a struggle to make their homes sanctuaries of refinement, were, for the most part, very hard worked themselves, and even if their formal morality, to which art had to conform, had allowed of their accepting so Pagan an ideal as that of the past century, they would have had neither the resources nor the training to realise it. When cheap and specious articles of domestic use were turned out of the new factories, economical housewives naturally jumped at such an opportunity of stocking their homes. A solid, mahogany cupboard—if one didn't look too closely at the way it was put together—was really quite as genteel as a Chippendale, while the patterns impressed on Messrs. So and So's carpets might be quite correctly copied from the Persian—and what more could you want?

The collapse of English interior decoration was not quite so swift and catastrophic as one would gather from some accounts. The great days of furniture had no doubt come to an end with Sheraton, but the old aristocratic tradition died hard and there was still much to be admired in some of the early Victorian productions. The classic grace of the Empire style still lingered—occasionally one comes across sets of chairs dating from about the thirties, with straight, fluted legs, and damask coverings. A great feature of social life at this time was the round table, at which the younger members of the party would often gather, and perhaps the young ladies' albums would form an excuse for a good deal of sly flirtation, while the old people chatted, or played cards, and turned a Nelson eye to the proceedings. These tables, often of rose- or satin-wood, are charming pieces of furniture, though they witnessed the encroachment of middle-class ideals in an ever-increasing solidity. The pianos, of a similar material, are another graceful relic of the Early Victorian drawing-room.

Not the least distinctive products of this time were the work of the ladies themselves, though it is only recently that this has come back into favour. The best of their needlework merits a higher praise than that of mere ingenuity. And even where it is merely quaint, it is seldom lacking in charm.

There was a great effort to revive the art of furniture making by applying to it the Gothic principles that were becoming fashionable in architecture. As nobody had any particular knowledge of what Gothic furniture had been like, the result was that the backs of chairs became like rose windows, and footstools like tabernacles. Prie-dieux with plush tops were dumped down, preferably, in the hall, where, if they did not come under the suspicion of popery, some use might be found for them at family prayers, though, as these involved sitting as well as kneeling, the best occupant was a child.

Towards the middle of the century, mechanical production was more and more coming to supersede craftsmanship, and the Victorians seemed to be fast losing both the desire and the capacity to surround themselves with beautiful things. Solidity and pretentiousness were the qualities chiefly aimed at. Everything in the house seemed to be playing a game of pretending to be something else. On the mantelpiece blossomed flowers of wax, in conservatories formed by hideous glass domes. The mirror, or the part of it that was not concealed by draperies, had become a garden for painted flowers. In the fireplace were brazen irons that some child would ruin by putting between the bars. The mania for draping things led to curtains flanking the fire-place, even when a fire was burning, an apparently dangerous practice to which there are *Punch* pictures to testify. In middle class homes appeared that horrid firstfruit of æsthetic standardisation, the oleograph portrait. Plush and horsehair were everywhere *en evidence*.

With the sense of fitness departed that of colour. It

is almost as if our grandparents had been stricken with colour-blindness. In dress and decoration the most hideous discords were received with joy. What the Victorians could put up with in the way of colour may be best seen to-day in their stained glass, which sometimes produces an agonising effect on the unwary visitor. Now that Dean Jenkyn's memorial window at Wells is mercifully removed, I should recommend the judicious iconoclast to devote his first attention to one of the parish churches at St. Alban's, where salmon-pink is joined in unholy wedlock with flaming magenta. But what the Victorians liked even more than this brutal sport of setting colours at each other's throats, was to dispense with them altogether. A reign of universal dinginess set in. The blues and bottle-greens of the dandies darkened into oblivion. The respectability of the age demanded that beneath the top hat all men should look as sober as clergymen—the sole exception being in respect of the almost sacramental ritual of the hunting field. Only young girls were tolerated in colours, and even their plumage steadily declined towards the drab fashions of the seventies.

Nevertheless, the mid-Victorian interior had an unmistakable, if not wholly a pleasant character, of its own, and for that reason even its tasteless solidity is an æsthetic cut above the ghastly resurrectionism that took its place. The idea of "period" decoration was in its Gothic infancy, people at least contrived to put something of themselves into their surroundings, other than an advertisement of their own snobbery. A solid and sober domesticity is in every line, and we might almost say in every pound and hundredweight, of that mahogany and plush furniture.

It is not for the clients of our Chesterfields of perpetual tick, who furnish homes from vans guaranteed not to display the firm's name to the neighbours—it is not for them to chide us for loving our grand-paternal armchairs.

CHAPTER XIX

THE GOTHIC REVIVAL

It was in architecture that the moralising tendencies of the Victorians had their fullest and most obvious scope, and it was also an art peculiarly subject to the conditions of a machine age. The mass production of buildings, in which beauty and convenience and soundness of construction were ruthlessly sacrificed to cheapness, had accompanied the transformation of human beings into "hands" in the new manufacturing towns. Those who travel out of London, especially by the Southern Railway, may mark some of the worst fruits of Victorianism in the shape of interminable rows of brick and slate boxes, all precisely alike, that seem better fitted to contain Robots than men. In the country you will see somewhat similar rows of very businesslike, plain-brick cottages, that form a queer commentary on the then fashionable sentiment about Merrie England. And yet the building of cottages had once been the occasion for as much display of charm and individuality as that of cathedrals. A new type of architectural shoddy, in the shape of the detached suburban villa, was evolved to meet the genteel and individualist demands of the middle class. We know how the heart of the representative philosopher, Macaulay, would leap up when he beheld a villa in a row.

But when the Victorians talked of architecture, they were not thinking of cottages and villas. For the manual worker a house was a means of keeping alive; for the office worker it was also a ticket of respectability—only for those who could afford not to work at all was it in any sense a thing of beauty, though even by them it was more often regarded as a thing of importance. The upper class were no longer arbiters of taste, and the putting up of big private houses had almost ceased to be regarded as an art. The architect's sole idea of beautifying a country house was to put it into fancy dress, and French châteaux and Tudor mansions everywhere affronted the landscape with their incredible pretensions.

It was round public, and particularly church architecture, that the enthusiasms and controversies of the time tended to centre. The great Gothic revival, which had started as a rich man's toy, had now gathered irresistible momentum, and the beginning of the Queen's reign witnessed the crowning triumph of its first, or decorative phase, in the erection of the new Houses of Parliament, a building which, though it sets out to match the perpendicular of Henry VII's Chapel over the way, has so distinct a character as almost to give it a style of its own. Associated with Barry, the architect, was the young Welby Pugin, who was shortly to champion a more serious ideal than the glorified picturesqueness of his colleague. For agreeably to the Victorian spirit and the Gothic tradition, architecture was to become not only formally moral, but formally religious.

This was largely the result of the new High Churchmanship. Pugin himself was converted to Catholicism, but he was at one with the Oxford leaders in casting back wistful eyes at the age of faith that had given birth to the

Gothic cathedrals. For with the new life that was given to the Emotional Revival in the thirties, a more serious view began to be taken of the Middle Ages. Even to Sir Walter Scott, these had hardly been more than a splendid pageant, while to lesser writers they had constituted a splendid setting for bogey stories.

But now more exact methods of enquiry were afoot. Historians like Hallam and Palgrave were already beginning to conquer Gothic mysteries by the rule and line of scientific research. And as the Middle Ages came to be more closely studied, it began to be suspected that they might provide the example of a social order to which, by comparison, that of the nineteenth century was as iron to gold. One of the first exponents of this view was Will Cobbett, whose *History of the Protestant Reformation in England* depicted the Protestant Fathers as villains not inferior to Pitt and Castlereagh, and the Reformation as the crime that had changed a good social system to a bad one. Carlyle, instead of indulging in sentimental generalities about the past, unearthed the memoirs of a twelfth century monastic Pepys, and allowed his readers to judge, by that unvarnished account, whether life under a mediæval abbot might not have been fitter for a human being than that dictated by the inhuman conditions of modern competition.

But not even Carlyle's account was so eloquent and convincing an indictment of the present in comparison with the past, as the architect Pugin's *Contrasts,* a book now strangely forgotten. For if Carlyle's method was to let you read for yourself, Pugin allowed you to see. In a series of contrasted drawings, he placed the modern environment side by side with that of a reconstructed past, a past—on the whole—skilfully and fairly reconstructed. The comparison was devastating. The mediæval treatment of the poor, in almshouses like New Cross, is contrasted with that of the Poor Law Bastilles, the only unfair point in the comparison being that the modern poor house has some of the features of a prison, though this is quite unnecessary to drive home the lesson that to the mediæval Church the poor man had a soul to be cherished, and to the modern Poor Law Commissioners only a carcase to be kept grudgingly alive and then dissected. The beauty of a mediæval town, with its battlements and gables and forest of spires, is contrasted with the spectacle of the same town modernised, with unsightly blocks of factory buildings, a forest, not of spires, but of chimneys, gas cylinders, poky conventicles, and all the accompaniments of utilitarian progress. The contrast of parish churches is cruel, the sugar-loaf affair at the end of Langham Place being put beside St. Mary Redclyffe, at Bristol.

That Pugin foreboded the mass production of imitative architecture, is evident from a delightful frontispiece, advertising a bogus competition—not so very unlike the real thing—for designing "a Church to contain 80,000 sittings, Gothic or Elisabethan, estimate not to exceed £1,500." Further designs are required for Moorish Fish Markets, Egyptian Marine Villas, Baronial Gin Temples, and so forth, while compo fronts are advertised as ready to be forwarded to all parts of the kingdom by steam conveyance at the shortest notice.

The notion accordingly gained ground, early in the

forties, of Gothic architecture as the expression in stone of an order of society directly opposed to the materialism and inhumanity of modern conditions. Not only were its buildings good in themselves, but there had been joy in their making. It had been the Gothic ideal that every craftsman should be a creative artist, or, according to the mediæval idea, a microcosmos, a little universe, as complete in itself as God's great universe:

"How each the whole its substance gives!
Each in the other works and lives;
Like heavenly forces rising and descending,
Their golden urns reciprocally lending."

The high priest of this ideal, though not its originator, was John Ruskin.

To Ruskin, as to Pugin, architecture was the outward and visible expression of a people's soul. In our own age of artistic specialism, public opinion—with the authority of one of our leading architects *—has labelled this belief the biological or some other fallacy. Architecture, and all the other arts, are to be isolated, like smallpox cases, from the main stream of a nation's life—the historian is to have nothing to do with them, unless he likes to tack on a chapter about æsthetic developments, in the consciously colourless style of one who is meddling with other people's business. The stones of Venice are to have no intelligible connection with the life of Venice; her buildings are but the highly technical product of such specialists as the Venetians may have been rich enough

* Mr. Geoffrey Scott in his *The Architecture of Humanism.*

to employ, and are to be judged according to technical standards by technical critics.

To Ruskin, or any of the Gothic revivalists, such a doctrine would have appeared not only stark blasphemy, but a *reductio ad absurdum* of materialism. To them it went without saying that art was the expression of a people's soul, though all of them might not have gone quite as far as Blake's aphorism, that any one can judge of a picture who has not been connoisseured out of existence. No doubt they prejudice their case by narrowness of outlook, and that lack of philosophic grasp that was a peculiar weakness of the Victorians. Ruskin himself, though at his best one of the most inspired writers that have ever held a pen, is, at his worst, one of the most inconsistent and tiresome, and the best and worst are often inextricably mixed up together.

It is not surprising, then, that like the Pre-Raphaelite painters, instead of seeing life, whose expression is art, steadily and whole, he should have taken sides with one period against another, and, in his eagerness to penetrate the soul of Gothic Christianity, have denied any soul at all to the Renaissance. In consequence, the most able of all modern attacks on the Ruskinian standpoint * consists ostensibly of a vindication of Renaissance architecture, a vindication that tacitly accepts Ruskin's indictment of Renaissance art as non-religious and non-moral. And hence the vindication is made to carry, as a necessary consequence, the degradation of art from a spiritual to a technical plane. But it is equally possible to allow Ruskin to have been right in principle, though wrong in failing

* Mr. Geoffrey Scott, *op. cit.*

to see that the human soul fulfils itself in other styles than Gothic, and that periods of art are not the heroes and villains of a historic melodrama.

It must also be remembered that Ruskin was in no sense a supporter, but rather an opponent of the Gothic Revival as it was carried out in practice. This, after 1840, derived its main stimulus from the Oxford Movement. The demand for ritual had naturally led to a demand for churches in which that ritual would have its proper scope and setting. The average church, at the beginning of the thirties, was not much better than an assembly room, with a gallery, as in a theatre, for the riffraff, and, for the gentry, private boxes, sometimes with a fireplace and a back door for unperceived escape. The parson sermonised in a black gown; there was no choir, though perhaps one or two fiddles in the gallery for music. The chancel was quite frequently closed altogether, or turned into a vestry.

Now all this was to be changed. The Churches of England were to be restored, as far as possible, to the functions for which they had been originally intended. Societies at Oxford and Cambridge were formed for studying the principles of Christian architecture, and the mediæval symbolism of which that architecture was the expression.* As a result, practically every church in the country, sooner or later, underwent a restoration, in the course of which a frightful amount of indiscriminate damage was done. Gothic became the only style for new churches, a Gothic more serious in intention than merely

* A good account of this will be found in Mr. Kennedy Clark's *The Gothic Revival*.

decorative experiments like St. Luke's, Chelsea, which had been put up in the early twenties as a counterblast to a Grecian temple-church at St. Pancras.

It is only fair to Ruskin to remember that he had neither part not lot in this work of restoration. To his mind, restoration was the worst form of destruction, a lie from beginning to end. Rather than restore a dilapidated church, he would have pulled it stone from stone, and constructed a wholly new one with the materials. Fortunately, his was not the deciding voice in the matter, and it is dreadful to think of what would have happened if this heroic principle of his had been put into practice.

The master restorer was a person of very different calibre, Sir Gilbert Scott, the designer of the Albert Memorial, a practical architect, who had served his apprenticeship putting up Poor Law Bastilles, and who—even by the standards of that laborious time—was a Gargantua for work. There is hardly an important Church in the country that does not bear the traces of his handiwork.

Sir Gilbert was not of the stuff of which martyrs, or fanatics, are made. He was a self-made man, with a *flair* for self-advertisement, and quite ready, at a pinch, to let his Gothic principles go by the board rather than lose a good job. But he was also an enthusiast, with a real love and reverence for old buildings, and, looking back on his own career, he can use language as strong as that of Ruskin about the way in which "the country has been, and continues to be, actually devastated with destruction under the name of restoration," though with charming candour, he admits "that the best of us have been blamable, and that even our conservation has been more or less destructive." But, considering what would probably have happened but for his intervention, Scott must be allowed to have a balance of good to his account, and to have handled his buildings with a reverence for which we can be grateful.

What the British Philistine was in the habit of doing with his ancient monuments may be seen at Canterbury. Here, during the thirties, the Cathedral was improved by having Lanfranc's beautiful Norman tower at the West End demolished, to make room for a twin to its Decorated sister, and the ruins of St. Augustine's Abbey were converted into an amusement park on the model of Vauxhall. As for the Norman Keep, that was made useful, as a coal shed for the adjoining gasworks. The climax came in 1859, when Wombwell, the menagerie owner, gravely petitioned the Mayor and Corporation to allow him to pull down the West Gate, one of the finest specimens of its kind in Europe, in order to clear a path for his elephants. It is perhaps less amazing that the city fathers should have gravely debated this modest proposal, than that the Mayor should finally have defeated it by his casting vote.*

Nevertheless the Church restorers had this to be said for them—that they were acting in the true spirit of the time in which the churches were built. Nobody in the Middle Ages could have conceived of Ruskin's idea that old buildings "are not ours. They belong partly to those who build them, and partly to the generations of mankind who are to follow us." To the mediæval builders,

* See *Highways and Byways of Kent* by Walter Jerrold, pp. 43-7.

as in a lesser degree to the Oxford and Cambridge reformers of the forties, a church was a church, and not a historical monument, and they had no hesitation in scrapping the whole, or any part of it, as occasion required. It was owing to this that the Middle Ages evolved the harmonious blend of styles that is the chief charm of our old parish churches, instead of leaving them plain Saxon or Norman. Ruskin's position—and that of most people to-day—can only be maintained on the assumption that the churches were alive till the Reformation killed them, and that all we can decently do is to embalm their corpses. And if this be granted, it must surely follow that the faith of Catholic Christianity, the soul to which these churches were once the living bodies, is a thing of the past, and that no movement or revival can reawaken it. It is hard to blame the men of that ostensibly devout time, for their unwillingness to accept so disquieting a conclusion.

As for the recovery, that was to give a new life to English architecture, of the Gothic principle, the results were singularly disappointing. It was not for lack of building—all over the country, and particularly in the swiftly expanding suburbs of great towns, churches sprang from the soil embodying all the most correct principles of the particular period selected, and designed with an erudition of technique to which no mediæval builder could have laid claim. It was simply that the churches refused to come alive. Let us take one of Sir Gilbert Scott's masterpieces, St. Mary Abbots, Kensington. Here you have all the proportions and features of the noblest decorated work—it would be hard to find definite faults, except just that it is uninteresting. I doubt whether any one regarding or entering it has felt that elevation of soul, that sense of awe and reverence, that the humblest village church so frequently inspires. It has less character about it than that rather preposterous toy put up to St. Luke in the neighbouring borough of Chelsea.

Even worse than the construction was the detail. The essence of Gothic, as Ruskin had conceived of it, was to give scope and joy to each individual craftsman. But Ruskin himself had a sharp lesson as to the meaning of Victorian Gothic, when he, and other intellectuals of the movement, concentrated all their enthusiasm on what was to have been a perfect example of Italian Gothic in the shape of the new Oxford Museum. Not only did the authorities, in that home of culture and mediævalism, deliberately starve the building of the funds necessary for its completion, but they procured the dismissal of an Irish workman, O'Shea, who displayed a truly mediæval genius in the carving of animals. It is pleasing to record that O'Shea had the last and annihilating word in the dispute, by going back to the building, after his dismissal, and chiselling, with furious energy, a festoon of parrots and owls, to represent members of Convocation.

If these things were done by Oxford dons, what could be expected of ordinary parsons, limited as to funds by the tight pockets of subscribers? Pious Victorians, though they might lay up for themselves treasure in Heaven, had sounder business instincts than to put all their eggs into one basket. They wanted to buy religion in the cheapest market, and in consequence created a demand, not for loving and faithful craftsmanship, but for the large-scale production of shoddy. The furnishing of Victorian churches became every whit as debased a trade as that of Victorian houses. Mawkish saints and smug monarchs smirked out of every niche and shouted from every window. Machine-carved substitutes were ordered down to replace long vanished rood screens. Mouldings and tracery, acanthus leaves and brass eagles, were multiplied with damnable reiteration. In the High and Catholic churches it was worst of all, for there the demand for tawdry imagery and all kinds of ecclesiastical junk was most expansive. The job of turning out such stuff must have been as soulless and mechanical as the product.

No doubt the Gothic Revival did here and there produce results that are not without value, and even at its worst it was—as any tourist by car may ascertain for himself—incapable of sinking to the horrors perpetrated, during this period, in French churches. Truro has a wonderfully good imitation of a Gothic cathedral. The new nave at Bristol has a grandeur that makes it no unworthy associate of the ancient choir. The Catholic Apostolic Church at Gordon Square aspires with something of the authentic mediæval fervour. An exception to the general poverty of Church adornments is occasionally to be found in monumental sculpture, though the best of this falls in the last quarter of the century. Secular buildings, like the Natural History Museum, have a fine, though not always appropriate, swagger, to offset the forfeited dignity and repose of such architecture as that of the British Museum. And the new Law Courts, the most ambitious effort of all, might produce a better impression, if their component members, like the German armies in 1914, had not got out of control of the Supreme Command and co-ordination with each other.

But after we have made every allowance, we shall find ourselves forced to the reluctant conclusion that the Gothic Revival was a failure, and not a very splendid failure at that. Its advocates founded their case on a simple fallacy of putting the cart before the horse. It was no doubt arguable that the original Gothic had expressed an ideal of civilisation saner and more spiritual than that of *laissez-faire* and devil-take-the-hindmost. But it did not follow that you could revive that civilisation by counterfeiting its effects, nor that such a counterfeit could be mistaken for anything else than what it was. Accordingly we find Ruskin and William Morris, who were, of all the reactionaries to mediævalism, the least bound by specialist limitation of outlook, turning their attention from the reform of art to that of society itself. Ruskin, despite the failure of all his practical schemes, did more than anybody else to bring the all-powerful middle class economics of his time into the hatred, ridicule, and contempt, in which they were destined to founder. His fame as an art critic has been long, and perhaps unjustly, eclipsed, but his dreams of social reform are the dominating realities of modern statesmanship. It is not with some little band of the æsthetic elect, but amid armies of the people, pressing towards the dawn, that his soul goes marching on.

We ask whether, such as it was, the Victorian civilisation could find no artistic outlet more natural than that provided by Gothic architecture, and Pre-Raphaelite painting? No doubt the desire for an escape, into a romantic dreamland, from the reality of intensive competition, was sincere enough. It was the Victorian decency not to look reality in the face until compelled to do so. But one wonders whether the most individual monuments of the age were not those that did not aspire to be artistic at all. The Crystal Palace is an experiment so bold as to be almost futuristic, and the possibilities of glass, as the material of a new, dynamic architecture, as opposed to the fixity of brick and stone, are more calculated to appeal to our own notions of relativity, than to the solid preferences of our grandfathers. The Clifton Suspension Bridge is lovely and satisfying to a degree that even the finest efforts of revived Gothic fail quite to attain.

Amid all the treatises on architectural principles of which the forties were so prolific, there is one that has probably been entirely forgotten. The author is a certain William Vose Pickett, whose name does not appear in *The Dictionary of National Biography*. He was probably set aside as a crank—perhaps he was one—but his little treatise, bearing an enormous title of which *New System of Architecture* must suffice, is certainly more original than anything that even a Ruskin could have produced. His idea is to make a clean sweep of the old traditions, and adapt our architecture boldly to the changed conditions of the time. He would go for his materials, not to the quarry, but to the foundry, he would use iron for building as it is already being used for ships and bridges and railways. He would explore the architectural possibilities of other metals, barium, for instance —that produces all the appearance of porcelain on the surface of iron—copper, brass, especially when lacquered, coloured glass, every description of woven or wire work. His "metallurgic architecture" would likewise avail itself of compositions, cements, *papier-mâché*, encaustic tiles, and make an extensive use of timber, which, it is pointed out, has greater architectural affinities with metal than with stone.

There follows a fascinating chapter on new architectural forms, based on the use of the curved instead of the straight line. Then comes another anticipation of the future, of more ominous import. "The indispensable concomitant of true excellence of architectural effect," that which the new architecture is destined to realise as never before, is, in the author's italics, *"the frequent and uniform repetition of its respective parts and features."* This is the vision, not of Victorian England, but of present-day Leningrad or Chicago—with mass production annihilating the individual. Mr. Pickett may yet be resurrected, when time has caught up with his imagination. As for Her Majesty's Government, when he submitted his schemes to them, he was told,

"It is not our duty or custom to encourage inventors." Which goes to prove that parrots and owls are not indigenous to Oxford quadrangles.

CHAPTER XX

CHARACTER AND CHARACTERS

THERE are certain works of genius that are less important for their own sakes than as historical landmarks. There was a play that appeared early in this century called *Man and Superman.* It might equally well have been called *Past and Future.* The Victorian Age had been, almost defiantly, as if in consciousness of a doomed ideal, an Age of Man. For us there would appear to be dawning the Age of Superman. A lover of Wagner would recognise in it the Twilight of the Gods.

Neither Mr. Bernard Shaw, nor his master, Nietzsche, realised to what unknown god they were constituting themselves high priests. They both thought of the Superman as of an individual, who, in some unexplained way, was to rise as much above the human as Man had risen above the monkey level. But two hundred years before either of them had burst on the world, the portrait of the Superman had been drawn—an awful and monstrous apparition, sprung, armed with sceptre and crosier, from the brain of Thomas Hobbes of Malmesbury. You can see it in the original edition, a man made up of men, packed together like worms in a carcase—the name of him Leviathan. For there is another biological analogy besides that associated with the name of Darwin. The human body has turned out, in the light of modern research, to be just such a Leviathan. It is a community more populous than the greatest nations, made up of living creatures inconceivably primitive as compared with the Republic Man, creatures specialised in accordance with the various services to the whole that it is the end of their being to perform, and who can be systematically starved, on occasion, that their bodies may form a sort of perpetually renewed Chinese Wall round about the community.

This last simile is borrowed, not inappropriately, from the most influential philosopher of modern England, Mr. H. G. Wells,* the arch enemy of individuality in this world and the next. Men are to the species what cells are to the man.

"The one remains, the many change and pass."

Nor is Mr. Wells alone in this opinion. It is gradually capturing the civilised world. Mussolini is annihilating the individual in the name of patriotism, the rulers of Russia in the name of the proletariat; the once sacred name of Liberty no longer commands even lip homage. Man, who deemed himself divine and immortal, sees his little day drawing to a close, and its last crimson beams strike upon the grim figure of Leviathan, breast high, as in Hobbes's frontispiece, above the Eastern horizon.

Sometimes we may be inclined to doubt whether it may not after all be an illusion, that an age of giants has been succeeded by one of pigmies. But men are not likely to rise above the level of their own ambitions, and where both the faith in individual greatness and the desire for

* The authorship, I think, is unmistakable, in spite of a son and a colleague collaborating.

it are on the wane, there is no god or destiny likely to thrust it upon us. We are content to be specialists, to concentrate our energies on as small a field as possible, that we may function with the precision of well-tested mechanical parts. That may account for the most striking phenomenon of the Great War—so far at any rate as England is concerned—in the extraordinary lack of outstanding personality among the leaders, after Kitchener, whose reputation had been made under Queen Victoria, had gone to his death beneath a cloud of disapproval, and the aged Fisher had departed in flaming revolt against the Lilliputian bonds by which genius was shackled. It was not only that there could arise no Iron Duke and no Corporal John, no Drake and no Nelson—but if we take such a comparatively small affair as the Indian Mutiny, where in the whole World War shall we find, for sheer individual personality, the peers of Havelock, Outram, the two Lawrences, Hodson, Strathnairn, Roberts, Neill, and the mighty Nicholson, the man whom an alien sect spontaneously worshipped as a god? Perhaps one Lawrence to stand as the equivalent of two—but after him? Well did Mr. Kipling modernise the old Wisdom into,

"Let us now praise famous men,
Men of little showing,"

to which Mr. Wells, followed by Mr. Lytton Strachey, would doubtless add,

"Let us now attack * great men, if there ever were any great men."

* But perhaps I wrong Mr. Strachey. He would, no doubt, prefer to call it "humanising" his victims.

Since the tallest and nearest figures make the best targets, the attack has been concentrated with peculiar violence on individual Victorians. And yet, cruelly as the Victorians have suffered from their biographers, we can place to their credit one enormous, though implied, admission, namely that they are eminently worth biographising. If it were not for the convention of good taste, on the one hand, and the law of libel, on the other, one could cite the names of eminent Georgians, whose reputations no future biographer will ever bring to earth, or, indeed, dig up out of it.

With all its faults, and they were many, the Victorian Age was one conspicuously rich in character—and characters. The cult of moral earnestness, the stress of competition, tended to foster those qualities of concentration and independence that are the basis of individuality. The very seriousness with which the Victorians took themselves, tended to foster personality. A habit of humorous self-depreciation may come not far short, in effect, of a craven fear of being great. Such men as Gladstone, as Ruskin, as Thomas Arnold, do undoubtedly invite the same sort of ridicule as the immaculate circus manager gets from the clown. But to reverence the highest when you see it, even in the looking-glass, is at least a potent means of auto-suggestion to live up to the highest standard.

What was most favourable of all to the development of character, was the love of liberty that in the middle class had the strength of a religion. There was nothing that aroused the enthusiasm of the reformed electorate so much as the idea of resistance to tyranny. Any foreign revolutionary, who sought refuge on English shores, was sure to be lionised. The Lancashire cotton operatives never wavered in their support of the anti-slavery cause, during the American Civil War, though multitudes of them were thrown out of employment owing to the blockade of the Southern Ports. Byron's

> "plain, sworn, downright detestation
> Of every despotism in every nation"

had become the normal, emotional reaction of the man in the street.

Nor was there ever a time when the sentiment of individual liberty was so strong at home. The average Englishman desired nothing more fervently than to be left alone to carve out his own fortunes. His economics were based on the free play of enlightened self-interest. His politics were biased by a watchful jealousy of state interference. His intellectual leaders, even when they were not individualists by profession, made up for it in practice. Carlyle, in spite of the Prussian discipline he came to worship in his old age, was the most intractable member of a family notorious for its aggressive independence even among Lowland Scots. And independence is the quality in a man that attracts Carlyle most, as in the incident he records of Samuel Johnson, a needy servitor at Oxford, pitching out of the window—"with what thoughts!"—a pair of shoes that some kind person had left at his door. And Ruskin, though he was perpetually talking about obedience, and though he made it a leading principle of his Company of St. George—where it meant obedience to him—was the most wayward and wilful even of Victorian individualists. The weakness, and no small part of the charm of his immense literary output, arises from its complete lack of intellectual discipline. What writer of our own day would dare to bring out a plea for a union of churches under the title "Notes on the Construction of Sheepfolds," a practical joke that increased Ruskin's royalties by the pence of certain earnest sons of the soil who expected a very different return for their money?

A raw and aggressive independence seems to have been the quality of all others prized, and displayed, by the Victorians. One of the secrets of Lord Palmerston's immense popularity was the impression the ordinary man had formed of old Pam, that he didn't care the straw that wagged from his mouth, what he said to any one. Nor, as a general rule, did he, even when conducting diplomatic correspondence, a fact that made his tenure of the Foreign Office a nightmare, not only to the rest of Europe, but to his Royal Mistress and his Premier, Lord John Russell. But the Queen found that Lord John could be just as blunt on occasion, for when she asked him whether it was true that a subject was, in certain circumstances, justified in disobeying his sovereign,

"Well," replied Lord John, "speaking to a sovereign of the House of Hanover, I can only say that I suppose it is."

But neither of "these two dreadful old men," as the Queen called them, could hold a candle to her for sheer domineering will-power. The young girl who could bolster up a defeated and discredited ministry for two years, rather than make the smallest change in the personnel of her Bedchamber, grew into the middle-aged widow, who isolated herself for long years at Balmoral, in the teeth of popular sentiment, and into the old lady, who, to the last, persisted in excluding her aging and gifted heir from the responsibility and inner knowledge appertaining to his rank. There is this to be said of the Queen's personality—you may like or dislike it, but you will find it uncommonly hard to belittle. It was no mere accident of position that she became, during her last years, the object of a veneration so unquestioning and universal, that only those whose memories run back to the Jubilee decade can realise what associations clung to the idea of "The Queen." Every volume of her letters that comes from the press confirms one's youthful prejudice, to this extent, at least, that among all eminent Victorians, there was none of more outstanding personality than Victoria herself. The idea of her as a mere puppet of the Prince Consort has been blown to the winds by the correspondence of her widowhood. And those late letters of hers that appear in Lord Lansdowne's recently published biography suggest that—contrary to the general belief *—the master hand was as sure as ever, and the grasp on the helm as firm, up to that last meeting with Lord Roberts, when, with the shadow of death already darkening over her, she fell to comparing his Lordship's experiences in South Africa with what another even more famous commander had told her of his difficulties in the Peninsula.

* My own included, and expressed in my *History of British Civilisation*.

The two great apostles of Victorian individuality were John Stuart Mill and Herbert Spencer, and of both of them it can be said that they lived their belief as eloquently as they wrote it. And this—at any rate as regards Mill—is saying a good deal. But where will you find a more robust display of independence than Mill's retort, when he was standing as Parliamentary candidate for the Borough of Westminster, to a working class heckler's

"Have you not said in your writings that working men are generally liars?"

"I did," replied Mill, simply, and it says worlds for the temper of Victorian England that the working men in the audience were highly delighted. We should not advise a repetition of this experiment to modern candidates, who have not previously secured a speedy and certain line of retreat.

Few of the books in which Mill's reputation was founded, when he occupied something very like the position of an intellectual dictator, have stood the test of time. But of the little treatise on Liberty, it is true now as when Morley said so, that to read it adds a cubit to a man's stature. It is a book whose full flavour can be best appreciated by one emerging from a boyhood of pious or sporting conventionality, into what seems to him the dawn of a new freedom. Opening the dingy and small-printed popular edition, after the lapse of many years, he will find it hard to recapture the joy scored, it may be, by dashes of red pencil in the margin.

"It is the privilege and proper condition of a human

being," runs one such passage, "arrived at the maturity of his faculties, to use and interpret experience in his own way."

Or again—

"He who lets the world, or his own portion of it, choose his plan of life for him, has no need of any other faculty than the ape-like one of imitation."

The message of dawn comes faint and distant on the afternoon breeze, like the horn-blast of Roland to the ears of Charlemagne, and yet he must be dull indeed whose pulse does not quicken on reading this noblest of all pleas for independence of thought, word, and deed, the more compelling from its restraint.

The whole essence of it was packed by Robert Browning into his one sonnet—an answer to the question "Why am I a Liberal?" of which the sextet runs:

> "But little do, or can, the best of us:
> That little is achieved through Liberty.
> Who, then, dares hold, emancipated thus,
> His fellow should continue bound? Not I,
> Who live, love, labour freely, nor discuss
> A brother's right to freedom. That is Why."

In Herbert Spencer, the individualist tendency of the age was exaggerated to the point of caricature. His philosophy is long out of date, except for its muscular and downright style, but he only lacks a Boswell to become as representative a figure of the nineteenth, as Dr. Johnson was of the eighteenth century. To some extent he himself has supplied the deficiency in his Autobiography, a wonderfully candid piece of self and family revelation.

In the Spencer family the soul of the British middle class, in the early nineteenth century, stands revealed in its hedgehog-like independence, its remorseless energy, its contempt for the pleasures and graces of life. There is that fine old grandmother, who survived into the forties, one of the first disciples of John Wesley, still, at the age of 83, wearing her plain Methodist cap, and of whom her son recorded that "her activity was so uniform that I do not recollect even the appearance of indolence. Her fault, if any, was in doing too much." There is Aunt Mary Ann, with "a strong sense of her own claims and not a duly proportioned sense of the claims of others." There is Uncle Henry, who ruined himself by speculation, and used to go out of his way to court insult by flaunting a white, Radical top hat. There is Uncle John, who was "entirely egoistic, and in pursuit of personal advantage sacrificed the interests of other members of the family without scruple"—Aunt Mary Ann knew him as "boasting John" and "blustering John," which her nephew gravely diagnoses as "descriptive names indicative of deficient sympathy." Uncle William, on the other hand, had "the desire to be facetious," but, in Herbert's doubtless expert judgment, "without the power of being so," and was "generally considered somewhat odd." Then there was Spencer's father, who refused, on principle, to address anybody as Esquire or Reverend, or to take the least visible notice of any question addressed him by his wife, that he did not consider to have been framed with sufficient clearness. Last, but not least, there was Uncle Thomas, the Simeonite parson and temperance reformer, by whom all public amusements were uncompromisingly tabooed, and who, being asked by a hostess why the youthful Herbert declined to take part in some waltzing, annihilated her with the awful finality of his pronouncement—"No Spencer ever dances."

The house in Exeter Street, Derby, in which the philosopher was born, was as austere as Uncle Thomas himself—Terpsichore could hardly have contrived to dance behind that façade of featureless brick. It was such an environment, and such an ancestry, as only the English middle class could have produced, such as alone could have rendered credible the phenomenon of Herbert Spencer. All the austerity and independence, all the pedantry and egotism, all the narrow, concentrated energy of these non-corybantic Spencers, were united and intensified in his one person. At the age of thirteen, he defeated even Uncle Thomas, to whose tutelage he had been entrusted, by leaving his uncle's parsonage, in the neighbourhood of Bath, and performing the really astounding feat of foot-slogging the whole way to Derby, with no more than two shillings in his pocket, concerning which escapade his Aunt, while still uncertain of his fate, records her "decided opinion that unless his parents punish him severely, and return him again to us *immediately,* it will not only be *insulting* to us, but *ruinous* to the boy himself."

Never was child more authentically father to the man. The fact that Herbert Spencer carried the family nonconformity a stage further by casting off the last rags of Christianity, only intensified his truth to the Spencer type. His hatred for any sort of authority fell not far short of an obsession. He strode through the Realms of

Gold like a Goliath, brushing Homer, Plato, Dante, Raphael, Michelangelo, Kant, contemptuously out of his path. He would hurry through Italy, not, like ordinary tourists, to admire, but to carp at old buildings and old masters and the very scenery. His egotism was untouched by either humility or humour. When he got tired of conversation, and did not want to leave the company, he used unobtrusively to plug up his ears. In spite of his portentous flirtation with George Eliot, he was frank enough to congratulate himself on his celibacy—"I am not by nature adapted to a relation in which perpetual compromise and great forbearance are needful." Nor, for that matter, was Carlyle, and it is not surprising that the two sages could not meet without violent disputation, culminating in a mutual and speechless glare.

The worst faults of the Victorian middle class were exaggerated in Spencer, its Philistinism, its lack of culture and urbanity, its incapacity to philosophise—for who but Spencer would have dubbed his God (the good, old, eighteenth-century Deity) unknowable, and then proceeded to know so much about him? Who but he would have succeeded in weaving his inherited prejudices so completely into the texture of the Universe? And yet the greatness of its blemishes does but serve to emphasise the greatness of Spencer's personality. There never lived a man more magnificently true to himself and his ideals. A chronic invalid, tortured with insomnia, and incapable of any prolonged exertion, indifferent to fame and contemptuous of honours, he never wavered through all the long years of his self-imposed task of formulating a universal philosophy. Carlyle might—or might not—have changed his attitude of defiance for one of worship, had he but realised that he was glaring into the eyes of a hero.

And it is remarkable concerning Herbert Spencer, that he, like another great Victorian, John Nicholson of the Mutiny, has become an object of worship among a sect of devotees. There are few forms of irreverence that any one dreams nowadays of resenting, but once let the name or philosophy of Spencer be blasphemed, and the stoutest of Victorian rulers will descend on the offender's knuckles. For there is still a sect of earnest and old-fashioned Puritans, strong in the faith of their grandparents' biology, to whom the Unknowable is God and Spencer is prophet. Long and immutably may they survive!

So far we have only dealt with one or two prominent names, and have necessarily conveyed a very imperfect idea of the extraordinary richness of that age in individual character. To do justice to such a theme one would have to write more biographies than ever Sir Leslie Stephen edited. For it is not only with eminent Victorians that we are concerned.

It is no accident that the period of middle class supremacy almost exactly coincides with the career of Dickens. It was only in such a time that Dickens could have found scope for his genius. It is impossible to imagine anything equivalent to the Pickwickian gallery of portraits in a modern novel. You might as well invite a party of Brobdingnagians into a ball-room. Nor, for that matter, could anything like the raw-blooded exuberance of Handley Cross society be conceivable in the wildest sporting novel of to-day. Even when they fly to the Arabian Desert for virility, our lady novelists no longer give birth to Heathcliffs and Rochesters. The Victorian was pre-eminently an age of characters in fiction. May we not be permitted to conjecture that this was because it was an age of characters in life?

It is an impression that deepens the more we study that life, from no matter what angle. Let that angle, for a moment, be academic. Where now is the old breed of Victorian dons, those "regal dons," of whom Mr. Belloc sang—can it be a generation ago? Nowadays we partially fill the old chairs with efficient specialists, gentlemen in the public school tradition, who would be as much at home in an officers' mess as at a High Table—worthier citizens, no doubt, than many a crusted old Victorian bachelor. But they themselves would modestly disclaim the style of "characters." To-day Mr. Belloc might look in vain—and I trust with regret—for the don capable of doing anything so unconventional as daring to attack his Chesterton.

But even at the beginning of the century, there remained only one or two survivors of the old school, living witnesses to the credibility of the legends from which the atmosphere of Victorian donhood may be partly reconstructed. There is the stately figure of Provost Okes, of King's, who died, at an immense age, in 1888, and who, during the long tenure of his Provostship, set his gnarled and parrot-beaked face like a flint against any suggestion of reform, and is said to have dominated his Council by stoutly refusing to allow motions of which he disapproved to be brought forward at all. When at last re-

form was forced upon him and his college by act of
Parliament, and King's ceased to be the closed preserve
of Etonian scholars, his official reception of the first non-
Etonian Fellow was overwhelming. After looking the
poor man up and down, with intense disapprobation, he
finally pronounced, in deep and measured tones, the
verdict:

"Let us hope that this new leaven will not leaven the
whole lump."

It helps us to visualise him, when we are told that he
was the last Provost who drove about Cambridge in a
gilded coach of state; also that many of his *jeux d'esprit*
are preserved—in the original, and no doubt correct,
Latin.

There were such paragons as Bradshaw, the University
Librarian, who, without having accomplished anything
specially notable in the way of scholarship, seems to have
towered above all his contemporaries by the force and
grandeur of his personality. There were, on the other
hand, such intractable characters as the old gentleman
who successfully defied even Okes, and who used to delight the undergraduates by marching round the court,
with a parrot on each shoulder, one trained to repeat
"Okes, Okes, Okes," and the other, "Brock, Brock,
Brock"—being short for Brocklebank, the Provost's chief
ally. One day, after all efforts had failed to remove him
from his Fellowship, he was discovered under the college
mulberry tree, with a spade, chopping malicefully at
worms, and muttering,

"Haven't got me yet, damn you! Haven't got me yet!"

After this, we are prepared for the legend of the some-

what similar old gentleman who lived above the gate of
his college, and used to mark his disapprobation of the
tutor by habitually belching on his head, until, that func-
tionary having armed himself with an open umbrella,
there came a bellow from above of "You coward! Be
a man and put that down!"

Or of the proctor who remarked to some undergraduates:

"Your conduct, gentlemen, has not only grieved Almighty God, but also seriously displeased Me."

It is not a bit more incredible than many of the remarks one has actually heard from the lips of Oscar
Browning, who was the last, and perhaps the grandest,
representative of authentic Victorian donhood.

The Victorian dons are not unworthy to stand beside
those dubious and intrinsic old men of Edward Lear,
who danced quadrilles with ravens, cut up their food with
scythes, walked through the streets of London brandish-
ing pigs, and looked out of windows to say, "Fil jomble,
fil jumble, fil rumble—cum—tumble." Such respectable
yet defiant individualists could only have been the product of a Victorian brain. In a sense, or nonsense, they
are the supreme representatives of the Victorian ideal.

We may shift our point of view from the academic to
the pedagogical, and turn our regard to the mighty headmasters, whose names will endure as long as, and perhaps
longer than, the schools they revolutionised—Arnold of
Rugby, Thring of Uppingham, and their peers. Or to
the parsons of the old, and perhaps—from the strictly
clerical standpoint—unreformed school, though no one
would use such an epithet in connection with Dean Purey

Cust of York, with his stately person, his magnificence of courtesy that would have graced a hidalgo of old Castille, and his vast stores of heraldic erudition. Affection even now clings to his memory, and justifies his epitaph in the Cathedral—"A man greatly beloved." As O. B. may be styled the last of the great Victorian personalities among dons, and Warre of Eton (almost as tough a reactionary as Okes) among headmasters, so I should be inclined to claim for Cust a similar position in the clerical world. But in such matters of opinion and necessarily limited knowledge, there can be no finality.

All one can hope to do is to convey some sense of the God's plenty of individual character by which the Victorian Age was distinguished. To sum it up as briefly as possible, I should say that its distinctive quality was one of earnest exuberance. The flood tide of personality was perpetually overflowing its banks, often with disastrous, nearly always with incalculable effects. The deified John Nicholson, to whom we have already referred, had not only been known to rush at a brother officer, under fire, and kick him in the direction of the enemy, but he was at one time for deposing, and at another, when himself mortally wounded, for shooting, out of hand, his own commander-in-chief, who probably deserved both. Gordon was another such incalculable genius, which accounts for the instinctive dislike of him in our own age—a dislike which has enabled the cock-and-bull story of his drunkenness to be propagated and accepted on evidence that it would be a compliment to describe as flimsy. It is only fair to say that it would take quite a considerable amount of strong drink to stimulate an average modern to the full-blooded exuberance that was soberly habitual in his Victorian equivalent.

Whether the balance of advantage works out in favour of the past, or the present, may be a matter for debate. We can best express the difference as that between a torrential river, mountain fed, and a canal, cut straight across a level plain. The analogy holds, in that the river requires a vast labour of artificial restriction to keep it from flooding, and is in that sense less free than the canal —the best defence of the Evangelical Lord being that, like certain ferocious school-masters, he had a wonderful way of his own in dealing with unmanageable boys. Finally, though the river is a more magnificent and soul-stirring object, and will generate a greater volume of transformable energy, the canal has the advantage when it comes to prosaic barge traffic.

Our desire to do justice to that earnest exuberance which the conditions of the Victorian Age tended to generate, must not blind us to its insufficiency, by itself, to level up the standard of character to requirements so exacting, beyond all precedent, as those of a revolutionised environment. A soul resembles a machine in this, at least, that the first of all things needful for it is energy. But that energy must be disciplined, and cunningly guided into the proper channels, if it is not to be wasted, or destructive. That, in the soul, is the function of the intellect, or, more precisely, of intellectual discipline.

It was just this element in which the Victorians were —perhaps fatally—deficient. Their energies seldom seem to have been co-ordinated in the best possible way towards the best possible ends. As we follow the steps of one after another of the giants who walked the earth in those days, our admiration is mingled with a certain bitterness of disappointment. They did much, it is true —but with that inexhaustible energy they might have done so much more, to make a world fit for their descendants to live in. Certainly of Darwin, perhaps of Browning, almost of Dickens, we feel that the whole best in the man was realised, that there was no wastage of energy. But of how many Victorians can we say this?

Can we of Ruskin, with his perpetual transition from the sublime to the eccentric, his lack of the synthetic faculty that resolves such a book as *Modern Painters* into a huge anthology of purple patches, his rigid limitation of outlook, that enabled Whistler to pillory him, before the world, as a High Priest of the Philistines? Can we of Newman, who, we feel, had it in him to have been as indisputably "the" philosopher for the new age, as Aristotle had been for that of the Schoolmen—had but the breadth of his vision been commensurate with its height, and depth? Can we of Carlyle, with his decline from hero-worship to something not far removed from Devil-worship? Can we of Gladstone, with his spiritual fervour that is never quite distinguishable from spiritual pride, his extraordinary inconsistencies, and his capacity for saying nothing whatever with the noblest eloquence that ever stirred the great heart of a people? Can we of Tennyson, of Shaftesbury, of John Bright, of Gordon? It is perhaps ungrateful, but yet hardly to be avoided, that our appreciation of what the Victorians have done should be clouded by the thought of what they had it in them to do—and did not.

Finally, we have to resolve what seems to be an inconsistency between the natural exuberance of the Victorian character, and the disinclination that we have noticed in the Victorians ever to give that exuberance full scope, ever to trust whole-heartedly and without reserve to their inspiration. The answer, I think, is that they instinctively dared not, because their natural exuberance was not informed by that harmony of the intellectual and spiritual powers that a Greek would have known as "eurhythmia" —something equivalent to Shelley's Intellectual Beauty. They dared not unchain forces so violent and so uncontrolled. Lacking a directive principle, they were bound to set up, and abide by, artificial checks. The only alternative to the Spirit is, in fact, the Law.

CHAPTER XXI

WERE THE VICTORIANS SNOBS?

OF all the charges that it is fashionable to level at the Victorians, there is none more constantly repeated than that of snobbery. It is generally repeated in such a form as to imply that snobbery was a special discovery of the Victorians, and something by which their age is conspicuously distinguished from our own. If it were *chic* nowadays to thank God for anything, we should most of us be doing so, with especial fervency, on the ground that we are not like the snobs our grandparents were.

This is surely an indiscreet attitude. Had the prosecution limited itself to saying, "the Victorians were snobs," it might at least have put up a plausible case. It is always possible to fall back on Thackeray, though even his evidence cuts two ways, for it at least shows that, in the forties, one of the foremost writers of the time was able to stand up and denounce snobbery, in all its forms, in a magazine which owed its success to the fidelity with which it expressed middle class opinion. Indeed, so popular were Thackeray's "snob" articles in *Punch,* that he was induced to keep the ball rolling long after it had lost its first and natural momentum, which accounts for *The Book of Snobs* rather outstaying the reader's interest in its latter stages.

The difference, in this regard, between Thackeray's time and our own, is best indicated by the fact that nowadays the magazines that cater for the middle class, instead of denouncing snobbery, devote their best energies to its mass production, on a scale that would have made the doughtiest snob of the forties stare and gasp. I doubt whether anybody of that time could quite have understood the mysticism that induces otherwise sane people to part with a weekly shilling for the rapture of gazing upon photographs of uninteresting but monied people in ungraceful attitudes, and frequently with open mouths, amusing themselves in rigidly stereotyped ways—"Sir Bors Boomgarden, at the Old Heavy Puppy Judging Trials, showing his programme to the Hon. Rosemary Stult." It is one form of mass production that was only stimulated by the catastrophe of a World War, as if the curse of Adam could not be fulfilled without the sniggerings of Eve. It lends an additional horror to the waiting rooms of dentists. And yet, so inured are we to this sort of thing, that not only does nobody ever dream of detecting snobbery in magazines of the kind we have described, but it is in their pages that we shall probably find the keenest strictures on Victorian snobbery. This would seem to indicate a standard of self-criticism worthy of the mate, who, returning greatly uplifted from a revival meeting, announced to the crew:

"Now, look here by ——! I'm going to have no more —— swearing on board this ship, and the next —— —— as I catch at it, I'll —— well give the —— Hell."

But the fact that snobbery has developed out of all proportion since the time that Thackeray wrote, by no means invalidates his diagnosis of this new, diseased growth in the social organism. In such a society as that visualised by Shakespeare, in which degree, priority, and place are scrupulously honoured, there can be no question of snobbery. His Coriolanus was as proud as Satan, but he was no snob. Neither were the tribunes who engineered his banishment snobs. As long as people are sure of their place in society, there can be no question of snobbery—it is only when degree is vizarded that it can arise. The eighteenth century, in spite of its sprinkling of adventurers and *nouveaux riches,* afforded comparatively little scope for the members of one class to ape the style of another. The Industrious Apprentice may have become Lord Mayor, but it is extremely unlikely that he ever boasted to his aldermen about "my friend, Lord Chesterfield."

The snob was, in fact, a by-product of the Industrial Revolution. The enormously increased importance and wealth of the bourgeoisie had had the effect of vizarding degree to an extent unprecedented since the dissolution of the monasteries had provided funds to start a new nobility. Now that fortunes were being made and lost so rapidly, even humble shop assistants, like Mr. Tittlebat Titmouse, began to ape the manners of swells, and to dream dreams of Ten-thousand a year. And had not the firm of Pitt and Company dealt even in coronets with those who could pay for them?

There was an element, even in snobbery, that was not altogether contemptible. Its rise was largely stimulated by the romantic enthusiasm that was at its height in the thirties and forties. There was an almost universal desire to escape from the brutal reality of the machine age into the dream of an idealised past. In spite of Macaulay, the neatest suburban villa lacked the attractiveness of a castle in Spain. But from an idealised past it is not a very far cry to an idealised present. The vanished glories of Barons on the Rhineland and Caliphs in Bagdad was scarcely more calculated to impress the clerk or shop assistant and his womenfolk, than that of the swells upon whom he could feast his eyes in the Row. There is a pathetic longing expressed in the old song,

> "I'd like to be a swell,
> A-roaming down Pell Mell,
> Or anywhere, I don't much care,
> So I could be a swell."

Samuel Warren made a masterly analysis of this trend of mind when he described the counter jumper Titmouse starving himself, in order that his miserable salary of £35. a year might run to enough cheap finery to enable him to have one weekly hour of glorious life, in the Park, on Sunday morning, ogling the girls, and lounging as nonchalantly as a d'Orsay. On such occasions, letters would marshal themselves before his mind's eye into the words, "Sir Tittlebat Titmouse, Baronet," or even "Lord Titmouse."

Tennyson's Lord of Burleigh, like the gallant lover he was, showed perfect comprehension of the feelings of a Miss Titmouse, when he suggested to his bride that they should

> "see the handsome houses,
> Where the stately nobles dwell."

Tennyson was, in fact, as much a romanticist of the modern country house as of the feudal castle. As for Disraeli, he was able to throw a glamour over the lives of his great gentlemen and ladies, which shows this most romantic of all adventurers to have had certain affinities with Don Quixote.

If we turn up the old annual, *Keepsake,* we shall find sentiment of this kind spread thick and luscious. Take *The Gardener of the Hall* by Monckton Milnes, afterwards Lord Houghton,

Thus eighteen summers every day I tended her (the daughter of the house) and them (the flowers),
I watched the opening of the bud, the shooting of the stem,
And when her childish laughter turned to silent maiden smiles,
I felt in heaven when e'er she passed, and scarce on earth the while.
How could I ever think to leave the old manorial hall?

This otherwise excellent girl makes a *marriage de convenance* with a rich lord:

"And now I wander up and down, I labour as I can,"

obsessed by the thought that even the young lady of the old hall may be no happier than a gardener. Where, in these degenerate days, are gardeners to be found so properly inclined?

Where the social order is in a state of such fluidity as it was during the nineteenth century, snobs are bound to arise. They were quite as much *en evidence* in the France of Louis Philippe as in contemporary England—if, indeed, we can use so breezy a word as "snob" to describe heartless and inhuman pushers like the Mme. de Marville, in *Cousin Pons*. And the English bourgeois, like other Englishmen, had a strong romantic streak in his composition, that made him rather inclined to idealise a lord, even to the extent of allowing lords to govern in his name. Dickens, that most redoubtable of Radicals, was more merciful to his gentlefolk than Thackeray, who, coming from a stock of Anglo-Indian civil servants, was less given to romancing about the gentlemanly attributes of gentlefolk. I do not believe that Dickens would ever have had the heart to describe so dirty, mean, and vulgar a squire as old Sir Pitt Crawley. Nor would Thackeray have let off Sir Leicester Dedlock so lightly, and even affectionately, as Dickens does. Lord Frederick Verisopht, in spite of his name, dies as valiantly as any knight-errant, in defence of a lady against a scoundrel. If we may borrow a phrase from Dickens's doughtiest modern champion, we may say that his typical member of the upper class—and we would not make a complete exception even of Twemlow—"though an ass is a gentleman."

No one would dream of calling Dickens a snob, and we may see in this great representative man of the middle class in the days of its supremacy, how Radical independence was not by any means inconsistent with that tendency—in him admittedly a slight one—to be sentimental about gentility, which, if pushed far enough, develops into snobbery. But—and this is the important point to remember about the early Victorians—this tendency was still held in check by a sturdy middle class self-respect.

We have already remarked on this quality in the Victorians. We are accustomed to laugh at them for their respectability, but it is a better and nobler ideal to be respected for what you are—be it merchant or tradesman —than to be furtively ashamed of it, and solicitous only to conform to the most approved country-house or smart-set standards. John Bright and Cobden were as proud of being honest business men, as any Hungarian Count of his forty ancestors in direct line. It was only towards the end of his life, when the first symptoms of change were beginning to appear, that Dickens got to describing a really snobbish atmosphere in the Veneering family. Mr. Dombey was proud, but he was proud of his money and commercial position, and his giddiest ambition was for the firm to become Dombey and Son. Mr. Podsnap has little to recommend him, but, in proclaiming his Gospel of Podsnappery,

"He speaks with an honest, triumphant pride."

Or let us pass from Dickens to Surtees. There are some of us who may think the idolisation of Mr. Jorrocks a little overdone, but in one quality the grocer Falstaff may fairly challenge the appellation of "great," and that is his superb absence of snobbery.

"You 'air-dresser on the chestnut 'oss," roars Mr. Jorrocks, during a check, to a gentleman with very big, ginger whiskers, "pray, 'old 'ard!"

"Hair-dresser," replies the gentleman, turning round in a fury, "I'm an officer in the ninety-first regiment."

"Then you hossifer in the ninety-fust regiment, wot looks like an 'air-dresser, 'old 'ard!"

Even Mr. Soapy Sponge, who is what his name implies, is not in any sense a snob. He is an adventurer, and, like his friend Facey Romford, more than a bit of a blackguard, but neither he nor Facey is out to improve his social position. Both are sportsmen to the backbone, and both, being men of insufficient financial means, are determined to get their sport by any means, fair or foul. But Sponge never dreams of toadying to his victims. The man who could fire a charge of shot into Mr. Jogglebury's poor, ill-trained Ponto, may have been a brute, but he was not a snobbish, but a sporting—which is sometimes the worst kind of—brute.

If the early Victorians of the middle class were in the habit of sentimentalising about the nobility and gentry, they were equally fond of standing up to and defying them on the slightest provocation. This may be seen in the career of *Punch,* whose note was then, as now, cunningly attuned to the mind of the fairly prosperous, black-coated citizen. The *Punch* of the forties was as sardonic and merciless an employer of the cudgel as his great original, but he had a generous hatred of oppression and sympathy with the bottom dog, and he did not in the least care how he expressed them.

Imagine a *Punch* of to-day publishing so savage an attack on the Game Laws as one, in 1844, representing a Duke in the act of sacrificing a kneeling peasant to a hare, or one, of the year after, entitled *Noble Poulterers,* in which a Duke is represented as hawking his game about the streets—which he can do cheap, it is explained, because they are nourished on the wheat, oats, and barley of his tenant farmers! And we must remember that this peculiarly unromantic practice of turning sport to profit is one pilloried also by Disraeli, for Disraeli is another instance of that Janus-like attitude to birth so character-istic of the time, and even Thackeray did not deal more mercilessly with his upper class than Disraeli in his *Sybil or The Two Nations.*

To return to *Punch,* we can imagine the horror and wholesale withdrawal of subscriptions among his modern clientele, were he to publish so positively Bolshevistic a cartoon as one to which we have already referred, con-trasting capitalist luxury with the horrors of the labour in the mines, or displaying such sympathy with crime as that entitled *The Home of the Rick Burner,* in which a demon with a torch is waving it before a poor fellow in a tumble-down hovel, sitting heart-broken beside the corpse of his starved wife, with his starving children be-side him, and the cupboard empty.

Nor is even the Royal Family spared, for we have Prince Albert's Beehives, "so constructed that the working bees within (that are a very curious species of bee and bear an outward resemblance to British mechanics and artificers), are carefully deprived of all the honey they elaborate, save the honey that is considered sufficient to afford them ample subsistence in all seasons."

We wonder what a Marx or a Lenin could have added to this.

Punch's tilts at Dukes did not end with the forties; for instance, in 1859, he attacks battue shooting, with special reference to the Duke of Rutland, remarking bluntly that "battue banging is not sport." In 1862 it is the Duke of Buccleuch, referred to disrespectfully as "Sawney," who mounts the pillory for offering resistance to the new line of the Thames Embankment. As late as 1880, the old fire is not quenched, for there are repeated attacks on the Duke of Bedford—or Mudford—for the disgraceful condition of Covent Garden, while in 1883 there is a shot at a royal Duke and Duchess for selling family portraits and furniture. But *Punch,* and the middle class with him, were by this time becoming too well schooled in gentility and good taste to go on with such unreasonable jesting, of which this is one of the last specimens.

That crabbed old *Punch* of the mid-nineteenth century was no doubt a Philistine, and an exponent of the worst John Bullish insularity, but his sins, which were many, may be forgiven him for the sake of his great heart. There was no humanitarian cause to which his support was not given. It was he who drove some of the last nails into the coffin of the duel; it was he who took up the woes of governesses; he who palliated the conduct of a poacher earning 8/-a week, and called for the informer on him to be put to Coventry; it was he who lashed the upholders of flogging in the army; it was he who denounced the virtual existence of one law for the rich and another for the poor; it was he who, as stoutly as Dickens himself, stood up for the victims of the new Poor Law. Nor were his sympathies confined to the human race, for he was, for a long time, one of the most fearless champions of animals, and not even aristocratic or royal sport was exempted by him from the ordinary criteria of humane conduct. The crowned head of Victoria herself shared the fate of Judy's, on account of her presence at one of her husband's deer-massacres in

Coburg, and, as late as 1878, stag baiting, by the royal pack, was contemptuously put on a par with badger baiting.

We have heard enough, and more than enough, about the defects of the Victorian bourgeoisie. I have no desire to minimise them, and there is a certain poetic justice in the fact that the enormous self-adulation of that class in the days of its supremacy should have given place to a reaction just as undiscriminating. But if the middle class were proud, they had a great deal to be proud of. It was they—and it would be but a slight exaggeration to say, they alone—who produced that harvest of genius and talent by which the Victorian Age has enriched all succeeding time. Their very critics and satirists were sprung from their own ranks. Mr. Podsnap and Mr. Bottles, those awful examples of the British bourgeois at his worst, were the creation of bourgeois brains.

What was remarkable about our middle class of that time was not its selfishness, for selfishness is a weed bound to flourish on such a soil as that provided by a life and death economic struggle for survival, it is not its occasional snobbishness, for that is bound to crop up in a time of social transition—what is remarkable and almost unique about it is its generosity and idealism, the extent to which it was ready to sacrifice its interests and class prejudices to what it held and felt to be right. What is remarkable about a man like John Bright was not that he—though himself a model employer—should have reconciled his conscience to his interests to the extent of opposing factory legislation, but that he should have put principle before class, to the extent of agitating for a franchise that was to break down the power of the bourgeoisie and enable the workers to prescribe the remedy for their own grievances.

The sentiments voiced by *Punch* in the forties are those expressed to-day in the columns of class-conscious publications catering for a proletarian audience. But few, if any, manual labourers in the forties could have afforded a *Punch,* and not all of them could have read it. Its contributors and cartoonists, men like Thackeray and Jerrold, Leech and Doyle, could not by any stretch of language have been described as lower class. What is remarkable about *Punch* is that he, a bourgeois of the bourgeois, should have established himself as a national institution, by catering for a middle class audience, whose blood was ready to boil at any spectacle of tyranny and oppression brought vividly before its eyes, in spite of its obvious interests and its scarcely challenged capitalist economics. The strangeness of the phenomenon will appear, when we think of Mr. Punch to-day—a hale and genial octogenarian, gentlemanly enough to know that the kind of thing he did in his youth is not done, and shrewd enough to recognise that, even if it were, the doing of it would constitute his own death warrant.

And when we speak of middle class insularity, it must not be in oblivion of the fact that, in his dealings with other nations, John Bull, if he had a narrow and insular mind, had also a big heart. Sometimes the narrow mind had the best of it, as in the shameful war on which England embarked, in 1857, under the guidance of her Victorian Darling, the evergreen "Pam," with the object of forcing opium on the Chinese. Here the situation is per-

fectly summed up in the *Punch* cartoon, which displays
Palmerston, with a pigtail in one hand and a "cat" in
the other, and a delighted Punch in the background calling, "Give it him well, Pam, while you're about it." Public opinion was almost as bad on the subject of Ireland,
and here insular and anti-Catholic prejudice played into
each other's hands, until the man in the English street
was quite honestly convinced that Ireland—with her
population halved by one of the most awful disasters on
human record—was the abode of murderous yahoos, with
no special grievances that were not of their own
creation.

But as a general rule, John Bull's heart, at least, was
on the right side. If he was offensively officious, and
wanted to have a finger in every pie, the things that he
hated were generally bad things—if tyranny and liberti-
cide are to be counted as bad. It was a fine and chivalrous
gesture of Pam's, when he got the French to join him in
strengthening the Sultan's hands, against the demand of
Austria and Russia that he should give up the Hungarian
patriots. It was certainly a noble and more effective gesture than that of chalking "Surrender the Kaiser!" on the
Queen of Holland's door, and then making an igno-
minious departure.

It may have been wrong of Barclay and Perkins's men
to have tanned the hide of a Field Marshal who had performed the same service for Hungarian ladies, and certainly highly improper for Pam to have been so jaunty
about it afterwards; but is there anybody, even now, who
does not harbour some sneaking regret that he was not

on the spot to add his contribution to the old hero's richly earned guerdon?

It is hard to justify the English tourists who, when French bayonets were propping up the Papal Government at Rome, could not be restrained from singing the Garibaldian songs of liberty in cafés and restaurants. Certainly no English tourist would be so indiscreet as to breathe the word "liberty" in Rome to-day. But the fact remains that the cause of Italian unity is not a little indebted to the sympathy of English Liberalism, and certainly Garibaldi would never have crossed from Sicily to the mainland, but for the silent acquiescence of the British navy, and the very decided line taken by the British government against the outraged despots of the Continent.

It was something, at any rate, to be proud of, that in a Europe in which a ruthless national egotism, whose high priest was to be Bismarck and whose culmination the World War, was steadily gaining ground, one nation should have stood—however waveringly and with whatever lapses—for the idea that a nation itself is a moral being, that the obligations of honour, duty, and principle are as binding in the Many as the One. Such a notion was latent even in the dry Whiggery of Lord John, and it was something more than latent in the bouncing knight-errantry of Palmerston. With John Bright, with Gladstone—in spite of all the latter's inconsistencies—it took on a religious complexion; they believed that a nation could not only be moral, but moral in a Christian sense. There were those who carried such principles even further, like the three Quakers who actually made a pilgrimage, just before the outbreak of the Crimean War, to St. Petersburg, in order to implore the Iron Tsar, in Christ's name, not to unsheathe the sword. They were received with all the courtesy of a great gentleman, though much derided and abused on their return to a war-fevered nation. And yet—though it is hard not to smile at their simplicity—one's fancy runs to speculating on what might have been the fate of Tsardom, had the miracle happened, and the iron heart melted. Certainly the grey hairs of the first Nicholas would not have descended in sorrow to the grave, and perhaps—who can tell?—the tragedy of his line might not have swept to the unspeakable horror of its final scene in the cellar.

The fault of Victorian policy did not lie in its idealism, as modern critics are apt to imply, but in the very reverse. Its great and basic defect was that of the Victorian nature, that defect imputed to the Church of Laodicea. The Victorian ideal was not coldly egoistic—like that of Metternich and Bismarck—but it lacked the fire of inspiration. It was moral on the principle of limited liability. Perhaps the greatest of all Victorian cartoons is that which represents Palmerston, slightly fuddled after a Cabinet fish dinner at Greenwich, saying to Lord Panmure—whom readers of Mr. Strachey will remember as the Bison—"What humbugs we all are!" And Pam was a humbug, not for standing up for the weak and for liberty, but for proportioning the stoutness of his attitude to the weakness, or distance, of his opponent.

The Crimean War was worse than humbug; not because of the generous impulse that prompted the man in the street to take on the big bully of Europe, but for the reason stated by Meredith's Nevil Beauchamp:

"He wished to know whether the English people would be so anxious to be at it if their man stood on the opposite shore and talked of trying conclusions on their green fields. And he suggested that they had grown so ready for war because of their having grown rather ashamed of themselves, and for the special reason that they could have it at a distance."

So too we can say of Gladstone, he failed—in so far as he did fail—by not being Gladstonian enough. His apostleship of liberty did more than any other thing, before the War, to make our name honoured in Italy, in Greece, and in the Balkans. His faith in freedom was of priceless value in building up the British Commonwealth of Nations; his faith in justice, even where we were the losers, in the matter of the Alabama arbitration, was a landmark in progress towards international peace, and one of the first links in a chain that may yet span the wide Atlantic.

But when he espoused the cause of slavery in America, when he played fast and loose with the Transvaal, when he drove John Bright in horror from his Cabinet by the bombardment of Alexandria, when he almost came to giving up the patriot Arabi to be done to death by the Khedive, when he sought the freedom of Catholic by the slavery of Protestant Ireland—then he was a Victorian in the worst sense in which the word is used, the self-righteous self-deceiver that his enemies would depict him.

Or take the ordinary middle class Englishman of the time. His insularity, though gross, is never quite contemptible, when he is voicing a principle. It was no doubt wrong for *Punch* to have represented the King of

Prussia and the Emperor of Austria as a couple of criminals had up before a very fat and ferocious John Bull on a charge of assaulting Denmark. But perhaps it is not a bad thing that even crowned bullies should be shown up as the criminals they are. What is wrong with the picture is the position accorded to Mr. Bull, who would certainly not have dared, and, in point of fact, did not dare, to lift a finger, or anything but his voice, to interfere. Again, there is nothing necessarily Philistine in Tennyson's talk about the "red, fool fury of the Seine." It was a point of view that, right or wrong, Tennyson was at perfect liberty to hold and defend about the French Revolution, and no whit more ridiculous than the snobbery that whitewashes the September Massacres, and almost canonises Marat, for no better reason than that they were French, and that the more we have of culture, the Frencher we will be.

Where John Bull was really vulgar and Philistine, was where he was making not the least pretence to principle, but instead of being, or even posing, as the champion of the little fellow against the bully, came forth as a bully and a braggart himself, loud-mouthed and unashamed. The national character was seldom seen to worse advantage than in the hysterical agitation that finally drove a peace-loving Premier, against his will, into a useless war with Russia. The send-off of Sir Charles Napier's fleet, that accomplished nothing whatever in the Baltic saw the wave at its crest—Palmerston uttering a farewell speech of incredible braggadocio and offensiveness, and the man in the street bawling forth his soul in the chorus

"England and France will soon pull down
The Eagle and Imperial Crown,
And his bearlike growls we soon will drown
With—'Let us give it to him, Charlie!' "

The seed thus sown was not long in producing its harvest of blood and tears, but other seeds were thoughtlessly dropped that took longer to mature. Prussia was, at the time, in the position of Austria as regards John Bull—he felt that he could insult her with glorious impunity. Some forgotten friction in the year 1855 moved *Punch* to suggest the following National Anthem for Prussia:

"If a blockade's in store
For Fatherland's poor shore,
If our Fritz * bring
On us the lion's claws,
We shall have ample cause
To sing with all our jaws:
God save the King!"

In 1861 we find *Punch* presenting a toy ship to a diminutive German, and advising him to cut away and not to get into a mess, and in 1864 the worst insult of all is levelled at the Fatherland, in a drawing of a jolly Jack Tar pointing to a typical German sailor—modelled evidently on the popular version of the comic Dutchman—and saying to his mate: "We can't be expected to *fight* a lubberly lot of swabs like him, we'll *kick* 'em, if that'll do!"

There is no such talk after Jutland—perhaps if there

* Frederick William IV.

had never been such talk, there might not have been Jutland.

We need not multiply instances of the narrowness, the arrogance, and fearful self-complacency that characterised the middle class, in this time of its supremacy. That has been done by Dickens, who loved them, and Matthew Arnold, who detested them. And no doubt, in the late sixties, when Matthew Arnold opened his attack, a decline was already beginning to set in; the idealism and generosity were wearing a little thin, and the self-complacency had become harder and more egoistic.

But it is the wildest injustice to treat the bourgeoisie of this splendid and prolific epoch as if they were only snobs and Philistines. The charge of snobbery is wildly exaggerated, that of Philistinism states less than half the truth. There was as much idealism, generosity, disinterestedness, to be found among the men of Dickens's time, as among those of Shakespeare's or Cromwell's. Their tragedy is at least not ignoble. They brought much to the solution of the great problem with which they were confronted, that of adapting their civilisation to the conditions of a machine age. But they did not bring quite enough. In that their tragedy consists.

In the four mid decades of the century, it would not be far short of the truth to say that the history of England is the history of the middle class. The middle class was the brains of England; her policy, her standard of civilisation, were the realisation of bourgeois ideals.

For the working class, after the final collapse of Chartism, the time was one of steady and fairly contented progress. No doubt conditions were shocking enough, judged by the standards of to-day, but contentment is relative, and there is no disputing the fact that after the repeal of the Corn Laws, and on to the seventies, the wealth of the country was increasing at a rate that eclipsed all previous records, and that the working man was getting at least some share—whether or not it was a just share—of the general prosperity. And progress, though unexciting, was not unfruitful. It was a time of necessary germination. Working men were learning how to combine in trades' unions; they were building up a vast organisation of co-operative stores. The Chartist mob was being drilled into an army, that might, when it had finished with the barrack square, some day take the field.

The upper class was more *en evidence*. Throughout the fifties and sixties its prestige and splendour were, to all appearance, undiminished. Agriculture continued to flourish in spite of free imports, and the great estates furnished their owners with lordly incomes. It was not, in fact, till the end of the seventies, that the sentence, so long deferred, was at last executed. A series of bad harvests precipitated a disaster that the competition of cheap foreign corn had made inevitable, and the landed interest received a blow from which it never recovered. The day of the old upper class, based on land and hereditary descent, was over. The new plutocracy rose, and has been in process of swamping it ever since.

It may be doubted, however, whether the fall of any people or class can be explained entirely on economic grounds. *Homo Sapiens* is a nobler animal than some of his latest specimens give him credit for being. It is usually the rotten tree that succumbs to the elements, and the body does not putrify before the soul has departed. What sort of a soul, we may ask, was there in the Victorian upper class in the days of its splendour? What part did that class play in the task of adapting civilisation to the new conditions?

I have tried to show what was the state of the upper class when the Reform Bill ended its long tenure of practically supreme power. One attribute that it shared with the bourgeoisie consisted of an almost demonic energy. If we may compare men with machines, we should say that the squire, like the business man, registered an enormous horse-power. But whereas, with the business man, this power was almost entirely devoted to work, with the squire, by far the greater part of it was put into an equally strenuous play. Now sport, or play, is a form of human activity in which the part of the intellect is overshadowed by that of the muscles. As sport came more and more exclusively to dominate the interests of the upper class, its capacity for leadership in other departments of life proportionately diminished.

The time with which we are dealing, from 1830 to 1870, was as fertile in outstanding genius as any similar period in our annals. The mediocre twenties—at least after the death of Byron—were succeeded by the brilliant thirties, nor did the fires die down during the next three decades. But in all this, the upper class had practically no part whatever. There was no sort of an intellectual awakening among their ranks, corresponding to that of the bourgeoisie. They remained, with unruffled complacency, in the trough of mediocrity into which they had sunk. Compared with their record in the eighteenth and early nineteenth centuries, their decline in every department of creative activity will be manifest.

Let us first take the field of statesmanship, for here the upper class held a position of overwhelming advantage. Not only were they still conceded almost a monopoly of cabinet rank in most governments, but their whole upbringing was supposed to fit them for such functions, and they had not to waste the best years of their lives in making fortunes. We have certainly Palmerston and Russell, statesmen whose minds were formed in the Georgian tradition—Palmerston had been a Lord of the Admiralty within two years of Trafalgar. Lord John's is a reputation that has not worn well, and we do not think that his warmest admirer to-day will credit him with genius. On the other hand, the reputation of Lord Shaftesbury has greatly increased since his death. There remains, among the major statesmen, Lord Derby, an excellent debater and a not particularly distinguished translator of Homer, but who is only remembered to-day as having been the Tory *roi fainéant* to Disraeli's Mayor of the Palace. Add to this that Lord Salisbury served his apprenticeship during these years, a younger son, who had, significantly enough, passed from Oxford into the stimulating atmosphere of Colonial life, and had subsequently been forced to make a living by his pen. And Salisbury did not come into the limelight until well on into the seventies.

It was the middle class Peel who revived the Conservative party on middle class lines, after the debacle of 1832; it was under his auspices that the tremendous gamble of a Free Trade policy was embarked upon; it was the middle class Cobden and Bright who made that policy inevitable; it was the middle class Gladstone who carried it to completion. The Tory party, overwhelmed by this second disaster, and bereft of ideas and leadership, was forced, in the teeth of its inclinations, to go for both to a middle class Jew. And when Queen Victoria's "two dreadful old men" at last dropped out of the Whig leadership, the party became Liberal under the auspices of Gladstone, with the middle class Carden, Forster, and Lowe, as his ablest lieutenants. And henceforth, till death intervened, Gladstone and Disraeli towered high above the throng of lesser politicians.

How easy it would have been for any competent aristocrat to have come to the front, is shown by the position and influence subsequently attained by the Duke of Devonshire, whose bovine mental lethargy was reinforced by an impressive honesty, and an even more impressive beard.

If the record of the upper class in its chosen field of statesmanship is disappointingly meagre, in other fields of creative activity it has even less to show. Surtees, Swinburne, and Bulwer-Lytton, for what he is worth, may be claimed as authentic scions of the English upper class; Lyell was of an old Scottish family, and Thackeray of Indian civilian stock. There was a scattered glimmering of minor lights, such as Lord de Tabley, Lord Houghton, Roden Noel, and that rather prosaic historian, Lord Stanhope. This is not much to show for the class that had produced Byron, Shelley, Scott, Chesterfield, Gibbon, Horace Walpole, Cavendish, and "Citizen" Stanhope. It would not be an exaggeration to describe the condition of the aristocracy and landed gentry as one of intellectual bankruptcy.

When Gilbert wrote a song to the effect that in good Queen Bess's time,

> "The House of Lords made no pretence
> To intellectual eminence,
> Or scholarship sublime,"

he quite misunderstood the spirit of the Elizabethan Age, but the words would exactly fit the Victorian aristocracy. It is extraordinary how small a part those who owned the stately homes of England played in her history. What were the orders of nobility doing to justify their existence? Where were the heads of our historic Houses? For the most part they were engaged in galloping furiously over the countryside in pursuit of vermin, or slaughtering game by means of powder and shot, or financing the training of horses to gallop against each other, and making this the excuse for the most unprofitable of all forms of speculation. To such pursuits was brought the same concentrated earnestness that in the middle class was applied to money-producing work, or to various forms of creative activity. The celebrated "doctor in boots," who informed his patients that they would shortly be dead if they did not immediately go hunting, would probably have been taken quite at his word in Shropshire or the Shires.

The atmosphere of English country society in the middle of the century requires a considerable effort of the imagination to realise. The importance of the various county magnates was something that would be almost inconceivable in our more democratic, or plutocratic, environment. A lord in those days was a lord, and made no bones about it, and a squire was one of the "minores barones," a little despot in his own sphere. Readers of Trollope will remember the dinner parties given by the Duke of Omnium, in which His Grace did not even deign to greet his guests individually, but after presiding at the head of the table during the meal, retired to his own apartments and left them to their wine. The lesser magnates were just as important in their degree. They lived on their estates, and their doings, and quarrels, which were frequent, were the talk of the whole countryside. One of the few scintillations of the aristocratic muse that have survived, is the couplet of Lord John Manners, which, be it remembered, was written and taken perfectly seriously in the forties:

"Let laws and learning, art and commerce die,
But spare us still our old nobility."

There is this, at least, to be said for these old county magnates. Whatever may have been their lack of brains, they had, in full measure, the rich individuality of character that was a special mark of the age. They lived out their own lives with a full-blooded assurance that the way they had chosen was the right one, that their status and privileges were rooted in the very nature of things. For this reason, they seldom asserted them in a way that was felt to be humiliating. The average squire was too sure of his dignity to be always thrusting it in people's faces, and even the proudest noblemen were often men of quite shabby attire and unassuming manners. Of the first Marquis of Abergavenny, Disraeli's friend, I have heard it said that one of his under-gardeners would have been more at his ease talking to His Lordship than to the head-gardener.

Let us go to Surtees as the most favourable witness as to the kind of character rife in the upper class during the early forties and fifties. Mr. Ralph Nevill, who is the most uncompromising admirer of this class and everything connected with it, tells us of Surtees, that his portrayal of English country life, during this period, is "of considerable historical importance." Very well, then, let us select from Surtees's gallery a portrait which Mr. Nevill, who certainly knows what he is talking about, assures us to have been taken from real life, and to have been easily recognisable by contemporaries. We refer to that of the Earl of Scamperdale.

This nobleman was the possessor of a magnificent estate, a splendid mansion in the Italian style, filled with all kinds of objects of art, purchased by his ancestors in the eighteenth century, and possessed a fortune of £90,000. But the Victorian Earl, who was "stumpy and clumsy and ugly, with as little to say for himself as could possibly be conceived," had no taste for beauty, or magnificence, or anything else but the pursuit of foxes. "He had the house put away in brown holland, the carpets rolled up, the pictures covered, the statues shrouded in muslin, the cabinets of curiosities locked, the plate secured, the china closeted," and he himself abdicated the main body of the mansion, and took up his quarters in the steward's room, with what used to be the muniment room converted into a bedroom for himself, and the plate room into another for a hanger-on, of uncertain origin, called Jack Spraggon, who did not turn up his nose at the cow-heel broth and almost raw beefsteaks that formed their daily fare, and who helped his Lordship with the hounds.

"The sitting-room, or parlour as his Lordship called it, had an old grey drugget for a carpet, an all-round black mahogany table on castors, that the last steward had ejected as too bad for him, four semi-circular wooden-bottomed walnut smoking-chairs; an old spindle-shanked sideboard, with very little middle, over which swung a few book-shelves, with the termination of their green strings surmounted by a couple of foxes' brushes. Small as the shelves were, they were larger than his lordship wanted—two books, one for Jack and one for himself, being all they contained; while the other shelves were filled with hunting-horns, odd spurs, knots of whipcord, piles of halfpence, lucifer match boxes, gun charges, and such like miscellaneous articles."

What were the two precious volumes that formed his Lordship's and Jack's sole reading, history does not relate, though we know that when Mr. Sponge produced his solitary volume, Mogg's *Ten Thousand Cab Fares* (price one shilling), Mr. Facey Romford remarked, in great surprise,

"What, you're a literary cove, are you?"

What sort of a literary cove Lord Scamperdale was may be judged from his unfortunate inability to write to Mr. Jawleyford an account of Mr. Sponge's misdeeds:

"Not being a great scholar, and several hard words turning up that his Lordship could not well clear in the spelling, he just confined himself to a laconic."

It would be impossible to conceive of a more vivid portrait of boorishness, Philistinism, and ignorance than that which the Dickens of the English countryside draws of this great English nobleman. Indeed, we may search through all his novels to find one of his numerous lords and gentlemen whom we can describe as being in any sense a man of culture.* The only way in which their tastes in any way differ from those of cave men, just emerged from monkeydom, is that they had not the cave's man desire for, still less his capacity for creating, beautiful works of art.

That Lord Scamperdale was by no means a unique specimen of his class will be evident to any one who cares

---

* Mr. Jawleyford certainly made a pretence, on one occasion, of reading Dizzy on Lord George Bentinck, but this was pretty obviously one of Jawleyford's many shams.

to study the record of individual families. The day of great collectors, who enriched England with the choicest works of foreign art—works which their descendants are now busy disposing of, for what they will fetch, to American lovers of beauty—had gone, never to return. By the Victorians, the heritage of their ancestors, still unsold, was recklessly trodden underfoot. This was sometimes true, in the most literal sense. In a certain great mansion, tapestries, of priceless value, were spread on the floors as carpets. In another country house a collection of prints, accumulated by one of the most celebrated of the old, Hell-fire intellectuals, was used to make a screen for the nursery, the prints being cut up into appropriate shapes, before being operated upon by a large family of children.

But the rakes of culture were no more, and as for the new owners and their houses, they served the Lord. Out of one great art collection, a certain picture, now among the Venetian masterpieces in the National Gallery, was kicked with ignominy because the noble and pious owner was not going to have the eyes of his womenfolk shocked by the spectacle of one of their sex naked. The same prohibition extended to babies, for a more recent painting of an infant but realistic Hercules was likewise disposed of, free, to the owner's brother, who, somewhat surprisingly, was a clergyman. He was, however, a man of resource, and procured an artist to effect certain cheap but essential alterations, so that to-day the picture stands displayed, in a form calculated to placate Mrs. Grundy, but somewhat to intrigue anatomists.

Nor was Lord Scamperdale by any means the only Master of Hounds to be troubled by problems of orthography. There was one, in Kent, whose deficiencies in this respect got him out of a serious scrape. There was a certain great lord in the neighbourhood who cared more for pheasants than foxes, and whose deer park was a sort of Tom Tiddler's Ground to the neighbouring packs. But a fox, who, having run from a considerable distance, was perhaps not aware of the local taboos, slipped through a hole in the park palings. The Master, deeming that in such a case of necessity the only course was to hack through, jumped off, and with the aid of one of his whips tore quite a considerable gap, through which the hounds and field passed. It was only when he got home that somebody pointed out to him the unforgiveable nature of the crime that he had committed, and advised him to make such timely amends as were possible. Accordingly he sat down and wrote,

"Dear Lord ——:
"I am afraid this afternoon I had to pull up some rotten old pailings (sic) in your park. I hope" etc., etc.

When he received this letter on the following morning, his Lordship, who was already on the verge of apoplexy and litigation, would almost certainly have crossed it on reading the word "rotten," had not the next word but one simultaneously caught his eye. Now he was by way of being a wit, and a wit of the ponderous and unhurried school that wages warfare by a process of sap and parallel reminiscent of the old siegecraft. The spelling of "pailings" was an opportunity not to be missed. The original grievance was forgotten, and for the rest of the morning his Lordship was engaged in the composition of a long and elaborate epistle, commencing somewhat as follows:

"DEAR MR. ——:

"When I was at Eton, I was under the impression, which would now appear to have been erroneous, that the spelling of the word 'palings',", etc., etc.

This incident, and incidents like it, were reported and discussed in all the country houses of the district, and from the dining rooms the fame of them spread to the servants' halls, and thence to the farms and cottages. The importance attached to the proceedings of these now wholly forgotten worthies is something hard for us to conceive of. But interests at that time were few, and life must have been terribly dull, apart from sport, in the country. Even the Assembly Rooms were robbed of their glory. The county families, as we learn from *Cranford,* no longer met together once a month during the winter to dance and play at cards—only "a musty odour of aristocracy lingered about the place" when the rooms were occasionally opened for some entertainment like that of the ex-sergeant conjuror, Brunoni.

The country houses themselves—such of them as have not been stripped of their old contents—bear silent witness to the disappearance, in Victorian times, of the old, aristocratic culture. There is scarcely a big house that has not a well-stocked library. There are ponderous volumes of the classics, in eighteenth century editions, there are calf-bound *Spectators, Ramblers, Tatlers,* and all the English and foreign classics with which a man of taste, in the reign of George III, could possibly have surrounded himself. But a modern visitor from Mars, if his experience were confined to a round of country house parties, would probably report, on his return, that earthly literature evidently came to an abrupt close early in the nineteenth century, to start again, in the twentieth, with an author called Edgar Wallace. Books had, in fact, become furniture, and that they might fulfil better their only conceivable function, were, by careful owners, locked up behind glass, and the keys taken away.

But it is not only to the library we need go for evidence. Everything, within and without, is in keeping, and produces just such an impression as we might have got from some rich patrician's dwelling, after it had been occupied by a generation or two of Goths. The objects of *vertu* have still been preserved, after a fashion, less from a sense of their beauty, than of the importance conferred by their possession. Even so the barbarian nature is revealed by such outrages as putting the best china under glass domes, or sheer ignorant destructiveness of the kind we have already alluded to. And the sort of pictures and furniture added by the Victorian owners forms a melancholy advertisement, that the class that had set so high a standard of taste during the past, and whose patronage had called for the making of so many kinds of beautiful things, had abdicated its functions, and degenerated into a mob of barbarians, who had reverted to the primitive routine of the chase.

We remember how *Punch*—that intransigeant *Punch* of the forties—had published a cartoon showing a kneeling peasant being sacrificed to a hare. He might have followed it by another, showing a country gentleman, in the act of sacrificing himself, and all his possessions, to a three-headed Moloch—a Trinity of Fox, Pheasant, and Race-horse.

And possessions were often cast away wholesale in the most literal sense. The gambling mania survived from the eighteenth century well on into the heyday of Victorian respectability. Gentlemen whose fortunes were so enormous that they might have been proof against any conceivable extravagance, contrived to dissipate them on the Turf. There was the last Marquis of Hastings,* one of the richest men in England, who started betting in hundreds at the age of sixteen, and in thousands at that of nineteen, and died a ruined man, and practically of a broken heart, at the age of twenty-six, having deliberately courted the society of the low parasites who battened on him—"Flash Fred" and his tribe. Surtees has given us a very similar type in his Sir Harry Scattercash, with his associates, Quod, Seedybuck, Spangles, Bouncey, Cutifat, and the rest of them.

Surtees seems to have been under no illusion as to the atmosphere pervading a Victorian racecourse. From his sympathetic account, and not from any Puritan propaganda, we should be justified in describing it as one of almost undiluted blackguardism. One of the most horribly realistic things in Victorian literature is where poor Jack Spraggon is killed at a jump, and lies unheeded by any one in the crowd except his patron, Lord Scamperdale, and some roughs.

" 'Oh, my poor dear Jack,' exclaimed his lordship,

* For the best account of him see *Fame and Failure* by Julian Ellis.

throwing himself off his horse, and wringing his hands in despair, as a select party of thimble-riggers, who had gone to Jack's assistance, raised him up, and turned his ghastly face, with his eyes squinting inside out, and the foam still on his mouth, full upon him . . . his lordship sunk overpowered upon the body. The thimble-riggers then availed themselves of the opportunity to ease his lordship and Jack of their watches, and the few shillings they had about them, and departed."

"When a lord is in distress," continues Surtees, "consolation is never long in coming," and come it does, in the shape of that arch humbug, Squire Jawleyford of Jawleyford Hall, who, "seeing the rude, unmannerly character of the mob," that comes pouring to the spot, as soon as it is realised that there is a dead man on view, leads off the Earl, who is blubbering incoherently about his friend having been "such a fine, natural blackguard." The scene is as grim as anything in Hogarth.

The Victorian Derby appears to have been just this sort of thing on a huge scale, those who could not afford wheeled conveyances hiring horses, and returning in different stages of intoxication, with the addition of such simple joys as those provided by false noses, pea-shooters, and so forth.

Of what strange doings were covered by the word "sport," we may judge by the fact that after the University boat-race of 1862, both crews joined for the purpose of setting dogs on cats in a shed, the shed being provided by Cambridge and the animals by Oxford.* As late as

* Woodgate's *Reminiscences of an Old Sportsman,* quoted in *London and Londoners* by A. R. Bennett.

the sixties, it was a by no means unknown thing for a badger to be brought home, by some sporting young fellow, for the purpose of being torn from his tub, with merciless reiteration, by the teeth of terriers.

The Victorians, as a general rule, managed to conceal the coarser side of their lives so thoroughly under a mask of respectability, that we often fail to realise how coarse it really was. Those fine old squires whose portraits more or less adorn the family dining room, would have fallen rather startlingly below our standards of refinement in certain respects. Though it was supposed to be very rude to associate with ladies in the clothes you had worn in the smoking room, I have good authority for stating that, in the days before water drainage became universal, a gentleman's clothes often bore unmistakable witness to quite another recent location. There was a lack of furtiveness about certain doings that would have delighted some of our younger intellectuals. Not having the honor to be one of them, I am unable to record the habitual use made by one great sporting magnate, after Divine Service and in full view of his fellow worshippers, of a mediæval and probably ancestral grave-slab.

Could we have recourse to the vast, unwritten literature of bawdry, we should be able to form a more veracious notion of life, as it really was in those not so very remote times. We are apt to forget that the refinement of mixed society was paid for by a compensating grossness of masculine intercourse. When the Victorian gentleman exchanged his dress coat for his smoking jacket, his act was symbolic. He was putting on a new man—or, perhaps, one might say, an old Adam. His smoking room humour was more direct and racy of the night soil than the elusive and rather perverted style in present vogue. Even Tennyson was noted for the Lincolnshire broadness of his anecdotage.

There was a great and flourishing underworld of vice. Mr. Ralph Nevill, writing in 1919, speaks of "the unblushing licence accorded to night houses and other resorts where, less than fifty years ago, the grandfathers of the present generation held high revel without, in due course, let it be added, becoming any the worse husbands and fathers." * Celebrated harlots, like "Anonyma," used to flaunt their charms openly in the Park and at race meetings, and were surrounded by bevies of fashionable young men. The era of respectability was also one of high play and fast living, though in both these respects the tendency was towards an improvement on pre-Victorian standards. This was even more the case as regards the still heavy drinking from which even clerical circles were not altogether exempt in the mid-nineteenth century.

It was only as regards intellect and taste that the upper class showed a decline from the level of the previous age. Here there is unfortunately no room for doubt—the evidence is overwhelming that Matthew Arnold's characterisation of them as Barbarians is no more than the truth. Nor did there seem any prospect of improvement in the future. The efforts of the great reforming headmasters had not extended to the intellectualising of the public schools. It is seldom that there is supply without any demand, and the parental demand was not for intellect, but for character. And character the public schools did

* *Echoes Old and New*, p. 229.

supply to an extent unapproachable anywhere else in Europe. The large amount of power delegated to the boys themselves, under the monitorial system, engendered habits of command and responsibility.

These are gifts of importance, but they require the guidance of a trained intellect to make them fruitful. What happened was exactly what might have been anticipated. The barbaric scale of values, that exalts physical prowess above truth and beauty, passed from the fathers to the sons, and the aim of public school discipline was more and more diverted from the production of scholars to that of sportsmen and athletes. Eton, the most aristocratic of all these schools, was also the most obstinately unintellectual. In the course of the traditional rivalry between Eton and Harrow, Eton "gentlemen" were habitually contrasted, by themselves, with Harrow "cads," but there was one contemptuous concession that no Etonian minded flinging to the men of the Hill:

> "Harrow may be more clever,
> Rugby may make more row!
> Swing, swing together!"

cleverness and noise being evidently valued equally. But no Harrovian has ever, so far as I know, showed the slightest desire to counter with the obvious repartee, that it is less discreditable, particularly in the absence of a river, to be a bad oarsman than a dunce.

The strength of the public school system lay in the training that it provided for the younger sons of the aristocracy. These sons had not yet begun to enter business to any considerable extent, but the power of command that the system engendered not only furnished the army commanded by the Duke of Cambridge with officers, who, if not much more intellectual than their chief, were at least brave, and popular with their men, but it was of inestimable value in the work of empire building, that was now proceeding apace. The squire's son easily adapted himself to the open air life of the colonies—and there was, in fact, a contemporary piece of advice to fathers which ran:

"If you have a son who's always on the dun,
   The sort of chap would ruin any family,
Take him by the heels, and never mind his squeals,
   And drop him right down in a colony." *

The younger son also played no small part in providing an incorruptible, if somewhat unimaginative, administrative staff for an India now removed from John Company's government, and under direct British control.

* I quote this from memory, but am unable to trace its source.

CHAPTER XXIII

THE SAINT MARTIN'S SUMMER OF ARISTOCRACY

WHILE it is difficult to exaggerate the disastrous nature of the surrender, by the upper class, of its functions of cultural leadership, at the very time when such guidance was more needed than ever before, we must not be blind to the useful functions that it still fulfilled. And first let us note that the barbarism into which it was sinking was softened and humanised, to some extent, by the influence of its womenfolk. And here the differentiation between the sexes, which has made the Victorian woman the target for so much modern depreciation, acted as an unmitigated blessing, by preventing her from being swept along the flood tide of muscular debauch. From Surtees, we gather that the sight of a lady, as apart from half-ladies, like Lucy Glitters, was, in his time, practically unknown in the hunting field, though no doubt in the sixties the equestrian lady, in a very long and dangerous habit, was beginning to figure at meets. But on the whole, we may say that the country gentry, if they had not risen above the standards of the primeval cave, had not yet fallen below them to the extent of mingling the sexes on their hunting forays. Woman, in her stronghold of the home, could at least see that it was not turned into a glorified pothouse, and that the life of the smoking room, like that of the brothel, should at least be so isolated that it could not contaminate the drawing-room.

Even Lord Scamperdale was drilled into some semblance of civilisation by the Miss Jawleyford who succeeded in capturing him. She got him to wear smart new clothes, and even to grow a pair of bushy whiskers. "She has marshalled a proper establishment, and got him coaxed into the long put away company rooms. Though he still indulges in his former cow-heel and other delicacies, they do not appear on the table."

Some allowance must also be made for the influence of religion. The success of the Puritan Low Church in capturing the descendants of Rupert's Cavaliers was extraordinary, though it was at the price of complete surrender of the old Puritan Radicalism. No doubt a good proportion of the old, openly flaunted viciousness, was merely driven into privacy, but it would be carrying cynicism too far, to doubt that the mass suggestion implied in a rigid outward respectability had not considerable effects in mitigating sexual incontinence. But the Low Church Lord, though a God of righteousness, had none of the attributes either of Athene or Apollo, and sport, provided it were confined to week-days, did not, as in the days of Cromwell, fall under the Puritan ban. As for the humanitarian aspect of it, it never crossed anybody's mind that the Friend of little children could take thought for the beasts that perish. Provided that Squire contributed generously to the plate, went to Church regularly, read family prayers to the servants and the Bible to himself, saw that sin was well cauterised out of his children, and that the third housemaid did not walk to Church with the second footman, the Lord's requirements were more or less fulfilled, and Squire might ride away and play with a clear conscience.

With all their failings, the landed gentry had at least this to be said for them, that they were—taking them for all in all—popular among their own people. They lived on their estates, they knew and were known by all, and where they did not employ agents, they also worked at the common business of agriculture. A farmer will be very polite to some rich, new, town-bred landlord whom he can exploit, but his real respect will be reserved for the rough-tongued and sometimes close-fisted old gentleman who can haggle with him on terms of perfect equality about the price of a bull. The proudest moment in the 8th Duke of Devonshire's life was when his pig took a prize at Skipton Fair. At the same time, it must be admitted that, even in agriculture, the landlords show a very marked falling off from the scientific ardour that had fired them during the Agricultural Revolution of the eighteenth century. We no longer meet with great innovating geniuses like "Turnip" Townshend and Coke and Bakewell. More and more we feel that play, and not work, holds the lion's share of the average landowner's affections.

It forms a not unimportant sidelight, that the shameful story of the depopulation of the Highlands by their chiefs begins with pasture and ends with deer forests.

The country gentry also played a not unimportant part as unpaid local administrators and magistrates, though with the growth of centralisation and of the elective principle, the once all-powerful Justices of the Peace found their powers gradually curtailed and their functions restricted.

But we are driven to the conclusion that the landed gentry, as a class, were ripe for the fall that was so shortly, though gently—as with leaves on windless November days—to be accomplished, there was also something corresponding to the October glory of their own park trees, a loveliness even of decay. There was, in the forties, a widespread romantic desire to restore the English countryside to what it was supposed to have been in a highly sentimentalised version of the Middle Ages. The landowner was to be the father of his people, just as the Church was their mother. The old feudal relations, the old amenities of Merrie England were to be revived in Young England. Maypoles were to appear on the village greens, the old dances were to be re-footed, everything was to be as different as possible from the soulless life of the new towns.

It was a generous ideal, though no doubt a great deal of absurdity was mingled with it. Trollope has shown us the comic side of the revival in his account of the Ullathorne Sports, organised on the most correct Gothic lines by Miss Thorne—in the course of which poor Harry Greenacre got his lance between his horse's legs, when riding at a Quentin. The Young England movement must also have afforded scope for such humbugs as Surtees's Mr. Jawleyford, another portrait certified by Mr. Nevill as drawn from real life. Jawleyford would preside over his biennial tenants' dinner, after Mr. Screwemtight had eased them of their cash in the steward's room.

Then Mr. Jawleyford would shine forth as the very impersonification of what a landlord ought to be. Dressed in the height of fashion, as if by his clothes to give a lie to his words, he would expatiate on the delights of such meetings of equality; declare that, next to those spent with his family, the only really happy moments of his life were those when he was surrounded by his tenantry; he doted on the manly character of the English farmer. Then he would advert to the great antiquity of the Jawleyford family, and so on.

But Jawleyford, one may hope, was an exception, and there seems no reason to doubt that the romantic—perhaps combined with the Low Church—spirit, did much to humanise relations between the squire and his dependents. Perhaps the mitigation of the still severe game laws, the disappearance of man traps and spring guns, may have had something to do with it, but we get the impression that the average landowner of the sixties was a very different sort of person from the hard and mercenary tyrants denounced by Cobbett—not an unprejudiced, but still a knowledgeable witness. Even the Jawleyfords found it expedient to pose as the fashionable type of benevolent landlord, and with better men there was no need to pose. A more searching wind of criticism was abroad than in past years. The local press was more outspoken and personal than it is to-day, and the landowner, from his very importance, was a mark for Radical inkslingers of what was then known as the "snarling" type. And the snarler was a hard opponent to counter, for if he was brought to book for libel—as in a case brought by the Hon. and Rev. E. V. Bligh against one of these gentry at Maidstone—he would, if defeated, prove to be a man of straw.

Nothing is harder to reconstruct than the village life of from sixty to eighty years ago—no records or statistics can give us the all-important personal touch. But old people whose memories run, or did run, back to that time, seem to have looked, as a general rule, with affection on the old families, and with regret on the coming of a new order of things in which even those families that are left are no longer rooted to the soil, but bring down their friends from Town, as Lady Dorothy Nevill puts it, "with the fish." A very old lady in a Guardians' Institute, not so long ago, told me she could remember "his lordship"— the Earl of Abergavenny who died in 1868—sending an ox all the way from his Sussex estate to his Kentish manor of Birling, in solemn state, preceded by outriders, to be roasted in the village. There was not always this pleasing ceremonial, but in those days when food was cheap and farming paid, there was not infrequently good cheer at the Hall for those who resorted thither on any possible excuse, and perhaps an occasional barrel of beer supplied at local cricket matches, besides warm garments for everybody at Christmas.

Whatever may be the verdict of history, there is no reason to suppose that the villagers had any criticisms to offer on the Squire's excessive addiction to sport. Very much the reverse—for they were addicted to it themselves, even when it took the form of poaching, and though crops were ridden over—nominally at any rate with subsequent compensation—and the life of a fox was preserved by the most awful of taboos, there is no reason to assume that this was resented, on a balance of advantages. I have, indeed, heard tell of a Radical farmer being horse-whipped by a certain Master of hounds, in front of the field, for shooting a hunted fox, and nothing further seems to have happened—in fact, when, long ago, I heard the incident related by the fine old Master in question, the story concluded with the sentence—on which I never dared to ask for elucidation—"And after that he became quite a good Conservative."

Cricket was in full swing during the fifties and sixties, in fact village cricket was at its best. That at least was a sport in which all classes could and did mingle on terms of equality, except that the squire's son, or sometimes the squire himself, would figure, as by right, as skipper of the local team. Wickets were none too good, and "hit hard, hit high, and hit often," was the order of the day, but this only made things more exciting, and encouraged a keener sportsmanship and good fellowship.

I would conclude this chapter by quoting from some old records of a Harvest Home, held in a Kentish village in 1871.* I think some idea will be conveyed of the still lingering romanticism that had once been Young England, and was even now a waning ideal.

These harvest homes had formerly been gatherings on a small scale, each master entertaining his people at his own home. This had now been superseded by gatherings on a large scale, all the neighbouring farmers sending their labourers free of expense, "men, women and children," says the local reporter, "whose attire betokened the

* There is a very full account of it in a book of press-cuttings, collected by the late Hon. and Rev. E. V. Bligh. The name of the paper is not preserved.

pastoral occasion." In one tent a feast was provided for the men, consisting chiefly of huge beef puddings and mugs of ale, while in another tent the women were treated to tea, bread and butter, and plum cake. The Rector, a Low Churchman of the best type, had departed from the then usual custom of ensuring attendance at Church by making the Service precede the meal. He preferred, he told them, to trust to their honour. Before the meal there were sports, organised by the ladies and guests of the Manor and a few helpers, and after it, speeches.

To two of these it may be worth our while to listen. The first was the Rector's. He started by referring to certain agitators, who had been round the district trying to form an Agricultural Labourers' Union. The Rector much regretted that these gentlemen were not there to take part in the proceedings, for "though we might possibly have enjoyed the fun of seeing them in the ditch by the hurdle jump, we should have picked them out with much pleasure." Striking a more serious note, the Reverend gentleman then went on to expound his, and the prevailing upper class, social philosophy.

These men, he said, had promised the Millennium. No doubt there was a blessed Millennium coming, but until that date, it was certain that no earthly millennium could ever be realised—a conclusion that seems to have been greeted with considerable applause. God had appointed, from the very first, that there should be different grades of society, high and low, rich and poor, and it was not for the rich to boast nor the poor to complain. An awful warning was contained in the fate of irreligious Paris, recently in the hands of the Commune, formerly prostrate before the Goddess of Reason. "Let us take warning by her fate, and as God has been pleased to constitute various ranks of society by placing some in the higher, some in the middle, and some in the lower ranks, let us cheerfully accept the position He has assigned us, and be thankful for His mercies."

That is a fair and honest translation, into terms of Low Church religion, of the Tory doctrine of degree, priority and place, advocated by Shakespeare, and before him, by Piers Plowman.

The last and most important speech was that proposing the health of the Lady of the Manor, a venerable dowager, and this was entrusted to a certain white-whiskered general, a Peninsular veteran, and a renowned "character" and speech-maker. He had previously given "the Army," taking advantage of the occasion to denounce those new-fangled manœuvres on Salisbury Plain, and the scandalous criticism of officers, as being too ignorant and aristocratic, but he had ended up with the consoling assurance that whate'er might betide "we shall find no difficulty, as heretofore, in beating our enemies."

His second speech requires no comment, except the assurance that it was the kind of thing that was considered graceful and appropriate at the time, and that no aspersion was ever cast upon the General's sobriety:

"I suppose it is owing to the extreme modesty of my friend the Chairman, or perhaps to my own impudence, that he has entrusted me with the toast I am about to propose. It is a toast, however, that I am sure you will all drink with enthusiasm, as would I with my whole heart, if I had one; but strange as the phenomenon may be, you see before you a man without a heart. I came into this country with one, I admit, but at present I am perfectly without one, and if I explain how I lost it, I think you will all discover that you are labouring under the same defect as myself. But to explain what I mean, I am at the Manor, partaking of Lady ——'s hospitality, and am continually under the refreshing eyes of her three amiable daughters.* [Hear! hear!] I will say nothing more in their praise, though I could speak out largely, but basking under their smiles and partaking of all their friendliness—as I have done for many years—I am proud of them, and at last I find that my very heart is gone. Now if such be the case with me, who have been here only a few days, what must be the desperate case of your own bosoms, living, as you do, under the eyes of Lady ——'s daughters, exposed to their warm, refreshing sunbeams, and partaking of all the bounteous kindness and sympathy of that noble lady and her amiable daughters?

"I know therefore that you will all drink the health of the Countess of —— with acclamation. I believe that that dear lady has been with you for upwards of fifty years. She likes to live here . . . because she finds the people are amiable, good, honest, sober and industrious. . . . Therefore I do not hesitate to introduce the toast to your notice, with the assurance that it will be received with acclamation."

And received it was, with boisterous but respectful applause—less than sixty years ago.

* The youngest of them was turned forty at the time.

CHAPTER XXIV

A TRAGEDY?

The new school of biography, from which most people derive their idea of the Victorian Age, is, from its very nature, bound to fall short, not only of the whole truth about that age and its achievements, but of the not essential part of it. For, as Mr. Clerihew Bentley so truly remarks, "biography is about chaps" and concentrates on personality. And no doubt a time so rich in personality forms the happiest of all hunting grounds for the student of chaps. But the Victorian Age was one not only of personality, but of work. To the middle class, that set the tone of civilisation, work was a gospel, and demanded a serious and concentrated enthusiasm that bore fruit, thirtyfold, sixtyfold, and a hundredfold, in most departments of national activity.

If we are to judge solely by what was done at the time, without any relation to what might or ought to have been done, a fair case could be made out for describing the four mid-decades of the nineteenth century as more fruitful than any similar period in our history. The only other period of equal length, that could enter into the comparison, is that extending roughly from 1580 to 1620, and would include, among its principal names, those of Shakespeare, Bacon, Byrd and Spenser. It is a rather childish, though an amusing occupation, to pit teams of geniuses against each other, but it would be especially fu-

tile, where, as in this particular comparison, the Elisabethans scored their most impressive triumphs in music and
the drama, in both of which the Victorians were at their
weakest. But we may perhaps hazard an opinion that
whereas one or two Elisabethans rose to greater heights
than any Victorian, the Victorians can claim a greater
abundance of talents and work of the first order. God's
plenty is the attribute of the age.

This impression is greatly strengthened if we turn our
attention from works of individual genius to the sum of
collective achievement. There was never a time when
the country advanced with such giant strides in the paths
of peaceful progress. After the Corn Laws and the Charter were disposed of, the figures of increasing wealth and
trade attained positively staggering dimensions. A period
of warfare on the Continent and in the United States
enabled England to improve on the start she had already
gained, and to confirm her position as the workshop, not
to speak of the bank, of the world. Such extra expenses
as those of the Crimean War and the Mutiny, John Bull
was able to take in his stride, almost without noticing
them. And in spite of the warnings of Mr. Malthus,
few people were seriously troubled about an increase in
population that merely meant more hands for the workshop. It was obvious that, for the time, at any rate, in
the race between population and wealth, wealth was
having the best of it.

In every department of life the reformer was abroad,
proceeding step by step, and guided more by British commonsense than by abstract theory. Even the classical
economics could not prevent enthusiasts like Lord Shaftes-

bury from forcing on to the Statute Book a steadily accumulating mass of legislation for humanising social conditions, until poor Herbert Spencer was moved to cry Ichabod at the triumph of the State over the Man. The condition of the prisons and the workhouses remained deplorable throughout the period, though by the standards the middle class set itself, the system adopted was a success, for crime steadily diminished, and the slow torture and starvation of the Bastilles proved efficient in keeping as many unfortunates out of them as was humanly possible. Education was held up by the bickerings of the godly, but by the end of the sixties the government was in office that was to make it universal.

The Victorian theory of social improvement centred on the idea of giving capitalist enterprise the fullest possible scope, and accordingly the whole capital of the country was mobilised for productive employment, the middle class being coaxed to venture its utmost savings by the principle of limited liability, and savings banks and even penny banks being formed to attract the coins of the poorest. We have already alluded to the great extension of self-help among the workers, by means of co-operative and friendly societies, as well as by the trades unions.

In no respect was progress more marked than in everything connected with health, and the prolongation of life. The revolution effected in surgery by Lister, and in nursing by Florence Nightingale, are merely the most conspicuous successes in the great war waged by mankind on Malthus's "positive checks" on the increase of its numbers. Hygiene and sanitation were becoming matters of state concern, and centralised control was being employed to break down the complacent filthiness of local authorities. Such drastic restrictions on the activities of the Old Man with the Scythe, who, after all, had his place in the evolutionary scheme, were in themselves calculated to add not a little to man's difficulties; for the more shareholders there are in the venture of civilisation, the more difficult it becomes to maintain dividends at subsistence level.

But space avails not to record, even in barest outline, what manifold and solid work, in the cause of human progress, stands to the credit of the Victorians. It was not only in England that this work was being accomplished, for it was thanks to the foundations laid during these years, that England woke up, about the time of the Jubilee, to find herself the senior partner in a Commonwealth of Nations, and her Queen the ruler over more peoples, nations and languages than little England held counties.

Nor must we forget those invisible fruits of progress that no statistics can measure. Surely we need have no hesitation in saying that England was not only greater and healthier and more prosperous in 1870 than in 1830, but that, taking all things into consideration, she had attained to a higher moral level—in so far as, nowadays, we may be permitted to call the lessening of grossness and brutality a good thing. Among all classes, in varying degrees, there was a movement away from the animal: men became kindlier and more self-controlled, cleaner, less drink-sodden, less crudely lecherous. There was certainly a long way yet to travel, but the day's journey must be measured from the starting point, and so measured, it must be acknowledged a good one.

When therefore we have tried the Victorian Age (within our defined limits) by the tests of individual achievement, collective achievement, and moral progress, we find that it passes all three with flying colours.

Again, as we have tried to show in the course of the preceding pages, most of the strictures, that it is now fashionable to pass on the Victorians, are either made in ignorance of the facts, or recall the old story of the mote and the beam. The legend of the Victorian woman boils down to the fact that the Victorians had a different ideal of womanhood from that fashionable to-day, but one that appears to have been excellently adapted to the circumstances of the time. The accusation of snobbery amounts to this—that the Victorians strove manfully against the first symptoms of a complaint that has so completely mastered our own age that we are no longer conscious of its existence. As for the alleged hypocrisy of the Victorians as compared with ourselves, we must remember that to an age that prides itself on its entire freedom from any sort of moral idealism, the moral earnestness that was the key-note of the Victorian character is naturally repellent, and, therefore, suspect. That does not prove it to have been any the less genuine. By its fruits it must be judged.

As for the gnat-like attacks on individual Victorians, that add such piquancy to up-to-date literature, their numbers make it impossible to dispose of them, except by the reflection that money is tight and reputations hard to come by, and—a man must live.

What more then, it will be asked, can we want? With what plausibility or justice can we talk of the Victorian drama as a tragedy?

The answer to this question has already been suggested. In judging of the achievement of an age, we are not concerned with applying some rigid and absolute standard, by which that achievement can be measured and compared with that of similar periods of time in the history of our own or other nations; what we have to consider is how far men have proved adequate to the requirements of their own time. An engineer, when he is designing a bridge, adjusts the strength of his materials to the weight he expects it to carry, and to the proposed span. It is no excuse for him, when a railway train has crashed into the river, to plead that other bridges, less strongly constructed than his own, have from time immemorial sufficed for horse traffic. He is dealing with railways.

Or let us look at the matter in another way, and regard Man in his capacity of the highest of animals. Neither his intelligence nor his machines have in any way relieved Man from the task imposed upon everything that lives, that of adapting himself to his conditions. That is the meaning of life, even in the most primitive cell. Matter submits to its environment—life has got to reply.

Environment is the Sphinx, that never ceases to put her riddles to everything that lives, and life must find the answer to each one of them, or cease to be. And as life rises in the scale of evolution, and becomes more opulent and complex, its burden is in no way lightened, for the riddles it has to answer become proportionately complex and difficult. It is the rule of the Sphinx that to whom much is given, from him shall much be required.

The most dangerous thing that can happen to any species is some sudden change in its environment. The riddle has remained the same so long that the reply has become habitual like the one played on an old-fashioned musical box. When the question is suddenly changed, the old answer is mechanically repeated, and then comes death. Some such tragedy must have overtaken those magnificent and gigantic lizards who, perhaps for as many millions years as Man has lasted thousands, maintained their lordship of creation. Perhaps it was some trifling change of climate, perhaps some cause more subtle still, but whatever it was, the small brains and huge bodies were unable to make the requisite change, and the result was death.

Or take another question, that is being put to mankind at this moment. The institution of war has grown up in response to certain primitive needs. It has been Man's habit, when faced with certain difficulties, to cut the knot, like Alexander, with the sword. Recent experience has plainly shown that, under modern conditions, this method is entirely out of date, and will, unless discarded in future, make an end of a civilisation that has outgrown it. It yet remains to be seen whether human institutions and habits of thoughts are capable of being well and truly demilitarised, or whether we are all destined to perish together miserably on the next breaking of the peace.

Now the conditions confronting the Victorians were just those which biology has shown to be the most dangerous with which living organisms can be faced. The environment of *Homo Sapiens* was being not only changed, but revolutionised, and—what had never happened before in the course of evolution—the species was itself responsible for the change. Without being in the least conscious of what he was about, Man, by means of his newly invented machines, was changing the conditions of his life with a rapidity that would have constituted an inevitable death sentence on any other animal. It remained to be seen whether discourse of reason, or whatever might be comprehended in the word "soul," would enable him to play the part of Œdipus in answering this last and most terrible riddle, that he himself had propounded.

If the answer was to be found anywhere, it was first and foremost upon England that the task devolved. It was she who had taken the lead and set the pace in this greatest of all revolutions, compared with which the one in France, with its guillotinings and cannon thunder, was a mere storm in a teacup. It was the machines that, in their infancy, had conquered Napoleon. It was by no means impossible that they might, in their maturity, end by devouring the civilisation that had given them birth.

Nor must it be forgotten that besides the peril that threatened mankind at large, England was faced with one proper to herself alone. If human resources should prove inadequate, in the long run, to cope with new demands made upon them, and a machine-made civilisation should break down, it was inevitable that England's fate should be the swiftest and most catastrophic of all. The very start that she had obtained had drawn her into staking everything upon the success of the new order of things. Unlike any other nation, she had multiplied her population out of all proportion to her capacity for feeding it. More than half of the human beings crowded within the limits of her shores, could not, by the utmost conceivable straining of her resources, keep soul and body together, unless by a never-ending stream of imports from overseas. Once let her fail to maintain her position in the world's markets, and death, in its most appalling shape, would, with mathematical certainty, bring down her population, million by million, to what it was before the days of the railroad and the power-loom.

That central problem was the theme of the Victorian tragedy. Could the people of this island, and, particularly, its dominant middle class, with its energy, its moral earnestness, and its seemingly limitless resources, bring about the miracle of adjusting human life and Western civilisation to the new conditions? If we are to limit our vision to that time alone, it would seem that the answer to the question would be a triumphant affirmative. For it is certain that England at the close of the sixties had—as far as statistics are any guide—not only maintained, but notably improved on her position at the beginning of the thirties. So far from population outrunning the means of subsistence, the tendency was quite the other way. There had never been a time when there had been fewer symptoms of despondency or discontent, and so far foreboding danger ahead, John Bull was a robustuous optimist, slapping his pockets, and calling the world to admire his prosperity, his constitution, his virtue, and everything that was his.

But had the riddle been answered after all, or had its solution been merely postponed? For if we look a little closer into the nature of Victorian prosperity, we shall see that it was due to merely temporary causes. England had taken the lead—thanks very largely to her accumulation of surplus capital during the eighteenth century—in the application of machine power to industry. The wars of the Revolution and of Napoleon had put her rivals out of the field for a generation. When they showed signs of reducing her lead, another generation of wars left England to have it all her own way in industry and commerce. She could easily maintain her position of workshop of the world, when rival shopkeepers were busy cutting one another's throats. The real test would come when, as was inevitable sooner or later, her rivals, the United States, Germany, and, ultimately, Russia, brought their gigantic resources into play, and when the "backward" peoples, who had been content to pay tribute for her capital, and to send raw materials in exchange for manufactures, began to set up shop for themselves. Sooner or later, too, it might come about that mechanisation would become world-wide, and that the nations that had supplied her with food would want it all at home for their expanding town populations.

What would happen when the coal, on which so much of her prosperity had been based, began to be used up—a danger that might perhaps be staved off for an indefinite time by improved mining methods? But what if another fuel, only obtainable from overseas, came to be substituted for coal, and the very foundations of her prosperity undermined?

There was another advantage, of a more intangible nature, that was already, during the Victorian Age, beginning to pass away. The early conditions of industry had peculiarly suited the English type of inventive genius. The fathers of the Industrial Revolution were eminently practical men, workmen for the most part, of slender education, but with a great fund of native commonsense. But as time went on, machinery became too elaborate and complex to yield its secrets to men guided only by the experience of the workshop. It was the trained mathematician or research worker, deeply versed in the theory of his subject, to whom the future of invention belonged. So long as Britain could produce men like Kelvin and Clerk Maxwell, she might fairly hope at least to hold her own, but in this new deal of the cards, trumps were no longer her strongest suit.

So far we have merely dealt with the narrower aspect of the question, as it affected England alone, and we have seen her multiplying her population, and diverting an ever-increasing proportion of it from agriculture to industry, in the confident assurance that the sun of prosperity would always continue to shine, and that where there were mouths to feed, God and the stranger would continue to supply her with food.

But even more important than the fate of England, was that of human civilisation, whose destinies, in the dawn of the machine age, were to so large an extent in England's keeping. How far did she, in setting an example to the world of how to transform human environment, at the same time show how it was possible to adapt life to the new conditions?

The only answer is that she made no serious effort at all. The Victorians decided, in effect, to concentrate on material progress, in the faith that every increase of human power over blind matter must be a good thing in itself. The eighteenth century had encouraged belief in a vaguely conceived of Deity, who would, in some unexplained way, take over the business of directing human progress. In other words, men had only to get on with their work, and all things would somehow be ordered together for good. That was an excellent excuse for the average Englishman to relieve himself from the uncongenial task of extending his vision to the whole of life, and, like Bunyan's citizen of Destruction, seeking, in the name of mankind, an answer to the question, "What shall I do?"

No doubt there were individual thinkers capable of perceiving that all was not well with the kind of progress to which mankind was committing itself. The chief of these was Carlyle, who denounced, in apocalyptic terms, the dehumanising tendencies of the new age. But Carlyle had not the patience nor the breadth of outlook to enable him to think out an adequate remedy. The God of his worship, before He degenerated into a Lord of Hosts buttoned tight in Prussian uniform, bore a suspicious resemblance to the old Deity. The Gospel of work and heroism was a rather more earnest and emphatic rendering of the prevailing belief of the age, that we had only to get on with the job in hand, and trust to the Powers that Be for the higher control. Tennyson, with his Larger Hope, Browning, with his robust confidence that you had only to march breast forward for clouds to break and right to triumph, the classical economists, with their faith that the conflict of egotisms would somehow be harmonised and made fruitful, were all, in their different ways, devotees of the Deity. This obliging Personage, whose message to mankind was, "leave it to me," was shortly to change his name to "Evolution."

His colleague, the Lord, was even more hopeless, though His methods were less insidious. He was frankly unintellectual, and clung to His taboos and His Genesis, with an incapacity for either learning or forgetting worthy of the Bourbon family. The majority of the clergy were too busy deciding whether to stand still with the Reformers, or to go back to the Fathers, to have any leisure to spare for the fashioning of adequate new bottles for the new wine.

The Victorians were, in fact, saddled with a religion that had ceased to respond to the demands of the time, and they were practically bankrupt of a philosophy, for the prevailing utilitarianism was only another method of cutting theory and getting down to the task in hand. Macaulay had voiced the view of the age, to the effect that philosophy had turned out to be windy humbug, and that the panacea for all human ills was science, the science that was producing such amazing results before all men's eyes, and whose capabilities for human betterment seemed unbounded.

But what neither Macaulay nor anybody else recognised at the time, was that Victorian science was dangerously lopsided and incomplete. Its most striking advances were in the direction of increasing the power of Man over things, and his knowledge of the material universe. It also enabled Man to understand and master his bodily processes, to the extent of adding another decade to his average life. But of the study of the inner man, of his mind and spirit, the Victorian age was strangely neglectful. Psychology was the one science that stuck fast in the ancient ruts. Galen had long ago ceased to be cited as an authority in medicine, but Aristotle, as a psychologist, was still almost as much deferred to by Victorian dons as by mediæval schoolmen. Even towards the end of the nineteenth century, the science of mind, such as it was, consisted mainly of barren analysis and resurrection of long deceased authorities, and it received little serious attention.*

Man, in his avidity to master things, had not even faced the necessity of mastering Man. The change in his environment was accompanied by no corresponding change in himself. It was as if he had trusted to that good-natured Deity of his to exempt him, somehow or another, from the law of all life, that the creature must adapt itself to its surroundings, or perish.

What the Victorians did, though without acknowledging it, was to patch up a compromise, that might, at any rate, last out their time. They deliberately avoided any vital or drastic solutions. They had no desire to reconstruct the foundations of society, or to take a new spiritual orientation. They were content to carry on from day to day, and to leave the future for Progress or the Deity to take charge of. They were practical men, and when

* Even in the new 14th edition of the *Encyclopædia Britannica* philosophy and psychology are lumped together sub-editorially, and the article Psychology is thoroughly in the old high and dry tradition.

everything seemed every day to be getting better and better, they did not see the sense of meeting trouble half way.

There is something about the Victorian Age that reminds us of that great mansion of Beckford's at Fonthill, with its vast proportions and the lavish magnificence of its decorations, but—without foundations. The edifice of Victorian civilisation lacked foundations, not because its builders were knaves, but because, being practical men, they did not bother about such things. Like the Fonthill workmen, who toiled, in relays and by torchlight, all the twenty-four hours, the Victorians went on, adding stone to stone, pausing occasionally to note the ever-increasing height and grandeur of the building, and trusting to some invisible architect for the soundness of the plan.

Even at the height of the Victorian noontide, ominous fissures and subsidences had begun to make themselves apparent, and, as the century went on, they got wider and deeper. The first great shock to Victorian complacency was given by an event that ought to have furished more food for pride than any other achievement of the age. This was the publication of Darwin's *Origin of Species*, as great a landmark in the progress of biology as Newton's *Principia* had been in that of physics. But Darwin had given the final push to the already shaky throne which the worshippers of the Lord had chosen to erect for him on a pile of Family Bibles. It became obvious to anybody who chose to think, that the seven days' creation, and the Adam and Eve story, were on a par of literal veracity with Jack the Giant Killer. Even the Victorian decency, which had tactfully closed its eyes to the havoc that German scholarship had already made with the literal interpretation not only of the Old, but of the New Testament, was no longer possible to maintain. A howl of orthodox fury went up when grave divines began to evacuate the old *ne plus ultra* positions. For, once the retreat was started, where was it going to end? To-day it was,

> " 'You can't,' said a Zulu,
> 'Believe that, you fool, you!'
> 'I don't,' said the Bishop of Natal."

To-morrow it would be Samuel Butler, remarking, "the carriage of Jesus Christ blocks the way." The faith that went no more than convention-deep, was dissolving in the twilight of no faith at all.

With the Victorian faith went the Victorian morality. A wind blew from France, heavy with strange passions, and it wakened the lyre of Swinburne. The spade that every one had agreed to call an agricultural implement, was now a bloody shovel. Solemn and scarlet sins were trumpeted with evangelical fervour. But fervour was too essential a part of Victorian morality to survive for long the breaking of the chief taboo. The intransigeance of Swinburnian passion, and the high seriousness of Meredithian comicality, were followed by a ripple of Butlerian and Shavian laughter, and the suppressed yawn of Oscar Wilde. The course of Victorian morality may be likened to that of a ship that leaves port with a hole in her bottom hastily patched over. There comes a time when she turns turtle, and is seen above the waters completely inverted. But after a few minutes neither deck nor keel appear—the good ship Morality has turned out to be a coffin ship, and there is nothing from horizon to horizon but a chaos of waters, and perhaps a boat or two battling with the waves, or a few black specks of swimmers.

That ship had treasure in her hold of more value, perhaps, than her own. For with the Victorian morality foundered the moral earnestness and concentration that had been the secret of the God's plenty of Victorian achievement. An age of mental stimulants, of hustle and journalese, had no taste for the semi-religious thoroughness with which the Victorians had carried their longest tasks to completion.

Perhaps the feeling against Darwinism had mingled with it some nobler impulse than that of a super-annuated Lordolatry. The Victorians had thought nobly of Man, and the discovery of his monkey ancestry symbolised to many of them a degraded view of human nature. Carlyle was disgusted even by the spectacle of monkeys in the Zoo. But however unjust it may have been to the biologists and primates to drag them into it, there can be no doubt that, as the century wore to a close, such bracing individualism as that of Mill, and such spirituality as that of the early Carlyle, passed imperceptibly but surely out of date. Man was no longer the image of God; he was no longer fully and completely a man, but a specialist, limited to his own field, a cell in a body, a cog or nut in a machine. His opinions were suggested to him by a press that scarcely made the pretence of convincing his reason; his vote was the weapon he carried in one of the vast caucus-controlled armies of party warfare. Emerson had proved wrong in saying that when the half gods go the gods arrive. Upon Heaven and Earth the twilight of the half gods had descended, but it was the twilight of evening and not of dawn. Above was the darkness of the Unknowable, below, the machines had made the Earth small, and on it hopped and blinked the Last Man of Zarathustra's vision, who made everything small, the Behaviourist Man, stripped of soul and personality, a mere temporary location for a routine of stimulus and response conditioned by factors that could be known and regulated by methods of exact science. In other words, Man, as the newspaper magnates, the political bosses, the advertising experts, and the amusement purveyors had anticipated the psychologists in concluding, was a machine constructed on rather simple principles. You had only to apply the right kind of stimulus to get whatever response out of him you chose.

To the great Victorians, the truth had been a matter of paramount importance. Tennyson had spoken of man as "battling for the true, the just"; Huxley had denounced "Soapy Sam" for using his great gifts to obscure the truth. But the Victorians would not have been Victorian had they given their whole heart and mind and soul and strength to the quest for the truth, wherever and whatever it might be. They had their reservations, their decencies, to which truth had got to conform. And so, after their time, truth itself followed God and the human soul into the darkness, becoming first a matter of pragmatic convenience, and finally one of complete indifference, a mere meaningless sound with no counterpart in reality, which appears to be the gist of the latest Huxley philosophy.*

It is a just nemesis on the Victorians, that any protests against the libels by which their biographies are so freely seasoned, is usually silenced by a reminder that, after all, what you want in a biography is not that it should be literally accurate, but a work of art—the art of fiction. If they had been better lovers of Truth, she would be guarding their memories now.

It was not the Victorian philosophy that was breaking down, but the Victorian social system. Even in the sixties, the middle class was beginning to lose prestige. A new generation of intellectuals was rising in revolt against everything that that class held sacred. Matthew Arnold branded it, indelibly, with the mark of the Philistine. Du Maurier, who had now more material to work upon than Thackeray, renewed the taunt of snobbery. Gilbert, in his songs and operas, was moved to such infectious laughter at little tin bourgeois gods, that the sting of his satire was hardly resented:

> "Morality, heavenly link,
>   To thee I'll eternally drink!
> I'm awfully fond of that heavenly bond,
>   Morality, heavenly link!"

By the eighties "bourgeois" was becoming a term of positive insult among middle class people with any pretensions to being advanced or genteel.

The fact is that the middle class had begun to lose

---

* As in Mr. Aldous Huxley's *Do What You Will*.

faith in its own ideals, and its sturdy self-respect was on the wane. The Dombeys and Pickwicks were yielding place to the Veneerings, and a mode of life was being evolved in the new suburbs, whose whole pride and ideal centred on the keeping up of appearances. The strenuous pursuit of conventional gentility, often on cruelly insufficient means, may have something heroic about it, and perhaps our great-grandchildren, when they unearth old copies of *The Maunderer,* and wonder what gluttony of toad-eating can have possessed its readers, may be guilty of the same lack of sympathetic understanding that our age has for the Victorians.

Certainly nothing became the middle class so well in the days of its supremacy, as the way with which, when the time was ripe, it laid that supremacy down. That some sort of a Reform Bill, letting the working class into the franchise, was due, was a matter on which most of the Whig-Liberals were agreed, but it was the genius of Disraeli that made him stake the fortunes of his party on the innate Toryism of the common people. He knew their responsiveness to leadership they could respect, and he divined that the old aristocracy of birth was likely to attract their suffrages more readily than the new aristocracy of money. He had judged rightly, for during the last quarter of the century the balance of power shifted decisively in favour of the Tories.

But like the Romantic he was, he had made one miscalculation. Just as Bolingbroke's ideal of a patriot king had failed to work in the previous century, owing to that king being George III, so Disraeli's ideal of a Tory democracy broke down from lack of leadership. The gentlemen of England had neither the intellect nor the imagination requisite for piloting the Ship of State through those dangerous and uncharted waters into which she had drifted. Such activities would have interfered too much with sport. We must remember that the very business of the nation, as transacted in Parliament, had to accommodate itself to the necessity of setting free legislators to slaughter grouse on the earliest possible day on which this could be done without the interference of the police.

The time was approaching when the old upper class would be scarcely distinguishable. The collapse of English agriculture, long deferred, had become an accomplished fact in the eighties, and the great estates no longer sufficed to maintain their owners in the old dignity. Many a country seat passed into the hands of the new rich, who treated it as an expensive plaything, and had no ties with the soil. The old Queen, as indomitable as ever, maintained her court as the last stronghold of aristocratic exclusiveness, but on the accession of her son, the last barriers were overthrown, and though a House of Lords still played its anachronistic part in the Constitution, its prestige had been fatally undermined by the putting up of the peerage to auction. The new plutocracy was in the driver's seat, and drove even Toryism.

And now the working class, having failed to find leadership outside its own ranks, was beginning to seek it from within. The political struggle of the future was to decide whether the resources of wealth, applied to mass suggestion by the great party machines, could counteract the preponderance of voting power in the ranks of Labour.

It was not only the upper class that was threatened. By the end of the century signs were apparent that the long period of Victorian prosperity was drawing to a close, that the curve of real wages had touched its highest point. Rival powers were at last beginning to bring their full resources into play, and England would have need of all her energy and imagination if she were to maintain her supply of those goods from abroad that were necessary to her existence. It was a premonition of coming peril that drove Joseph Chamberlain to seek, in tightening the bonds of Empire, new markets for old.

Peril of a more catastrophic nature was threatening not only English but human civilisation. The principles of free government and free trade, for which the Victorian foreign policy had all too fitfully stood, were not those destined to prevail in the new Europe. It was not Cobden but Bismarck who was to call the tune to which the nations danced—and that dance was the Dance of Death. After the fall of Napoleon III, Liberalism was a discredited cause in Europe, and ideals went out of fashion. Even in England there was a reaction to force and Jingoism, until the humiliating experience of the South African War deflated her self-esteem.

But now it was becoming apparent that Nietzsche had been too optimistic when he opined that the Last Man, the product of mechanical civilisation, was indestructible like the ground flea. That creature's machine-created environment had provided him with the means of improving his condition, gradually and by the exercise of a wisdom beyond that of his fathers, but it had also provided him with the means of easy and rapid suicide. And these means—not having adapted his mind to that new environment—he was determined to put into operation. Happily progress had not gone quite far enough to make war the complete suicide it would have been a decade or two later. It was decreed that mankind should have one more chance, at the eleventh hour, to make good the failure of its fathers to effect the inward and spiritual counterpart of the revolution brought about by the coming of a machine age.

Those of us who are still old-fashioned enough to retain a working faith in free will, have no need to despair. We are not behavouristic automatons, but men, with souls to save and destinies to command. "Rejoice not against me, O mine enemy!" cried Bunyan's pilgrim, when Apollyon had beaten him to his knees, "for when I fall I shall arise." And instead of wringing impotent hands over the downfall of that edifice which our fathers wrought so nobly in all but the foundations, let us learn from their failure and take counsel from Goethe:

> "Mightier
> For the children of men,
> Brightlier
> Build it again,
> In thine own bosom build it anew!
> Bid the new career
> Commence,
> With clearer sense,
> And the new songs of cheer
> Be sung thereto!"

INDEX